Garden Bulbs
for the South

Also by Scott Ogden:
Gardening Success with Difficult Soils

Garden Bulbs
for the South

Scott Ogden

TAYLOR PUBLISHING COMPANY
Dallas, Texas

Designed by Deborah Jackson-Jones

Published by Taylor Publishing Company
          1550 West Mockingbird Lane
          Dallas, Texas 75235

Library of Congress Cataloging-in-Publication Data

Ogden, Scott.
     Garden bulbs for the South / Scott Ogden.
        p.   cm.
     Includes bibliographical references (p. 241) and
index.
     ISBN 0-87833-861-6
     1. Bulbs—Southern states.   I. Title.
SB425.O44   1994
635.9′44′0975—dc20   94-7931
                                              CIP

Printed in the United States of America

10   9   8   7   6   5   4   3

Contents

Introduction

The flowers come forth like the belles of the day, have their short reign of beauty and splendor, and retire like them to the more interesting office of reproducing their like. The hyacinths and tulips are off the stage, the Irises are giving place to the Belladonnas, as they will to the Tuberoses.

Thomas Jefferson, May 26, 1811,
in a letter to Anne Randolf Bankhead

Bulbs have a bewitching quality that sets them apart from ordinary flowers. They resurrect gardens from drab dormancy and appear suddenly, heralding the season of growth and bloom. Some exude the exotic glamour of orchids; others radiate the freshness of fields and meadows. Through their succulent, crystalline textures, they convey the charm and intimacy of woodland or the brilliant iridescence of mountain heights.

Nearly all bulbs share in the miraculous habit of reawakening to growth and bloom. Many are so precocious they seem to appear overnight, as if by magic. The lively blossoms emerge from hiding to selflessly spend their substance on the air. After a few weeks of vigorous growth, the plants disappear below ground to sleep, leaving gardeners to await their return.

Because of their hardy, easy growth, bulbs are among the most democratic flowers. They present their glories within reach of casual gardeners and can be shared easily over the garden fence. The entire routine of growth, bloom, and dormancy pursued by tuberous plants ensures survival in the most difficult circumstances. With only modest encouragement, these flowers succeed famously. They travel readily, multiply swiftly, and endure in almost any garden.

All this is well known in cold climates, where springs have long been enlivened by bulbs from Holland. These imports are ideal for the gardens of the North, but have limited application in warmer climates. South-

1

ern gardeners participate in the tradition of bedding spring bulbs, but only through contrivance. A few dedicated flower lovers purchase fresh bulbs each autumn to deposit in their refrigerators. After a few weeks of chilling, they exhume their prizes and inter them in the cold winter ground, along with a sprinkling of bonemeal.

These ministrations are intended to trick the bulbs into thinking they are back in the Netherlands. The technique works surprisingly well, and in March or April the dutiful bulb gardener will usually be rewarded with a handful of lovely, fleeting blossoms. However, this imported glory soon yields to the grim task of yanking out spent plants and sending them on to the compost pile. The same destination awaits the gruesome remains lying in the refrigerators of the forgetful.

This is not to suggest that Southerners should not enjoy growing the hardy bulbs of the trade. These can be showy and successful in warm climates, if properly treated. Modest plantings of tulips or narcissi tucked here and there among other border flowers are certainly worthwhile. Even in the North such bulbs are more often used as seasonal bedding than as honest perennials.

For public gardens this kind of bedding display can be justified, but for the average home dirt dauber there are more rewarding activities. The effort and expense invested in temporary bulb displays might as readily be employed on something new, exotic, or extraordinary—even on flowers that like the South. There really are bulbs that blossom in warm climates without spending the fall in the icebox. Quite a few return on their own and increase in beauty from season to season.

Numerous references describe the needs and wants of the common hardy flowers of the Dutch trade, and there is little reason to repeat such information here. Our concerns are the historic, neglected, and little-known bulbs whose beauties belong rightly and traditionally to the South. Warm-climate bulbs are part of an ancient horticultural legacy, connecting Southern gardens with predecessors dating back to the beginnings of settled life.

❧ Naturalizing

Bulbs that establish themselves as perennials are said to naturalize. Like living plants everywhere, naturalizing bulbs must successfully grow, flower, and multiply (either through seed or through vegetative division). All of these stages must occur if the bulbs can truly be said to naturalize.

Some failures take several seasons to reveal themselves. A planting of daffodils may return faithfully, yet remain hatefully barren of bloom. A patch of crocuses might diminish gradually over years, rather than collapse in a sudden catastrophe. As a rule, if flowers don't show clear signs of increase, they are wasting away toward a certain end.

❧ Bulbs and Other Devices

At what must have been a very early moment in the natural development of plants, the storage of food and water became an important convenience. This permitted survival during periods of cold or drought and hastened growth and reproduction when favorable conditions returned. Even such primitive examples of greenery as the cycads (*Cycadaceae*) display swollen stems and leaf bases that serve to store starch and moisture. Gardeners refer to any such devices as bulbs.

The proper botanical names for these reservoirs vary, depending on which components of plant tissue have been enlarged to serve the storage function. True bulbs develop from the swollen bases of leaves, as may be seen at an early stage in the barely developed bulb of a leek. The primitive bulbs of lilies (*Lilium* spp.), wood sorrels (*Oxalis* spp.), and magic flowers (*Achimenes* spp.) retain the separate scales formed from the leaves. These types of bulbs resemble artichokes.

More advanced, tunicated bulbs like onions, daffodils, and amaryllises have scales that completely encircle the growing axis. Stems of these plants frequently are reduced to mere disks known as basal plates, from which roots may sprout and offsets may bud.

Quite a few of the flowers that gardeners categorize as bulbs depend on storage organs developed from the bases of stems. These stem tubers, known as corms, are common to such members of the iris family as *Crocus* and *Gladiolus*. While true bulbs may grow and increase in dimension over several years, corms completely replace themselves each season, often forming new tubers atop the shrivelled remains of the old.

Rhizomes are swollen stems that creep along horizontally either at or below-ground level. Unspecialized, yet effective, storage structures, they belong to some of the most common bulbs: irises, cannas, gingers, aroids, and other favorites possess these easily divided rootstocks.

Tuberous roots are also widespread. A range of plants, such as *Anemone*, *Ranunculus*, and *Cyclamen*, depend on miscellaneous storage organs developed from the roots. Clear-cut distinctions between root tubers and rhizomes often are wanting, so these classes tend to blur.

These storage strategies, all enabling their possessors to compete in cold or semi-arid climates, appear to have evolved many times in the history of growing things. The single genus *Iris* includes within its ranks species with true bulbs, corms, rhizomes, and fleshy roots. The onions (*Allium* spp.) are also varied in their choice of storage mechanisms. The unique rootstocks of tuberoses (*Polianthes* spp.) combine swollen roots, fleshy rhizomes, and true bulbs together.

Many of the best-known bulbs form a natural group centered around the lilies. The three big bulb families, *Liliaceae*, *Iridaceae*, and *Amaryllidaceae*, are all monocots and probably share a common ancestry. However, many flowers that gardeners know as bulbs are only distantly related to these.

What unites all of them from the gardening standpoint is ease of handling. Unlike most of the world's flora, bulbs may rest contentedly in a paper bag on a shelf for as long as three-quarters of the year, or be shipped thousands of miles packed only in dry sacking. As long as they can be replanted in time to complete annual growth and flowering, they seem none the worse for their journeys. This fantastic portability opens wide possibilities for the gardener to acquire rare blooms from distant lands and permits fully mature flowering effects the first season after planting.

❧ *A Bit of Botany*

Surprising as it may seem, many bulbs are meagerly known to botanists. Fleshy bulb flowers preserve poorly and leave little to study in herbaria. Few professionals receive opportunities to learn about these plants in a living condition, so gardeners may often observe characteristics unrecorded by scientists. Several bulbs popular in Southern gardens have never been adequately studied or designated with a Latin name.

Latin names often tell useful information about a plant's character, habit, or history. Many of the botanical names of bulbs allude to classical or mythological figures, while others are charmingly descriptive. The rain lilies, which are the subject of the first chapter, have an especially lovely name, *Zephyranthes*, which translates as "flower of the west wind."

Nevertheless, to avoid bludgeoning readers with such matters through the text, botanical commentary has been reserved for the Appendix. Those who have an interest will find a taxonomic review of Southern bulbs there, along with notes on bulb origins and culture.

❧ *Acknowledgments*

Of numerous people who assisted in my writing this book, several deserve special recognition. Larry DeMartino offered helpful reviews and shared his informative enthusiasm for the gingers. Thad Howard endowed me with a wealth of experiences and information on subtropical bulbs of all kinds. Steve Lowe, Paul Cox, Margaret Kane, Joe Tocquigny, and other able plant folk all shared with me freely. For these unusually gifted people and for the support of my family, I give humble thanks.

Rain Lily Day

As August fades, the worn-out fields in the Southern countryside come to life with late-season wildflowers. Thistle-leafed eryngo (*Eryngium amethystinum*) blushes steel purple, while snow-on-the-prairie (*Euphorbia marginata*) casts a milky bloom over the landscape. The summer sky responds in kind, as the relentless blue of the heavens softens to hazy amethyst. It's still hot as the devil, but we may begin to hope for the cooling rains of fall.

Sometimes it's a short wait, and occasionally a hurricane in the Gulf of Mexico or some other cloudburst intercedes to make things tolerably moist and pleasant. In most years, though, the meadows parch to tawny brown, and gaping cracks appear in the hardened clay. It's often mid-September before relief arrives.

As the first norther of the season approaches, a great wall of thunderstorms moves in and drenches the earth. The soaking rains initiate a floral miracle peculiar to this region. Northerners search longingly for the first crocus in the melting snow. Here it's rain lilies thrusting from crusted earth that bring special joy.

Plants that have sulked through summer heat veritably jump into growth with the autumn drenchings. The electrical storms bring nitrogen from the atmosphere in the spattering drops of rain. Rain lilies know the difference between this thunderstorm water and the bland effluent from the hose. They have patiently reserved their blooms for the real thing.

These miniatures have sputtered in flower all summer, but nothing like what is to be. Five days after the deluge comes a miracle of the floral year: rain lily day. On this prodigal morning every unspent *Zephyranthes* and *Habranthus* in the garden explodes in blossom.

The rains restore freshness to the air, and the coolness of the passing front lingers. The mushroomlike growth of these little amaryllids slows, and their warm colors deepen. It has been five days since the autumn soaking stirred the bulbs from dormancy. With patient progress the tiny scapes have steadily risen from the ground.

Now starry bouquets of pink, gold, copper, and cream dance along the edges of paths and borders. In meadows and fields beyond, the wild rain lilies are in flower, and the air is filled with their musky perfume. You need to shrink down and stroll among the grassy leaves to find the true measure of the brightly colored trumpets and goblets proffered by these little bulbs.

It seems certain that every Southerner who knows them holds the rain lilies dear, yet most meet only a handful of these beauties. Few realize the vastness of the rain lily clan or how many jewels and treasures it holds.

The rain lilies, fairy lilies, zephyr lilies, or atamascos are tiny kin of the tropical amaryllises. Botanists have assigned these bulbs to *Zephyranthes* and to such related genera as *Habranthus*, *Haylockia*, and *Pyrolirion*. Most are native to the American tropics, but a dozen species range into the southern United States. Wherever rain lilies grow, they count on thunderstorms to stir them into bloom.

Garden culture for these little bulbs is simple, and most varieties thrive throughout the South. You can keep weed pulling to a minimum by employing a good, nonaggressive groundcover companion. Some of the best are sedums. Several adapt to Southern gardens and have shallow roots, which won't compete with the bulbs for food. Little gray sedum (*Sedum potosinum*) and Texas sedum (*S. texanum*) are two of the most heat-tolerant.

❧ *Old Favorites*

The most familiar rain lily in cultivation, *Zephyranthes candida*, is a true autumnal. It just begins to bloom with late summer rains. Instead of the flattened grassy foliage typical of its clan, this species produces tapered, rushlike leaves. The dark green foliage stands through winter frost and offers a foil for the starry, white autumn blooms.

In much of the South, *Z. candida* is a roadside wildflower. It's common to see the immaculate flowers fluttering over pools of coffee-colored water. In South America these little amaryllids line delta shores along the Rio de la Plata. A romantic Spanish explorer named this "river of silver" and the "silver republic" (Argentina) beyond for these modest, white blossoms.

In the garden *Z. candida* is not at all particular. It flowers happily on gumbo clay or flour sand and luxuriates as an aquatic in the bog garden. It's a favorite for borders, where its stiff, upright foliage shows smartly. *Z. candida* benefits from a little extra water to help carry it through summer and some vigilance to exclude moisture-thieving roots of trees from the plantings. Otherwise, it's absurdly easy and prolific. Every storm from September through November stirs the clumps to flower.

The tiny bulbs of this rain lily suffer from drying, so it's always best to obtain *Z. candida* in a growing condition. In most parts of the South, nurseries offer this species in pots swollen with bulbs ready to divide. If by some misfortune all you succeed in finding are dried bulbs, be prepared to wait a year for flowers.

Zephyranthes grandiflora

Zephyranthes candida

Zephyranthes chlorosolen

Zephyranthes rosea

Zephyranthes atamasco

Zephyranthes insularum

After this prolific variety, the rain lily most often met in cultivation is the lavish pink *Z. grandiflora*. Succulent, rosy blooms over three inches across rise above its grassy foliage following summer downpours. The six or eight gracefully expanded petals are complemented by yellow anthers and an opulently long, white stigma.

Mystery surrounds the origin of *Z. grandiflora*. It's certainly a native of tropical America, but nobody seems sure about where. The cultivated strain of this flower is sterile and refuses to seed, yet it may be found naturalized in many warm countries, including our Gulf Coast. Generations of affectionate gardeners are to blame. They have spread this species far and wide, for it is among the best-loved subtropical flowers.

If rain lilies ever become popular entries for flower shows, this variety could certainly set standards for judging. In size, proportion, texture, and depth of coloring, *Z. grandiflora* reigns supreme. Only a half-hardy constitution limits its popularity. In the middle and upper South, a good mulch of hay or pine straw will help carry the semitender bulbs through winter.

Like most subtropicals, *Z. grandiflora* covets rich ground and gives its best when fed generously. This requires continuous effort from Southerners, for organic matter swiftly decays in our warm climate. On very chalky or limy ground, a pocket of acid sand mixed with compost affords a practical home. Gardeners with heavy clay will receive gratifying results from annual dressings of compost or manure.

A third rain lily common to Southern gardens is the startlingly golden *Z. citrina*. It's one of the easiest varieties in the drier gardens of Texas, as it accepts impoverished soil and droughty summers. It's also remarkably cold-hardy, considering its native range in the Yucatan; zero-degree weather is no threat.

If the rains are willing, *Z. citrina* begins flowering in early summer, but its best shows wait for fall. Then the bright golden goblets rise in masses above narrow, sage green foliage. The collective impact of several hundred of its glowing blossoms on a sunny September day is truly heartwarming.

This rain lily makes a lot of seed, which may be gathered and planted straight away or left to fall and naturalize. As with most amaryllids, the flat, black seeds of *Z. citrina* store poorly and lose viability if not sown immediately. They grow easily in pots if scattered thickly and barely covered with sandy compost, however. When well fertilized, they grow to flowering size in eighteen months or less.

The abundant seed of *Z. citrina* invariably comes true to its golden mother, even if the blooms are dusted with pollen from another species. This is due to what botanists refer to as parthenogenesis, an ability among certain plants to clone themselves. This reproductive strategy enables some species to aggressively multiply and colonize disturbed habitats. Such common garden weeds as dandelions and familiar trees as mayhaws (*Crataegus* spp.) and citrus have this capacity. Even if bees fail to bring pollen to the blossoms, the seeds mature and grow into genetically identical copies of the mother plants.

There is an old, pale yellow rain lily called 'Ajax' whose parents seem to have been *Z. citrina* and *Z. candida*. It's likely that *Z. candida* was the seed parent, or "mother," of this hybrid. *Z. citrina* must have been the pollen parent, or "father," of 'Ajax', for parthenogenesis would have blocked its ability to cross if tried as the mother.

For reasons that defy explanation, the bulb trade commonly markets both *Z. citrina* and *Z. grandiflora* under patently erroneous names. *Z. citrina* usually reaches shelves as *sulfurea*. This seems simple enough to decipher, since both citron and sulfur indicate yellow. The confusion comes with *Z. grandiflora*, which often arrives as *Z. rosea* or *Z. robusta*.

The true *Zephyranthes rosea* is a charming, deep rose rain lily from Cuba. Its rounded, often eight-petalled, blooms are only a third the size of *Z. grandiflora*'s. Wide, green foliage and low stature also set it apart. *Z. rosea* is popular in Florida gardens as an edging plant, where its colorful, chocolate-scented blooms brighten the hurricane season. Unfortunately for gardeners elsewhere, the shallow, clustered bulbs have poor resistance to frost.

The same tenderness afflicts *Z. rosea*'s white-flowered cousin, *Z. insularum*. This is another Caribbean species that often appears in Florida gardens. The original plants came from an old home in Key West, hence the botanical name, which means "of the island."

Z. insularum makes a thrifty clump for foregrounds of tropical borders. It thrives on almost any soil, including barren chalk. Where frosts visit regularly, these tender bulbs may be kept in pots plunged in the ground for summer. Dazzling white blooms appear above their dark, strappy foliage from August through October.

What is called *Zephyranthes robusta* in the nursery trade is actually *Habranthus robustus*, a lavender-pink amaryllid from Argentina. This species matches size and stature with *Zephyranthes grandiflora*, but it has blooms that nod and face outward from the stems like a little amaryllis. It's this character that leads botanists to place this rain lily in the separate genus *Habranthus*.

Established clumps of *H. robustus* make fine shows in gardens of the lower South. At regular intervals through summer, the gray foliage disappears behind masses of lilac bloom. Although comparable in hardiness to *Zephyranthes grandiflora*, the fast-multiplying bulbs of this *Habranthus* grow shallowly and need winter protection, except in the lower South.

❧ *Atamascos*

The common rain lilies of Southeastern wilds are the atamasco lilies (*Zephyranthes atamasco*). Their curious traditional name comes from a Native American word. To many Southerners these showy spring blooms are familiar as "wild Easter lilies." Atamascos inhabit swampy forests and coastal prairies from Florida west to Alabama, and northward to Virginia and Pennsylvania.

For woodland gardens, atamasco lilies afford ideal early-season accents. In the South their white funnels appear in March or April. The trumpet-shaped blooms emit a sweet fragrance and make pleasant companions for the azaleas and Louisiana phlox blooming at the same season.

The broad, grassy foliage of atamasco lilies comes up in early winter. The bulbs prosper under deciduous trees, whose bare branches allow sun to reach the ground. The rich leaf mold and acid soils found under hardwoods favor these flowers, and damp or boggy conditions are accepted eagerly.

Where soils are alkaline or drought-prone, atamascos may be grown in pots. On a sheltered patio or a cool greenhouse, they often sputter in flower through the entire winter. In the summer the bulbs go dormant, but you should not allow them to dry out entirely.

In addition to the typical broad-leafed atamascos, there are two variants native to Florida, which botanists sometimes list under separate names, *Z. treatiae* and *Z. simpsonii*. Both have narrow foliage and favor sandy pine flatwoods or roadside meadows, rather than the swampy woodlands enjoyed by *Z. atamasco*. Typical *Z. treatiae* blossoms are smaller than those of *Z. atamasco*, with slender petals that recurve like little tiger lilies. *Z. simpsonii* produces funnel-shaped blooms flushed pink on the exterior. All three types grow readily in gardens and may often be found around old homesteads in the South.

Arnold Puetz, a Jacksonville, Florida, nurseryman, advertised them this way:

A NEW LILY OF GREAT PROMISE.

The Easter Lily of the South.

Zepheranthus Treatae.

One of the most charming spring and summer flowering bulbs, whose slender stems bear a large, pure white sweet, lily shaped flower.

To introduce these Fairy Lilies everywhere, and to give every lover of flowers a chance to try them with very little outlay, I will forward during the year 1881 by mail postpaid one dozen for 25 cents or five dozen for $1. After January 1st, 1882, 5 cents each or 50 cents per dozen will be charged. It is worth double the money.

❧ Zephyr Gardens

Personal Note: Many years ago I received a copy of a catalog belonging to an enterprise run under the delightful name of Zephyr Gardens. By the time I got the list, the proprietor, Dr. Thaddeus Monroe Howard, D.V.M., had long since retired from the bulb business. Yet the plants described were so extraordinary and full of promise that gardeners had continued to pass along his catalog years afterward.

When I came to live in San Antonio, I introduced myself to Dr. Howard, and we began a long discussion concerning the bulbs he had collected and the hybrids he had created. Over several seasons Dr. Howard related his work with bulbs of many kinds. What follows is a tale about rain lilies and the marvelous discoveries of Dr. Howard and others.

When Thad Howard began collecting rain lilies in San Antonio during the early 1950s, the *Zephyranthes* world was still rather small. His garden included the "old" species described above and several of the wild rain lilies of South Texas. The only hybridizing that had been done with the group had taken place in faraway India.

Early in the century Sydney Percy Lancaster, secretary of the Agricultural and Horticultural Society of India, crossed several rain lilies into a strain known as × *Cooperanthes*. These were hybrids of *Z. grandiflora*, *Z. citrina*, and a species obtained from a German plant collector in Austin, Texas. In deference to this source, a Mr. Peter Henry Oberwetter, Lancaster referred to these bulbs in his notes as "*Cooperia Oberwetterii*."

Oberwetter's activities will be discussed further in a later chapter. For now, what merits attention is the essential direction of Lancaster's hybridizing. He had united the colorful tropical species of *Zephyranthes* with a fragrant, hardy rain lily from central Texas. The resulting offspring grew robustly and displayed a range of warm pastel colors.

Dr. Howard tried importing Lancaster's crosses from India to Texas. The bulbs were shipped but never arrived, and Howard resolved to make his own hybrids from scratch. Along with breeding, dedicated collecting in Texas and Mexico soon expanded his rain lily garden to undreamed-of proportions.

❧ Cooperia

A number of the bulbs Howard listed in his catalog fall into a group long known as *Cooperia*. These are essentially night-blooming *Zephyranthes* with white, ivory, or sulfur-colored blooms and sweet, primrose fragrances. Their long-tubed blossoms attract visits from night-flying moths, who pollinate them with equally long tongues.

Flowering from early summer to fall, the most widespread of these is *Zephyranthes chlorosolen* (*Cooperia drummondii*). This hardy flower ranges through Texas and into adjacent Louisiana, Oklahoma, Mexico, and New Mexico, with outposts scattered from Brazil to Kansas.

Through most of this territory, *Z. chlorosolen* presents a homely aspect. Typical strains bear small-cupped blossoms rising above bunches of wiry, olive drab leaves. The occasional fine specimen offers wide blooms that open to flat stars. The best shimmer with a satiny sparkle. In cool weather the blooms assume a pink tinge.

Even modest strains of this *Zephyranthes* have the capacity to transform barren fields and vacant lots into floral wonderlands. It's impressive to see the multitudes of tiny blossoms magically emerge from hiding. They rise over the dormant summer grass, expand their waxy petals as the sun sets, and fill the night air with heavy fragrance.

In gardens *Z. chlorosolen* thrives in a variety of situations, from flower borders and rockeries to rough turf. The thick-textured blooms show well among annual overplantings of sweet alyssum (*Lobularia maritima*) or moss rose (*Portulaca grandiflora*). For raised positions low, ground-hugging evergreens such as Longwood

Zephyranthes traubii

Zephyranthes pulchella

Zephyranthes "Labuffarosea"

Zephyranthes macrosiphon

Zephyranthes drummondii

Zephyranthes primulina   Howard and Odgen

creeping thyme (*Thymus glabrescens*) or carpet germander (*Teucrium aroanium*) make good drought-tolerant companions. The robust bulbs propagate readily from capsules of flat, black seed and self-sow where offered mulches of grit or pea gravel. They soon offset into large clumps.

Very similar to *Z. chlorosolen*, but with elegant, floppy-petaled blooms, is *Z. traubii*. This species luxuriates in the moist ground of coastal prairies between Houston and Victoria, Texas, where *Z. traubii* flowers in bar ditches and roadside swales each autumn. Tiny, clustering bulbs and narrow foliage give this species a delicate character.

Farther south, in eastern Mexico, *Z. traubii* shows up in a summer-blooming race that favors savannahs or rough woodland. These Mexican traubiis (if that's what they are) are easier growing and more drought-tolerant than their Texas cousins but lack some of their size and grace.

Within the city limits of Brownsville, Texas, and up the coast near Corpus Christi, grow two curious rain lilies with pale sulfur blooms. The first is *Zephyranthes smallii*, an apparently natural hybrid of *Z. chlorosolen* and the bright yellow, day-blooming *Z. pulchella*. It looks like a lemony version of *Z. chlorosolen* and seems even more amenable to cultivation. Its charmingly fragrant flowers appear continuously through summer and fall, opening in early afternoon.

It is fortunate that *Z. smallii* makes such a congenial garden plant, for it seems destined to oblivion in the wild. Nearly all of the natural habitat of these small flowers has disappeared in suburban development. The bulbs persist mainly in yards, vacant fields, and baseball diamonds in the city of Brownsville, Texas. Gardeners can do this plant a favor by sharing bulbs and seed and maintaining it in cultivation.

The other yellow cooperia is called *Z. jonesii*. It has round, solitary bulbs and straw-colored flowers, tinged russet in bud. *Z. jonesii* also seems to be of hybrid origin but is less prolific in gardens than its Brownsville cousin. It flowers from September to November, in company with *Z. traubii*, *Z. chlorosolen*, and three yellow, day-flowering rain lilies.

❧ Drummond's Legacy

The common white cooperia (*Z. chlorosolen*) makes a useful garden plant but has never attracted the following of a similar rain lily growing alongside it in central Texas. This other cooperia casually resembles *Z. chlorosolen*, but it is really very distinctive. One nineteenth-century botanist actually proposed a separate genus (*Sceptranthes*) for this unique amaryllid. Today it's known botanically as *Zephyranthes drummondii* (or sometimes as *Cooperia pedunculata*) and horticulturally as the giant prairie lily.

Before this discussion goes further and readers tire of tripping past names like *Cooperia* and *Sceptranthes*, it's appropriate to review the origin of a bit of taxonomic chaos. *Zephyranthes drummondii* and *Z. chlorosolen* first found their way to scientific attention through the efforts of Scottish plant collector Thomas Drummond. Drummond collected widely in Louisiana and south-central Texas during the early nineteenth century, and the botanical names chosen for many

Southern wildflowers commemorate his work. Unfortunately for students of rain lilies, both of these night-blooming *Zephyranthes* have been honored with Mr. Drummond's title, one as *Cooperia drummondii*, the other as *Zephyranthes drummondii*.

If botanists class these flowers together as *Cooperia*, then *Z. drummondii* becomes *Cooperia pedunculata*. If both are regarded as *Zephyranthes* (the route chosen here), then *Cooperia drummondii* becomes *Zephyranthes chlorosolen*. Either interpretation generates a measure of confusion, for *Cooperia drummondii* (*Zephyranthes chlorosolen*) and *Zephyranthes drummondii* are distinct plants.

🌸 Giant Prairie Lilies

One may only hope these entanglements will not dissuade gardeners from enjoying these fine flowers. *Z. drummondii* produces its good-sized, milky blooms as early as March and then on through midsummer. If rains are sparse, flowering continues into the fall. The broad, grayish leaves remain active and lush most of the year but may die away briefly in late summer. The globular, brownish black bulbs approach the size of tennis balls when grown in rich soil.

With lush, swirling, sage green foliage to set off its sweet-scented blooms, the giant prairie lily makes a good border citizen, ideal for edging a bed, filling a planter, or nestling among rocks on a slope. It accepts most types of soil and any watering regime from drought to deluge. The bulbs are hardy throughout the South. Few summer blossoms offer a more pleasing fragrance than these waxy, white blooms.

Giant prairie lilies differ from other cooperias in several curious ways. They exhibit an earlier blooming season and generally seek higher ground than the other night-blooming rain lilies. Small stems (pedicels) appear beneath the ovaries at the base of the blooms. The three longest of the six stamens may just be seen protruding from the mouth of the flower tube. The other three stamens and the very short stigma are completely hidden from view. This arrangement gives the flowers a ghostly appearance reminiscent of moonflowers.

In most of its range, *Z. drummondii* produces blooms with blunt, rounded petals. These look like coarse white crocuses and are common from central Texas west into eastern New Mexico. Some large South Texas strains of the species have more star-shaped flowers with pointed petals, which may spread to over three inches across. They make an impressive sight dotting a rugged hillside.

In northern Mexico *Z. drummondii* inhabits rough and little-known deserts and brushlands. Dr. Howard visited these regions in the summer of 1964 and discovered a curious new rain lily blooming near the town of Iturbide, Nuevo Leon. The coarse, pale pink flowers of this *Zephyranthes* opened in midafternoon and seemed intermediate between the night-flowering *Z. drummondii* and a pink, day-blooming rain lily native to adjacent mountains. Howard named the unusual find *Zephyranthes morrisclintii* and noted its relationship to the giant prairie lily.

Z. morrisclintii usually has frosty pink blooms, but occasional white forms may also be found in the rugged sierras of northern Mexico. With a little effort, these may be distinguished from true *Z. drummondii* by their more upright, dull blue foliage and funnel-shaped blooms. Both the white and pink strains of *Z. morrisclintii* make hardy, successful plants for Southern gardens.

In the neighboring state of Tamaulipas, John Fairey and Carl Schoenfeld of Yucca-Do Nursery recently found another interesting ally of the giant prairie lily. This variant also occurs in pink and white editions but has glossy, green leaves and bulbs that are small and brown-skinned. The discoverers of this lovely plant have nicknamed their find *Zephyranthes* "Labuffarosea," the pink rain lily of La Buffa.

In their native San Carlos Mountains, these rain lilies make a stunning show in varied shades from white and blush to pink and rose. Especially fine flowers have snowy centers with cerise flashes on the petal tips. Although the long-tubed blooms have the same odd construction as the nocturnal *Z. drummondii*, "Labuffarosea" opens in the morning like ordinary day-blooming rain lilies.

These Mexican relatives of the giant prairie lily may be natural hybrids, or they might represent evolutionary links between the nocturnal *Z. drummondii* and its day-flowering ancestors. Whatever their origin, they offer fine material for gardens. Their large, colorful blooms and robust habits of growth are sure to win many followers.

❧ *The Laredo Yellow*

Nature is remarkably complex at times, and sleuthing among old gardens occasionally turns up a puzzle that takes years to unravel. In April of 1949 Texas plantsman Fred Jones happened upon an odd rain lily growing in a garden in Laredo. The plants had large, turnip-shaped, black-skinned bulbs, strappy, gray leaves like *Z. drummondii*, and funnel-shaped, greenish yellow blooms.

Jones wondered if these Laredo plants might be hybrids between *Z. drummondii* and the golden *Z. pulchella* that grew in marshes nearby. He set about crossing these two species to test his hypothesis—no mean task, since the long-tubed blooms of *Z. drummondii* had to be sliced open and de-anthered to prevent self-fertilization. After several seasons a few seedlings flowered. Most were maternal (parthenogenic) and resembled one or the other parent, but two were a beautiful primrose color. Jones's hybrids were lovely and showed that *Z. drummondii* and *Z. pulchella* could cross. Nevertheless, they weren't quite the same as the curious Laredo plants.

Several years passed before Dr. Howard encountered what appeared to be the 'Laredo Yellow' growing in the wild, brush-covered mountains of northern Mexico. This region is home for many unusual flowers, among them yellow rain lilies of the *Habranthus* group. These grow along with *Zephyranthes drummondii* near a rugged ridge called *Cuesta de Mamulique*.

Dr. Howard sent specimens of the yellow rain lilies to Dr. Hamilton Traub, who named the new species in Howard's honor as *Zephyranthes howardii*. The species has since been transferred to *Habranthus*, so its proper name today is *Habranthus howardii*. This rain lily is similar to the cultivated plant from Laredo but makes smaller, solitary bulbs and flowers less freely. The blooms also differ on technical points such as tube length and anther placement.

After years of puzzling over these curious plants Dr. Howard realized that the 'Laredo Yellow' probably originated as a natural hybrid between *Zephyranthes drummondii* and the yellow *Habranthus howardii*. Someone must have brought it down from the mountains years ago. Since then, its large, black-skinned bulbs have passed into many gardens. Through the 1960s Dr. Howard distributed these bulbs as Fred Jones's 'Laredo Yellow'. In 1990 he described them botanically as × *Coobranthus coryi*.

This chartreuse hybrid of the giant prairie lily thrives in both arid and humid regions of the South, multiplying steadily with offsets and seed. Although the strangely colored blossoms are more curious than beautiful, 'Laredo Yellow' adds interesting variation to the nocturnal cooperia group. It's also considerably easier to grow in gardens than the yellow *Habranthus* presumed to be its parent. The late Florida rain lily enthusiast Alek Korsakoff successfully crossed 'Laredo Yellow' with *Z. grandiflora* to create a lovely hybrid named 'Hjalmar Sandre'.

❧ *True Yellow*

The richest gold among the rain lilies belongs to a relative of *Z. citrina* from the western Gulf Coast. It's aptly called *Z. pulchella*, which means "pretty" in Latin. The species is a fall bloomer with slender leaves and long-necked, black-coated bulbs. The golden blossoms, further gilded by fat anthers dusted in orange pollen, glow like jewels set among the green grass.

Z. pulchella grows in scattered groups over the coastal prairies and fills swales and bar ditches with spritely colonies. After fall rains, blooms appear over standing water under the guard of swarming black mosquitoes. The brilliant flowers and bright green, rushlike leaves illuminate grasslands in Texas and eastern Mexico from August till November. Although commonly small and crocuslike in appearance, good forms of the species have nice-sized blooms with well-formed, wide-spreading, waxy petals.

Z. refugiensis is a unique localized relation of *Z. pulchella* with greenish gold blooms and a neat, clumping habit. This species grows in a small area where the ranges of *Z. pulchella* and *Z. jonesii* overlap. Theorists have suggested that the lemon-tinted *Z. refugiensis* originated as a hybrid between these species.

Z. pulchella and *Z. refugiensis* both need damp conditions to flower successfully in gardens, but otherwise are easily accommodated. Their half-hardy foliage grows through the winter months and dries off in early summer. They enjoy rich, heavy soils but get along on sandy ground if well watered.

❧ *A Rain Lily Safari*

A favorite autumn adventure is a rain lily safari to the soggy Texas coastal prairies where these yellow varieties abound. If you visit about five days after a drenching shower, you may see six or seven different rain lily species at once. This makes quite an exotic bouquet.

Proceeding east from the old presidio at Goliad, the land flattens out in a broad plain dotted with stunted live oaks. Along the roadside the common white cooperias (*Zephyranthes chlorosolen*) show among the tall grasses. Soon these

Habranthus concolor

Zephyranthes 'Laredo Yellow'

Habranthus brachyandrus

Zephyranthes bella Howard and Odgen

Zephyranthes fosteri

Zephyranthes lindleyana

are joined by large-flowered *Z. traubii* and sulfury *Z. jonesii*. An occasional giant prairie lily or Texas copper lily (*Habranthus tubispathus* v. *texensis*) may join these. By the time the road reaches the town of Refugio, *Z. pulchella* and *Z. refugiensis* dot the fields with their golden chalices.

🐚 *Mexican Yellows*

In eastern Mexico Dr. Howard discovered a number of colorful rain lilies with good drought tolerance and everblooming habits. One of the best is the queen's rain lily, *Zephyranthes reginae*. Howard found this light apricot species on one of his early collecting expeditions near Valles, San Luis Potosi, and he distributed it for many years as "Valles Yellow."

Like *Z. citrina*, this species happily self-sows and multiplies into thrifty patches. A handful of seed is all that's necessary to start a thriving population. It's one of the most rewarding rain lilies for Southern gardens and flowers steadily from early summer till frost. *Z. reginae* seems quite hardy to cold.

Near the town of El Naranjo, San Luis Potosi, grow two more yellowish *Zephyranthes*, one with bright lemony blooms and another with pale ivory-colored petals. These varieties occur together on prairies thick with black clay. The yellow-green species is *Z. nymphaea*, a Mexican ally of *Z. pulchella*. Its long-necked bulbs root deeply in the muddy soil. Slender leaves and stems raise cup-shaped flowers above the meadows. Its cream-colored companion, *Z. subflava*, expands starry, two-inch blossoms. Both of these species succeed in the lower South, but they need protective mulching where winter temperatures drop below 20 degrees F.

Near Tamazunchale ("Thomas and Charlie") on the old Pan-American Highway grows an elegant, long-tubed rain lily with wide, channeled, dark green foliage. This is *Z. primulina*, a beautiful species whose light primrose blooms carry a pronounced pink tinge on the backs of the petals. As it comes from a subtropical section of Mexico, *Z. primulina* appreciates some protection from hard freezes.

🐚 Mayitos

In the same region where *Z. primulina* grows, there are also rain lilies with large, pink blooms and lush green, keeled foliage. These beauties rival *Z. grandiflora* in size, and they surpass it in precision and symmetry of design. J.G. Baker christened this species *Z. macrosiphon* in reference to the long tubes of the flowers.

In the wild these showy flowers are most often a rich rose, but light pink forms occur on occasion. Whites have never been reported, yet other Mexican rain lilies have pale forms. There is probably a pristine white *macrosiphon* awaiting discovery on some remote mountainside.

Z. macrosiphon responds to good culture and enjoys rich soil. It declines rapidly, however, when subjected to drought, extreme heat, or serious cold. Although less reliable in gardens than *Z. grandiflora*, *Z. macrosiphon* grows quickly and easily from seed. It makes a fine subject for a pot on a terrace or windowsill. Its tidy clumps of foliage bear a succession of rose blooms through the growing season.

Other pink rain lilies in Mexico come mostly from regions seasonally beset with drought. The most common ones tolerate a range of growing conditions and adapt to gardens where frost does not penetrate the soil deeply. In cold regions they may be potted or dug and stored over winter like gladioli. They bloom promptly when replanted in early summer.

Botanists usually assign the variable *Zephyranthes* of central and western Mexico among three roughly defined species. In the valley of Mexico and nearby central plateau, the common pink to white variety is *Z. verecunda*. It's a modest little flower, on average about six inches or less in height; occasional individuals may reach twice this size. Some of the most beautiful are white with delicate streaks and pencilings of pink.

An ally of *Z. verecunda* from near Morelia, Guanahuato, has been tongue-twistingly described as *Z. latissamafolia*. The name means "wide-leafed," for this variety has broad, green foliage that spreads across the ground. Katherine Clint, the discoverer of the species, nicknamed this little bulb "the lady-in-green." This seems especially appropriate when the blushing blooms nestle among the foliage in early summer.

The famous Florida bromeliad collector Mulford Foster discovered *Z. fosteri* on a trip through the Mexican territory known as Nuevo Galicia, or Tepic. This rain lily grows near Guadalajara and through much of west-central Mexico. Although the original plants Foster collected were deep rose, shades from pink to blush white may be found as well. *Z. fosteri* is a short rain lily with spoon-shaped petals and tufts of narrow, grassy leaves. Its colonies look like emerging crocuses as they flower among brown grass in late June.

On the plateau near the city of San Luis Potosi and through much of the eastern Sierra Madre, the local rain lilies are known as *mayitos*, or "may flowers," for their early-summer blooms. One of the most common is *Z. lindleyana*. It has a short pedicel like *Z. drummondii* and comes in a variety of sizes and colors from pink to white. Dark rose selections have been called *Z. clintiae* by some authors.

Near Monterrey, *Z. lindleyana* appears in a distinctive, robust strain, approaching *Z. drummondii* in size of bulb and width of foliage. These rain lilies bloom early in the year, often around the first of March, and then on into May and June. Dr. Howard distributed these for many years as 'Horsetail Falls'.

This variant of *Z. lindleyana* makes an excellent garden plant and seems fairly hardy to cold. It develops large, solitary bulbs crowned with wide, pale green leaves and good-sized, light pink blooms. In the South it flowers along with atamasco lilies and thrives in sun or part shade. 'Horsetail Falls' grows readily from seed.

❧ Desert Denizens

A desert seems like an odd place to find something as delicately beautiful and fragile as a rain lily blossom, but the arid parts of Mexico are well endowed with a variety of *Zephyranthes*. Beyond truly dry regions like the American Southwest, these species are unlikely prospects for garden cultivation, but most do well in pots and make interesting additions to a rain lily collection.

On the outskirts of the booming industrial city of Saltillo, Coahuila, one may find occasional clumps of rain lilies with distinctive, goblet-shaped blossoms. These are white with a pink flush and appear in clumps scattered through desert scrub. Their name, *Z. crociflora,* is suggested by their crocuslike form.

On discovery *Z. crociflora* looks much like another desert species, *Z. erubescens,* which grows farther south, in the state of San Luis Potosi. Despite the superficial resemblances, a quick look down into the center of its blossoms reveals distinct arrangements of anthers and stigma. *Z. erubescens* usually grows as a solitary bulb or with only a few offsets, in contrast to the clumps typical for *Z. crociflora.* In addition to a pink-on-white color scheme, *Z. erubescens* also appears in a lovely deep rose.

After rain showers in early summer, the barren creosote flats in southern Nuevo Leon brighten with tufts of a tiny, pink rain lily. The blossoms seem to sparkle like ice crystals in the high desert air, for they have enlarged water storage cells in their succulent petals. This gives them special radiance, so that they resemble certain orchids or Guernsey lilies (*Nerine*). Their name, *Zephyranthes chichimeca,* recalls the Chichimec Indians who formerly roamed the northern Mexican desert.

The tiniest and most charming of the desert species is *Z. bella,* a refined ally of *Z. fosteri.* This elfin amaryllid grows in the barren countryside of San Luis Potosi and is hardly larger than a quarter. Its colonies look like fields of pale pink-etched crocuses.

Throughout the deserts of northern Mexico, and through most of Arizona, New Mexico, and West Texas, visitors are liable to encounter tiny, greenish gold rain lilies with wispy blue-green foliage. These have been aptly named *Z. longifolia* for their narrow leaves. The small, cup-shaped blossoms appear following early summer rains and offer a welcome bonus to bleak desert gardens. Unlike other desert species, *Z. longifolia* is rather hardy to cold.

❧ *Mañanitas*

Following the May rains which awaken the *mayitos,* heavy June thunderstorms arrive and bring forth *mañanitas.* These larger rain lilies ("tomorrow flowers" in the local vernacular) belong to *Habranthus* and have the graceful inclined blooms that give this genus its special character.

The best known *mañanita* is *Habranthus concolor,* a species found in the cactus-filled deserts surrounding the city of San Luis Potosi. Its large blossoms are accompanied by broad, gray foliage. As with the slightly smaller *H. howardii* from the brushland south of Laredo, the flowers of *H. concolor* come in a peculiar shade of desert green, a chartreuse yellow shared by a number of flowers common to arid regions.

H. concolor is certainly worthy of cultivation for its showy blossoms. To assure proper flowering, the bulbs should be given a dry winter rest. This may be accomplished by annual lifting and storing or by planting in raised beds. The large, black-coated bulbs should be protected from penetrating frost and not allowed to remain overly damp during cool weather.

On a trip through Guanahuato in July 1954, plant collectors Morris and Katherine Clint found rain lilies in leaf that they presumed to be robust specimens of *H. concolor*. They took the big bulbs home and grew them on in their Brownsville, Texas, garden. The next spring they received a delightful surprise when their planting produced several huge, snow white blossoms with rich yellow throats. They had discovered a new species, *Habranthus immaculatus*.

H. immaculatus is a good grower in gardens and soon offsets to form large clumps. When the Clints discovered it, they were especially impressed, for it looked for all the world like a pure white amaryllis. *H. immaculatus* grows and flowers in ordinary garden loam and adapts wherever it receives protection from penetrating frost. The Clints once succeeded in crossing this species with a beautiful salmon *Zephyranthes* from the Caribbean, but the delicate hybrids proved difficult to maintain. *H. immaculatus* would be well worth crossing again.

In addition to these large white and yellow *mañanitas*, Mexico also has several smaller *Habranthus* species in shades of pink or white. In Oaxaca there is even a species with peppermint stripes, *H. vittatus*. Although lovely, most of these lack the vigor needed to recommend them for garden use.

Along the roadsides of central Texas, the common yellow rain lilies of summer and autumn are borne by a small, hardy *Habranthus*. These "Texas copper lilies" (*Habranthus tubispathus* v. *texensis*) range over dry fields and prairies. Flattened, grassy foliage appears through the cool season, and diminutive, glowing blooms follow in summer. The thimble-sized flowers have streaks and stains of bronze, which make them look orange when sun shines through the translucent petals.

This little rain lily seeds and naturalizes in neglected areas and rough turfs. It seems to accept any amount of drought or abuse but seldom tarries in well-tended or -irrigated gardens. This wildling apparently resents such attempts to settle it down.

H. tubispathus ranges throughout central Texas and also turns up in northern Argentina and Uruguay. This is a very curious natural distribution shared by several American bulbs. In addition to forms resembling Texas plants, the South American populations of *H. tubispathus* occur in a lovely pink strain, v. *roseus*.

South America seems to be the headquarters for *Habranthus*, and many beautiful sorts grow there on red clays like those of Georgia or Oklahoma. Most of the species thrive in the southern United States if offered rich, acid soil and mulch to retard frost.

'Russel Manning' is a select variety often listed as a form of *H. robustus*. Enormous, funnel-shaped blossoms top its twelve-inch stems, suggesting a light pink amaryllis. This selection makes a striking accent for subtropic borders. It flowers freely through summer.

The orchid trumpets of *Habranthus brachyandrus* darken romantically to deep burgundy throats like blooms of the old-fashioned rose of Sharon (*Hibiscus syriacus*). These medium-sized blossoms complement soft pink tropical sage (*Salvia coccinea* 'Bicolor'), shrub morning glory (*Ipomoea fistulosa*), salt marsh mallow (*Kosteletzkya virginica*), or old-fashioned, frost pink China roses. They resonate

Habranthus gracilifolius

Habranthus tubispathus var. *texensis*

Zephyranthes 'Starfrost'

Zephyranthes 'Teddy Buhler'

Habranthus martinezii

Zephyranthes 'Apricot Queen'

against the strong foliage of purple heart (*Setcreasea pallida*) or purple wood-sorrel (*Oxalis regnellii* 'Triangularis').

H. martinezii accents its creamy petals with a dark olive throat. Small stature and graceful aspect give it considerable charm. It looks like a pale *H. tubispathus* top-heavy with blossom.

H. juncifolius produces narrow-petaled blooms suffused with pink. These autumn flowers appear in small clusters atop ten-inch stems. True to its Latin epithet, which means "rush-leafed," *H. juncifolius* bears distinctively round, stiff foliage.

Habranthus gracilifolius (*H. estensis*) makes flattened foliage that grows through the winter. Its elegant, rosy blossoms appear in clusters at the end of summer.

🐚 *South American* Zephyranthes

With the exception of *Zephyranthes candida* and the several *Habranthus* discussed above, the remaining South American rain lilies have been slow to enter cultivation. Jose Alberto Castillo of Buenos Aires, Argentina, has introduced a few choice varieties in recent years, a couple of which seem admirably suited to the reddish, acid clays of the South.

Zephyranthes minima is a tiny curiosity with white blossoms no larger than an onion floret. Its threadlike foliage reveals a kinship to *Z. candida*, but the scale of the plant is unique. This little Argentinian bulb would be a wonderful choice for a pot or trough planting, where its miniature charms could be appreciated close up. *Z. minima* is vigorous and multiplies rapidly from seed.

Zephyranthes flavissima is a golden beauty from Argentina and Brazil whose tongue-shaped petals spread into small stars. It lacks the drought resistance of the North American yellows, but otherwise seems easy to grow, with flowers appearing from spring to late summer. Like *Z. pulchella*, this bulb makes winter foliage that tolerates light frosts. The bulbs may also be potted for immersion in a garden pond.

Another rain lily from Argentina and Uruguay is so original and odd in its design that botanists have placed it in another genus, *Haylockia*, distinguished by a subterranean ovary. This gives these nocturnal blossoms something of the character of a crocus. The most widespread species, and the one most likely to do in the South, is *Haylockia americana*. Its cream or primrose yellow blooms appear in late summer. Three or four weeks later the underground seed pods emerge and shed papery, black seeds. These may be planted immediately for increase.

The bulbs of *H. americana* are large, with thick, black coats like rain lilies of the cooperia group. They send up several narrow, sprawling, green leaves over winter. Haylockias come from hot, subtropical regions, so they should be offered a good baking in summer.

The fire lily or flame lily of Peru (*Pyrolirion flammeum*) is an exotic ally of *Zephyranthes*. Its shocking tangerine blossoms appear in early summer with the first warm rains. The similar golden flame lily (*P. aureum*) produces orange-yellow blooms that rival daffodils. Both of these bulbs are rare and entirely tender. Except in frost-free regions, they should be dug and stored for winter.

🐚 *Hybrids*

When Dr. Howard began to hybridize rain lilies, he started by crossing *Zephyranthes rosea* and *Z. citrina*. He envisioned creating a vibrant orange bloom from the mix; but the child of this union was 'Ruth Page', a rich pink, starry flower with a white throat.

'Ruth Page' grew vigorously and proved a good parent. By mixing in turn with *Z. smallii*, *Z. traubii*, *Z. pulchella*, *Z. reginae*, and *Z. lindleyana*, Howard generated a series of beautiful miniature amaryllids in a rainbow of colors, including, eventually, the orange tone he had hoped for. He grew and distributed his best crosses, as well as a number of fine hybrids from other breeders. Several of these may be found in the gardens of fortunate Southerners today. All are rare treasures.

'Starfrost' is a lovely, soft lilac-rose with a contrasting white star. This is overlaid by a silvery sheen, as if frosted. Since it is descended from *Z. smallii*, 'Star Frost' inherits some of the sweet fragrance of that parent, as well as its free-blooming habit.

'Big Shot' is a remarkable selection producing flowers up to five inches across. These are pale cream, lightly tinged rose, and, despite their size, quite graceful. This one descends from the Mexican strain of *Z. traubii*.

'Apricot Queen' reserves her warm-colored blossoms for late summer, just as does her parent, *Z. pulchella*. The medium-sized flowers open widely to rich apricot with a yellow throat. The dark green foliage grows vigorously. Seedlings usually come true, so 'Apricot Queen' may be multiplied readily.

'Libra' is a robust child of 'Ruth Page' crossed with 'Horsetail Falls'. It answers the need for a vigorous garden rain lily with good rose-pink flowers. These are goblet shaped and appear from midspring through early fall. The wide foliage is an attractive asset. The big, black bulbs multiply swiftly, and this is another hybrid that comes true from seed. 'Libra' seems to resist cold as well as *Z. drummondii*.

'Grandjax' descends from a Ray Flagg cross of *Z. grandiflora* and an old, creamy yellow rain lily, 'Ajax', which is itself presumed to be a hybrid between *Z. candida* and *Z. citrina*. The light pink blooms of 'Grandjax' resemble candida in form and have white throats with a green central star. They bloom furiously all summer and fall and quickly multiply into thrifty patches.

'Aquarius' is a parallel hybrid produced by E.L. Brasol from 'Ajax' and *Z. candida*. When the fall rains arrive, its grassy leaves are smothered by masses of creamy yellow funnels. Like 'Grandjax', it's a rapid multiplier.

'Ellen Korsakoff' is a creation from Florida breeder Alek Korsakoff. The clone has the same parentage as 'Ruth Page', but instead of a pink flower, it's a lovely pineapple blend. It's rather tender but responds well to good culture. Rich, acid soil is best.

'Teddy Buhler' is a unique Korsakoff offspring from *Z. albiella*, a tender rain lily from Colombia with white, funnel-shaped blooms. The other parent is *Habranthus martinezii*. 'Teddy Buhler' looks much like a little, white *Habranthus* with wide, grass green foliage. It offsets quickly and provides gorgeous masses of white bloom all summer.

Another *Habranthus* hybrid of garden value is *H.* × *floryi*, a cross between *H. robustus* and *H. brachyandrus*, with a lovely mixture of characteristics from each parent. Korsakoff's hybrid of *H. martinezii* and *H. robustus* is also worthwhile. It flowers shyly when first planted, but soon multiplies into a thick patch, covered several times each summer with carpets of medium pink blooms.

On a trip through Panama, Louisiana plantsman Ira Nelson discovered another hybrid of *Z. albiella*. He introduced these tender, pink-flowered rain lilies through the Louisiana Society for Horticultural Research. They have since spread widely through Gulf Coast gardens under the name 'Panama Pink'. The tiny bulbs of this tender variety multiply and flower prolifically. The other parent of 'Panama Pink' is presumed to be *Z. rosea*. Botanists have named the hybrid *Z.* × *flaggii*.

On the island of Dominica, Padre Julio Cicero has actively grown and hybridized the native scarlet-flowered rain lily, *Zephyranthes bifolia*. This unique species occupies an anomalous position somewhere between *Zephyranthes* and *Habranthus* and also goes under the name *Habranthus cardinalis*. Padre Cicero's crosses involve *Zephyranthes rosea* and the white-flowered *Z. puertoricensis*. His hybrids are known as *Z.* × *bipuertorosea* and come in delectable shades of scarlet, salmon, and apricot-pink. Alas, all are woefully tender. North of Florida they must be restricted to pots.

❧ *The Jacala Rainbow*

Not long after Dr. Howard began hybridizing, his collecting trips to Mexico took him along the Pan-American Highway south through the state of Hidalgo. Near the town of Jacala, he stumbled upon a rain lily bonanza he could scarcely have anticipated.

The region is mountainous and lies about six thousand feet above sea level. The hillsides are filled with pockmarked outcroppings of limestone. The lush jungle of lower elevations gives way to open meadows with scattered pines, junipers, and oaks and herds of wandering cattle. This beautiful upland country-side projects a fresh and pleasant aspect.

When early summer rains freshen the moss-covered slopes, the rain lilies appear from every nook and cranny. On some slopes they are golden, on others pink. In many places the blooms are peach-colored, or yellow with red flashes on the petals. In the dry valley south of Jacala, most of the rain lilies are porcelain white. In a few places the flowers are deep blood red, a true carmine undiluted by rose or burgundy, set off by flaming golden anthers.

Katherine Clint collected in this region about the same time that Dr. Howard made his discoveries, and she sent some of these red and yellow rain lilies to botanists for determination. Eventually, the bicolored form was described in her honor as a new species, *Z. katherinae*.

It seems likely that these flowers are hybrids between the various reds and yellows growing nearby. All the different color forms share certain characters:

Zephyranthes 'Prairie Sunset'

Zephyranthes 'Grandjax'

Zephyranthes x *bipuertorosea*

Zephyranthes katherinae 'Jacala Crimson'

Zephyranthes 'Libra'

Zephyranthes 'Aquarius'
with *Manfreda undulata*

Their foliage is narrow, their bulbs small and globular, and their petals rounded or spoon shaped. Most of the flowers have long tubes.

It would take years of research to determine the true relationship of these complex forms, but it takes only a glimpse to appreciate the tremendous beauty of their warmly mingled colors. The hand of nature has gardened as well here as anywhere on earth.

❧ *Cooperanthes at Last*

As sometimes happens with avid plantsmen, a few rain lilies appeared by surprise among Dr. Howard's collection. These had probably come from a mislabeled assortment received years earlier and had taken several seasons to come to flower. When they finally revealed themselves, Howard realized he had acquired at least two clones of Lancaster's Cooperanthes hybrids.

One was a large, snowy white, like an all-white *Z. grandiflora* with an icy sparkle. This he nicknamed 'Bombay'. It seemed to be a slow grower and set no seed, but it was hardy and long-lived. The other clone looked to be one of Lancaster's pastel-colored hybrids. Howard christened it 'Prairie Sunset' for its yellow, pink-stained blooms. Unlike 'Bombay', this variety bloomed prolifically all season and ripened large pods of seed. It turned out to be one of the hardiest and most dependable *Zephyranthes* hybrids in Dr. Howard's collection, and it became one of Zephyr Gardens' favorites for its warm blend of colors.

On the long journey from Texas to India and back again, this lily had indeed been "gilded." Like a precious gem, 'Prairie Sunset' continues to grace Southern gardens today. It's a true treasure, as are all the rain lilies you may meet.

2

Petite Afrique

In the South, fall comes like a second spring, but with decidedly tropical overtones. Long-blooming salvias seem reinvigorated by the shortening days, their flowers enlarging and deepening in color. Marigolds, both annual and perennial, ripen aromatic, golden blossoms. Clear blue Cape plumbagos sag under the weight of phloxlike trusses. Cigar flower (*Cuphea micropetala*), shrimp plant (*Justicia brandegeana*), and candle bush (*Cassia alata*), swell in exotic late-season bloom.

The freshened air and moderating temperatures invite a whole array of plants into renewed activity. It's as if a gentle breeze from Africa had blown into the garden to awaken the inhabitants. This rich and rewarding season includes a surprising number of bulbs. Their exceptional flowers grace gardens at a time when they can be specially savored.

❧ Guernsey Lilies

The best known of the late bloomers belong to a group of Asian amaryllids that Southerners have long called Guernsey lilies. In standard horticultural references, this common name refers to the African *Nerine sarniensis*. In the South it often applies to the oriental *Lycoris radiata*, and Southerners are chided unfairly for their ignorance in these matters. The origin of the confusion lies properly in early botanical history.

Guernsey is one of the Channel Islands, lying between France and England in the straits of the English Channel. Bathed in the mild waters of the Gulf Stream, the island has long been a haven for plants. Since Elizabethan times, flowers raised on Guernsey have been taken to the markets of London.

One of the popular cut flowers produced on the island is *Nerine sarniensis*, a crystalline pink amaryllid originally from the Cape of Good Hope.

28

Known as Guernsey lilies in the flower trade, they became an important export early in the 1700s. According to tradition, these unusual plants arrived on the island as storm-tossed wreckage from a broken ship. The bulbs washed ashore, took root, and naturalized among the dunes.

In 1753 the Swedish naturalist Carl von Linné (Carolus Linnaeus) published descriptions of plants in the collection of his patron, George Clifford. The sumptuous account, *Hortus Cliffortianus,* included many of Linnaeus's first attempts at plant classification (he is remembered today as the founder of our modern system of plant and animal taxonomy).

His entry for the Guernsey lily is especially curious. Linnaeus relates an account of the fabled shipwreck: "Radixes ex Japonia allatae & ex nave naufraga ejectae in littus arenosum insulae Sarniae." (The bulbs were brought out of Japan and thrown from the broken ship onto the sandy shore of Guernsey Island). Linnaeus goes on to list *Lilio-narcissus japonicus* and *Lilium sarniense* as synonyms. Clearly, he thinks that the Japanese *Lycoris radiata* is the same plant as the Guernsey lily, *Nerine sarniensis.*

It's easy to see how Linnaeus erred with these two similar bulbs. *Nerine* and *Lycoris* share the habit of autumn bloom, and both flower on slender, naked stems. Strap-shaped leaves follow and grow through the winter. Both have spidery umbels of narrow-petaled flowers. The most obvious differences come from the long, projecting stamens of the *Lycoris* and from its color, a warm orange-red, rather than the sparkling pink seen in *Nerine.* Linnaeus mentions both *"genitalibus longissimis"* (very long stamens) and *"rutilo flore"* (reddish flowers) in his entry for the Guernsey lily, which leaves little doubt that it is *Lycoris radiata* he is describing.

Certainly, the bulbs grown on Guernsey Island for so many years are *Nerine.* Their lasting qualities as cut flowers far surpass *Lycoris.* Linnaeus must have assumed that the spidery flowers in George Clifford's garden were the same as the cut blooms he knew from stalls in the flower markets. The confused identity of *Lycoris radiata* perpetuated in the American South appears to be a genuine inheritance from Linnaeus. The bulbs, along with their mistaken appellation, probably came to the New World with early colonists from Europe.

As for the true *Nerine sarniensis,* its success in America has been limited, so far, to California and Oregon. In Florida and the Gulf states, *Nerine* bulbs safely winter, but the sweltering Southern summer seems to do a poor job of preparing them to flower. It is rare to get a bloom from a *Nerine* in the South and fortunate that we have several lovely *Lycoris* to take their place.

Lycoris has a fascinating denomination of its own, as the title commemorates a famous and intriguing mistress of the Roman general Marcus Antonius. Since this is a true Latin name, *Lycoris* follows the rule of receiving the accent on the antepenultimate, or third to last, syllable. You may say this name correctly (*Ly'coris*) when you are alone or among botanists, but if you wish to be understood by other gardeners, you will probably need to mispronounce it with the accent on the middle (*Lycor'is*), as with *Clematis* and *Oxalis.*

For a common name distinct from "Guernsey lily," *Lycoris* species are often called "spider lilies." This risks confusion with amaryllids such as *Hymenocallis* and *Crinum*, so careful gardeners usually amend the name to "fall spider lily" or "red spider lily." The summer flowering *L. squamigera* is sometimes called "surprise lily" or "hardy amaryllis," and the golden-flowered *L. africana* appears frequently as "hurricane lily." Since *Lycoris* come into bloom without accompanying foliage, they are also known fancifully as "naked ladies."

Lycoris radiata probably came to North America before the beginning of the nineteenth century, although there are few early records of its cultivation. The heirloom strain found in gardens is, in any case, distinct from the imported types currently available from Japan.

Studies performed by geneticists make clear that this old Southern variety has an extra dose of chromosomes. Researchers call this a triploid condition: The plants have three sets of chromosomes, rather than the diploid, or double, set of typical species. It's a state of affairs that frustrates would-be hybridizers, since the extra genes make the bulbs sterile. For gardeners, however, it's a windfall. Triploid bulbs have tremendous vigor and hardiness, and many types make especially reliable perennials. Such plants grow and flower under conditions ill-suited to ordinary forms.

Through the first half of the twentieth century, most of the *L. radiata* sold in the United States were this old triploid clone, but after World War II commercial growers in Japan began supplying American dealers with native *Lycoris*. The oriental nurseries introduced many fine bulbs at inexpensive prices, while domestic supplies simultaneously dwindled. The old triploid strain now has become difficult to obtain, although each autumn it flowers by thousands in gardens throughout the South.

If you are offered offset *Lycoris* bulbs from someone's garden, chances are they will be progeny of this prolific triploid variant. These bulbs may become nearly as large as daffodils. On heavy clays they bloom more readily than diploid types.

Where soils are well drained and on the acid side, the commercial strains of *Lycoris radiata* succeed nearly as well as the old garden variety, but their smaller bulbs produce flowers a couple of weeks earlier. If both kinds are planted strategically through a garden, the *Lycoris radiata* flowering season may be stretched over a month.

Lycoris rate among the choice bulbs for woodland, and nearly all the species associate well among trees or in borders of shrubs. Their early-ripening foliage matures as growth commences in spring, so they may be planted under leafless hardwoods and even under briefly deciduous live oaks. All *Lycoris* enjoy soils enriched with leaf litter and humus, and the more delicate species require them. Their fragile, spidery flowers are at their best in sheltered groves where wind and sun cannot reach in to cause premature withering.

With their long, feathery stamens, many *Lycoris* recall deciduous azaleas, and their blossoms issue a similar impression of grace and wild woodland beauty. The elegant "bird cages" formed by the clustered flowers attract butterflies, who stop to sip from the quiet blooms as they migrate southward each autumn.

These graceful, slender-stemmed flowers practically arrange themselves in gardens and combine happily in a variety of settings. Dark-leafed aucuba or cream-variegated pittosporum make good glossy foliage companions. To soften the bareness of the tall, leafless stems, *Lycoris* may be positioned among over-plantings of Southern shield fern (*Thelypteris kunthii*), maidenhair fern (*Adiantum capillus-veneris*), Japanese anemone (*Anemone* × *hybrida*), or other shade-loving perennials. A simple backdrop of mossy boulders or leaf-littered earth also affords a lovely, dramatic contrast.

Bulbs of *L. radiata* and other *Lycoris* are usually available in late summer. If set immediately in the ground, the larger bulbs may flower the first season, but most *Lycoris* test the planter's patience and take a year of settling in before blooming. These flowers resent frequent disturbances and will punish gardeners by exacting a similar waiting period following division and replanting. These slow starts are one reason for the *Lycoris* reputation of erratic and unreliable flowering. Another cause stems from susceptibility to winter cold.

Lycoris may be grouped in two broad hardiness categories: "evergreen" types, which send up leaves in autumn, and late-leafing varieties, which emerge in early spring. Since the first group keeps foliage through the winter, leaf damage from harsh freezes sometimes prevents bloom the subsequent autumn.

Although tenderness limits a few *Lycoris* to culture in the lower South, several are thoroughly hardy. In their native homelands the species range through upper Burma, China, Japan, and Korea, where many experience severe cold. In American gardens *L. radiata* regularly endures five degrees F without damage, and less if protected by leaves or snow cover.

🌸 *Winter-Green* Lycoris

In addition to *L. radiata,* several colorful species and garden hybrids retain leaves through the winter. Their foliage is an attractive feature, helping to give otherwise dormant gardens a lush, lively appearance. The dark green leaves come to blunt tips and have distinctive milky stripes down their centers.

The first *Lycoris* cultivated in American gardens may well have been the golden *L. africana* (*L. aurea*). These bulbs are common about the ancient Spanish city of St. Augustine and presumably have grown there since colonial times. In spite of its botanical name, *L. africana*'s homelands are the subtropical provinces of China. Floridians know these flowers as hurricane lilies, and their spidery clumps of bloom are a September feature of many Gulf Coast gardens.

This golden spider lily is one of the truly magnificent flowers of the subtropics. Its two-foot spikes bear whorled umbels of cadmium blossoms, each with gracefully recurved and undulating petals. The airy groups of flowers have a jaunty, upright tilt, which gives them special flair.

After blooming, the bulbs throw up lush fountains of dark green, pointed leaves with a bluish cast. These leafy masses resemble giant *Liriope* clumps and persist through winter if protected from frost. The foliage withers in any hard freeze, however, and such disasters inhibit blooming.

As with the old garden strain of *L. radiata, Lycoris africana* has disappeared from modern nursery sources. Its place has been taken by an imposter, *Lycoris traubii,* which Japanese nurserymen discovered on the island of Formosa (Taiwan). These bulbs are invariably sold as *L. aurea,* but reveal their true identity upon blooming. *L. traubii'*s saffron blossoms have wider, more flattened petals than the orange-toned *L. africana,* and the blooms are disposed symmetrically at 90-degree angles from the stem. The winter foliage of *L. traubii* is dark green and comes up about two weeks later than that of *L. africana.*

For most gardeners the substitution goes unnoticed, as both species have essentially yellow blossoms. The exchange is welcome in frost-prone regions, for *L. traubii* has greater cold tolerance. It flowers regularly in plantings as far north as Memphis, Tennessee, and may endure temperatures down to twelve degrees F with little damage to the foliage.

Frost-hardiness for both yellow-flowered *Lycoris* improves when they are planted on sand, since such soils hold warmth better than clays. Gardeners in marginal regions may create raised beds of sandy soil to accommodate their bulbs. A small nook near a sheltered south wall offers a suitable home for several of these flamboyant golden blossoms. Where winter cold is not a threat, *L. traubii* and *L. africana* relish culture on heavy clays and may be treated to plentiful applications of compost and manure.

At the same time that Japanese importers began shipping *L. traubii* to America, they also began distributing bulbs of cream-colored varieties that they labeled *Lycoris alba.* These resembled *L. radiata* but had milky blooms tinted various shades of yellow, salmon, or pink. Botanists identified several strains among these "white"-flowered *Lycoris* during the 1950s, and various plants received such names as *Lycoris albiflora, L. straminea, L. elsiae, L. howdyshelii,* and *L. caldwellii.*

Today these "species" are regarded as hybrids derived from crosses between the scarlet *L. radiata* and the golden *L. africana,* saffron *L. traubii,* or other oriental species. The hybrids make fine garden subjects and flower usefully along with the red and yellow types in early September. They seem nearly as hardy as *L. radiata* and show excellent vigor. Their pale blossoms offer just the right tones to light up dark places under evergreen oaks, and the bulbs seem not to mind heavy competition from tree roots. They are still marketed by importers today as *Lycoris alba.*

Hybridizers in Japan and the United States have introduced a handful of artificial *Lycoris* crosses bred along lines similar to these wild plants. Most remain rare in the bulb trade, but practically any named *Lycoris* is worth obtaining for trial, if opportunity arises.

One fall-foliage type shows special promise. It's a cross of the warm red *L. radiata* and a hardy, pink-lavender-flowered species. The hybrid, *Lycoris* × *Jacksoniana,* grows readily through the South and Southwest, flowering in September with rich peach-wine blooms touched blue on the petal tips.

❧ *Spring-Foliage* Lycoris

The lavender and pink tones seen in *Lycoris* × *Jacksoniana* come from *L. sprengeri,* a species in the spring-foliage section of *Lycoris.* These late-leafing types are the

Lycoris aurea

Lycoris traubii

Lycoris radiata

Lycoris x *Jacksoniana*

Lycoris albiflora

Lycoris squamigera

most cold-hardy members of the group, many thriving in the middle and upper South.

Along the Gulf Coast and in Florida, these same *Lycoris* are mysteriously unreliable. They refuse to flower even when their bulbs thrive and increase. High soil temperatures are the apparent culprit, as this seems to inhibit bud development. Careful siting in shaded beds of leafy groundcover helps to keep bulbs cooler and may permit blooming in warm regions.

The most popular of the spring growers is *L. squamigera,* an old garden selection known as the magic lily. One rarely finds a more beautiful flower possessed of such an undemanding disposition. It's nearly ideal for gardens in the middle and upper South and even into the cold climates of the Midwest. On both sandy acid soils and heavy alkaline clays, *L. squamigera* thrives.

This species makes some of the largest bulbs in the genus, and it multiplies swiftly into substantial clumps. Its broad, gray leaves look like extraordinarily robust narcissus foliage and appear and disappear in concert with spring daffodils. This tremendous herbage can become something of an embarrassment, as it looks especially untidy while dying away in late spring. Naturalistic treatment in a woodland setting is the usual solution.

Sometime after the Fourth of July, rainfall triggers the thick scapes of the "surprise lilies" to bolt upward from the ground. They rise swiftly, in four or five days expanding to crowns of succulent, lilac-pink buds. The clustered blossoms open to look like small amaryllises and shimmer with lavender highlights on their broad rounded petals.

Like the triploid *L. radiata,* this strong-growing species enjoys an extra set of chromosomes, which fuel unusual vigor. Genetic evidence suggests that these were acquired through hybridization. *L. squamigera* appears to be an unusually lovely garden "mule" descended from a cross between the straw-colored *L. straminea* and the rosy pink *L. incarnata.* Whether this mixing occurred in nature or in the forgotten garden of some oriental flower lover, no one knows. *L. squamigera* reportedly came to America with a certain Dr. Hall of Bristol, Rhode Island, who had grown the flowers in his garden in Shanghai, China, prior to the American Civil War.

Several other spring-growing *Lycoris* have made their way to North America, but none approach *L. squamigera* in prominence or widespread adaptability. The most commonly available in the trade are *L. sanguinea,* with rather small clusters of orange-red blooms, and *L. sprengeri,* with light pink flowers. *Lycoris incarnata* is occasionally offered as well; its rose blooms are accented by electric blue petals.

All of these have gray-green spring foliage and produce flowers in late summer along with *L. squamigera.* They perform well in the upper South but seem to dislike the heat of the Gulf Coast states. *Lycoris haywardii,* a natural hybrid imported by Wyndham Hayward of Winter Park, Florida, is exceptional in this regard. Although it produces its foliage in the spring and grows well in cold regions, its orchid pink blooms appear generously even in the deep South. It remains unfortunately rare in the bulb trade.

❧ *Hardy Golden* Lycoris

Shortly before the 1949 Communist takeover of China, the United States Department of Agriculture received bulbs from the Sun Yat-sen Memorial Garden in Nanking. Among them was a *Lycoris* with golden yellow blooms like *L. africana* and gray spring foliage like *L. squamigera*. These proved hardy at Glen Dale, Maryland, and Dr. Hamilton Traub described the new plant as *Lycoris chinensis*. Unfortunately, this variety proved slow to propagate, and importations from China remained closed for decades.

In the 1950s Nashville garden expert and *Lycoris* fancier Sam Caldwell invited listeners to his radio talk show to share information about the spider lilies in their gardens. One called in to describe a yellow *Lycoris* she had collected while working as a missionary in the region between Huchow and Hangchow, China. This woman, a Mrs. Henry Sperry, had shared the bulbs among several gardeners in central Tennessee, where they were thriving. Caldwell dubbed the bulbs *"Lycoris sperryi"* in honor of their collector.

Both of these hardy yellow spider lilies propagate at a snail's pace from seed or offsets. They remain regretfully rare in gardens. The recent reopening of China to horticultural exchange with the West makes it likely that they and their kind may become more available in the near future.

❧ *Mediterraneans*

Many of the bulbs growing in the countries around the Mediterranean Sea choose to blossom in the fall, for this is the beginning of the growing season in these climes. Several derive from meadows of *terra-rossa*, a peculiar reddish, claylike earth similar to many soils found in the South. Bulbs from these regions often perform famously on dry, raised rockeries.

Chief among these autumnal bloomers is *Sternbergia lutea*, a golden flower suggestive of a large, waxen crocus. Its luminous goblet-shaped blossoms appear soon after the arrival of September rains. These living drops of sun brighten gardens for a fortnight. As the brilliant flowers fade, the dark green foliage rises in their place. Narrow and distinctively keeled, it makes short, leafy clumps with the somber, pedestrian appearance of mondo grass (*Ophiopogon*). *Sternbergia* leaves last through the winter and die down with warm weather.

The scientific name of these bulbs commemorates an accomplished German botanist, Count Caspar Sternberg (1761–1838). Early references, such as Parkinson's *Paradisus* and *Hortus Floridus* of Crispin de Pass (1615), identify these bulbs as "autumn daffodils." Gardeners ever since have puzzled over the comparison of this *Crocus*-like flower to a *Narcissus*.

The analogy is actually a sound one from a botanical standpoint, since *Sternbergia* and *Narcissus* both belong to the amaryllis family. Crocuses are members of the iris tribe, growing from corms instead of the true bulbs shared by amaryllids. Still, this hardly satisfies most gardeners.

It may be helpful to understand the origin of the term "daffodil," for this name did not always belong to the golden trumpets of spring. The word derives through corruption from the Greek *asphodel,* which in classical times applied to almost any lilylike plant. As a Mediterranean native, *Sternbergia*'s claim on this title seems as valid as any narcissus'.

Nevertheless, those uncomfortable with calling these goblet-shaped blossoms "daffodils" have added several additional sobriquets. Some contend that *Sternbergia* is the biblical "lily of the field." Indeed, this may be, for it is a common wildflower in the Levant. Other names applied to these bulbs are "Mt. Etna lily" and (of course) "yellow autumn crocus."

Modern planters may take their pick of these, for each seems suitable. Unfortunately, none of the monikers applied to these beautiful flowers can really be called a "common" name, for the bulbs themselves remain relatively obscure. These brilliant flames of autumn ought to be widely planted, yet *Sternbergia* resides primarily in the neglected borders of old homesteads.

These golden blossoms are among those mysterious, sensible flowers that seem to choose the gardeners for whom they will prosper. Invariably, their happiest homes are around the humble bungalows of honest folk, rather than in the well-tended borders of aristocrats. Leave these flowers benignly to their own devices, and they bloom faithfully for decades. Transplant and pamper them to feature as some conceit of grand design, and they modestly die away.

There is a tradition in the South that Thomas Jefferson was the first to import *Sternbergia* to America, and that the bulbs passed along in gardens descend from his original planting at Monticello. If this is true, then his bulbs must have prospered mightily, for there are antebellum *Sternbergia* plantings scattered from Virginia to Texas. In several gardens they spread like fantastic golden carpets beneath the dark, sprawling branches of ancient oaks.

These old bulbs have slightly smaller blooms and narrower leaves than the types offered in the Dutch trade; otherwise, they seem similar. Their Mediterranean origin would seem to imply a love for dry, sunny slopes and fast drainage, but in the middle and upper South, *Sternbergia* thrives on heavy clays. In warmer gardens along the Gulf, some shade will be appreciated, and the bulbs usually prove more permanent if given raised positions.

In addition to the Dutch and "Jeffersonian" strains of *Sternbergia,* specialists occasionally import a handful of other types. All are worthy of trial, especially in more temperate sections of the South.

S. sicula is a narrow-petaled species from the stony hills of Sicily and Greece. It flowers freely in September with starry, golden blooms. *S. fischerana* offers its large, light yellow flowers on six-inch stems accompanied by gray-blue, upright foliage. These December blossoms seem none the worse for exposure to zero degree F temperatures. *S. clusiana* flowers earlier and holds its blooms close to the ground.

A great rarity discovered in 1978, *S. candida* has already been endangered in its native Turkey by overly zealous collectors. This is no wonder, for the flowers sound particularly enticing. The cream-colored blooms break sternbergia traditions not only in their color, but also by blossoming in spring. These bulbs remain expensive and hard to come by, but they may be more available in the future. They would be well worth trying in Southern gardens.

 *Autumn Narcissi*

Along the Strait of Gibraltar and the adjacent western Mediterranean, the brush-covered hills provide homes for three odd little bulbs that flower in the fall. These aren't *Sternbergia*, but true narcissi. Their tiny blossoms hardly afford the show we envision from daffodils, but these novelties succeed in the South and add diversity to our list of autumn blooms.

The first species, *Narcissus viridiflorus*, makes a slender, little plant with narrow foliage. The clusters of star-shaped, tubular flowers have tiny, practically nonexistent cups, and, as you might expect from the botanical name, they are green. You could miss the little blooms altogether, but for their powerfully sweet fragrance.

The others, *N. serotinus* and *N. elegans*, face upward like rain lilies and have rounded, white petals centered around small, yellow cups. The flat-faced flowers are mostly solitary and only an inch or so wide. *N. serotinus* flowers before the appearance of its solitary leaf. This distinguishes it from *N. elegans*, whose bulbs produce several leaves prior to flowering.

B.Y. Morrison, horticulturist, bulb fancier, and resident of Pass Christian, Mississippi, reported success with all of these species in his Gulf Coast garden. The biggest challenge faced in growing them seems to have been getting enough of the tiny things to create some garden effect. Such miniatures warrant spots near paths or on raised beds, where their small October blooms can be seen and admired. They also make fine choices for trough plantings.

In the same regions of the Mediterranean where the autumn narcissi proliferate, their distant relatives, the snowflakes (*Leucojum* spp.), have also experimented with fall flowering. Of the handful of species, the most likely to succeed in Southern gardens is *Leucojum autumnale*, the autumn snowflake. Like *Narcissus viridiflorus*, these are plants of slender build, with narrow, winter-growing foliage that resembles clusters of emerald knitting needles. Tiny, white, bell-shaped blossoms appear before the leaves on top of bright green, threadlike stems.

Autumn snowflakes adapt to beds of sandy soil, but these miniatures are so frail and delicate in appearance that they are customarily reserved for pots. They make fine companions for the little narcissi and will continue in bloom over a surprisingly long season if sheltered from hard frost.

Autumn Crocuses

Although there are a number of true autumn crocuses, including several garden varieties to be discussed shortly, the plant most often met under this name is not a *Crocus* at all, but a *Colchicum*. These lilylike perennials form large, fleshy corms, which have the novel ability to flower while still unplanted. Bulb dealers have found them to be a popular item in garden centers.

Colchicum autumnale, the meadow saffron, is the most frequently offered. The stemless, lavender blooms appear in September, often while yet on display at the nursery. Several weeks afterward, the gray, boat-shaped leaves follow. This foliage looks like oversized tulip leaves, which should come as no surprise, since both flowers belong to the lily family.

Unfortunately for Southerners, the commonly available colchicums are as ill-suited to our warm climate as most of their tulip cousins. Only in the damper, cooler parts of the South will they remain more than a season. For any hope of success, they must be given shady sites in rich woodland where they will never be subjected to drought.

Colchicum has a wide distribution around the eastern Mediterranean, and there are probably several varieties suited to warmer sections. *C. psaridis*, a native of the *terra-rossa* pasturelands of Greece, is one that might do. Unfortunately, the varieties in the trade come mostly from the high Alps. For Southern gardeners it seems better to forget these lilies and concentrate on genuine fall-blooming *Crocus*.

The most famous autumn crocus is celebrated less for its beauty than for its value as a colorful spice. This need not be, for it is as lovely as any of its tribe. The medium-sized, purple-veined, lavender flowers of *Crocus sativus* have been cultivated since classical times for their long, crimson stigmas, the source of saffron. These are picked and dried to make the flavorful powder used in the famous Spanish *paella*. Saffron remains among the most costly seasonings, due to the tremendous labor required to process the tiny stigmas. If a gardener enjoys cooking, a homegrown patch of saffron will provide a cost-effective source of culinary flavoring, as well as a warm show of autumn blooms.

Crocus sativus occurs wild in several forms scattered from Italy to Turkey. Present-day commercial production occurs mostly in Spain but also extends through the Middle East to India. The clone in widespread cultivation is a centuries-old selection chosen for its prolific flowering.

Corms of this crocus respond to rich soil by enlarging to the size of gladiolus tubers, each producing several November blossoms. In Spain the saffron growers customarily divide plantings each season and apply a generous manuring. In the humid South, feedings such as this might invite summer attacks from soil fungi. Any fertilizer given should be modestly applied during the cool season of the year.

Under garden cultivation the corms soon break up into a multitude of smaller tubers. These need to be reset every two or three years to keep them flowering, but they otherwise persist and multiply indefinitely without additional aid. The large flowers, with their netlike patterns of violet, arrive welcomely just as the garden seems to be giving up for the season. The blooms appear sporadically from the end of October through November, depending on weather.

After flowering, these crocuses send up long, grassy foliage. If the garden receives visits from mice or rabbits, these tender leaves will need protection, as they are a favorite winter browse. A few prickly branches taken from a juniper, pine, or other tree may be laid over the crocus patch to defend the plants from hungry marauders. The foliage will continue to grow through the twigs without ill effect. Thus guarded, the leaves may perform their service of collecting sunlight to feed next year's blossoms.

One of the most valuable fall crocuses in Southern gardens is still making its way around the horticultural world. Although now thoroughly established in the bulb trade, *Crocus goulimyi* was described as a new species from Greece as recently as 1955. Its excellent vigor and free-flowering nature have won it many friends in warm climates.

The soft lavender blooms of this variety hoist themselves above the ground on long, slender perianth tubes. This sets *C. goulimyi* apart from other fall crocuses and gives the plants a particularly elegant appearance. The small corms multiply into large patches and seem to accept many kinds of soil. In their native habitat on the Mani Peninsula of the Peloponnesse, they grow in *terra-rossa* fields among stones and at the foot of old rock walls.

The delicately tinted blooms of this crocus combine with groundcovers of prostrate gray sedum, silvery dianthus, or the lime green *Origanum vulgare* 'Aurea'. They also naturalize happily in a sage-toned carpet of unmown buffalograss, along with sternbergias, rain lilies, and other low-growing fall flowers. *C. goulimyi* offers an ideal underplanting for a many-stemmed witch hazel (*Hamamelis virginiana*), whose golden froth of autumn blooms line pliant twigs at the same season.

In the cooler portions of the South, the favored crocus of autumn is the showy crocus, *C. speciosus*. This Turkish variety can be generous with its large, violet-stained blossoms, and the corms are usually inexpensive and widely available. The big flowers are colored a silvery gray on the exterior and glow inside with yellow throats and large, reddish stigmas like the saffron crocus.

'Cassiope' is a vigorous clone developed by the Dutch firm of Van Tubergen from the old variety 'Aitchisonii'. Its aster blue flowers appear in late October or November. This seems to be the most heat-tolerant variant and is more reliable in the lower South than other cultivars.

Crocus medius bears lilac flowers, with a purple star in the throat made by dark veins in the petals. This species derives from hillsides along the French and Italian Riviera and performs well in much of the South. It looks a great deal like the saffron crocus but remains smaller. *C. laevigatus* is a choice Grecian variety with silvery purple blooms, blessed with a honey-lemon scent, appearing late in November and December. Although harder to find and slower growing than some, it's worth seeking out.

Several other fall crocuses are less easily coaxed into settling down. Leafy woodland soils offer the best opportunities. The white-flowered *C. ochroleucus* and the lavender *C. kotschyanus* and its white-throated form, *leucopharynx*, bloom successfully almost anywhere for their first season or two. They become finicky after that. If your garden proves not entirely to their liking, beds will need replenishing after three or four years, as the old corms dwindle away.

🌸 *Cyclamens*

In the upper South some of the most beautiful fall flowers come from hardy cyclamens. These are Mediterranean relatives of the tender florist cyclamen (*Cyclamen persicum*). They come from regions where at least some frost can be expected in winter and summers are long and dry. The easiest and most prolific in Southern gardens is the ivy-leafed *Cyclamen hederifolium*, still found in many catalogs under the name *C. neapolitanum*.

Crocus goulimyi

Sternbergia fischerana

Allium stellatum

Schoenocaulon drummondii

Rhodophiala bifida: var. *bifida* and
   var. *spathaceae*

Rhodophiala bifida var. *granataflora*

The pale, turned-back petals of these fragile blooms might be overlooked if seen only one or two at a time. Where these tuberous flowers are satisfied, though, they continue to swell and multiply over years until fifty or more rose, white, or carmine blossoms rise from each four-inch corm. The individual blooms are borne on long, corkscrew-like stems that creep briefly under the leaf litter before turning upward toward the November sun.

The places cyclamens like best are shallow, lime-filled soils under oaks or other trees whose roots sop up excess moisture and whose canopy of foliage rains down a gentle manuring each autumn. Here the shallow tubers should remain unmolested, with a natural covering of fallen, brown leaves. In such favorable positions, the plants will seed themselves into large patches. After the flowers appear, the tubers send up masses of succulent, dark green leaves marked attractively with gray and silver. This winter foliage is a feature lovely enough to warrant cultivation of cyclamens all by itself.

In the lower South, where soils remain warm year-round, the tubers of cyclamens are liable to melt away from rot if not kept absolutely dry over summer. The hardy species are probably best forgotten near the Gulf. However, if the garden includes sheltered positions where frost is rare, the tender *C. persicum* may be used for winter bedding. The delicate roots of these corms should be disturbed as little as possible, so small cyclamens may be plunged into the ground pot and all, then removed to dry out over summer. *C. persicum* is one of the few cool-season flowers that blooms happily in the gloom beneath a live oak.

🌸 Oxblood Lilies

Rotting timbers and sagging porches mark the sites of many farms in the South. The old frame houses were once homes of folk who raised cotton. After only a generation of productivity, the greedy crops combined with shortsighted farming techniques to destroy fertility. The worn-out land was abandoned and the populace moved away, leaving homes to molder and decay.

Hard freezes usually kill back the weeds in December, so if you visit the old houses in January or February, it's not unusual to find rows of bright green, strap-shaped leaves shining among the brown grass. Usually, the leaves mark the line of a former path or drive. Sometimes they make circles on the lawn, or edge some old property line or foundation. They are often the only remainder of the garden that once grew around the house.

If you return in early autumn, you may see the flowers of these bulbs. They are not likely to be mistaken for any others, though they bear a strong family resemblance to amaryllises. The deep crimson blossoms appear in small clusters on top of slender stems less than a foot tall, so that the ground seems smothered in red. They are known by several quaint names, but the one most evocative of their singularly brilliant appearance is "oxblood lily."

Botanically, these little amaryllids have shifted about under several titles and still are the subject of modest debate. In British and American literature, they usually appear under the label *Hippeastrum advenum*. Recent South American floras are more likely to name them *Rhodophiala bifida*. Since the bulbs are natives of Argentina and Uruguay, it seems proper to defer to the Latin American specialists, who presumably know them best.

The waxy, green, two-valved spathe of the oxblood lily is a characteristic it shares with *Hippeastrum*. The narrow foliage and winter growth habit of *Rhodophiala* are more like *Habranthus*. This relationship seems confirmed by the capacity of these two genera to hybridize. The oxblood lily crosses fairly easily with *Habranthus juncifolius*, although the offspring are sterile.

There are several additional *Rhodophiala* scattered down the narrow country of Chile, many with lovely blooms in cream, yellow, and vermillion. None has successfully entered Southern gardens, for these species are denizens of bitterly cold mountains, barren deserts, and windswept Patagonian prairies. They loathe the heat, humidity, and horrendously poor soils on which *R. bifida* thrives.

No other Southern bulb can match the fierce vigor, tenacity, and adaptability of the oxblood lily. Whether planted on worn-out gumbo clay or on impoverished sand, the long-necked, black bulbs make themselves at home. The plants send out thick, white roots, which contract and pull them deeply into the soil, sometimes as far as eighteen inches down. Safely hidden in the cool earth, they multiply steadily into healthy clumps. Although probably best divided while dormant, they seem to grow along even when disturbed during their winter growing season.

The brilliant crimson flowers appear along with the first autumn rains. During hot weather, blooms last only a few days, so the bulbs are of most value when shaded from strong sun. Since their foliage grows through the winter, oxblood lilies make good woodland companions for *Lycoris* and *Sternbergia*. If used in a sunny border, these vibrant flowers make a happy contrast to the soft gray and lavender of catmint (*Nepeta faassenii* 'Six Hills Giant') and a dramatic complement to the smoky filigrees of bronze fennel (*Foeniculum vulgare* 'Rubrum').

Like the old horticultural stocks of *Lycoris* and *Sternbergia*, the oxblood lilies in Southern gardens constitute a special strain. These heirlooms rarely seed, but they do multiply quickly from offsets. New bulblets form in a curious twisting pattern about the mother bulbs. As the oxblood lilies increase, divisions may be passed from garden to garden. In this way these plants have slowly spread across the South.

A few connoisseurs raise a pink variety of oxblood lily, *spathaceae*, but this color form is likely to remain rare in gardens. The pinks lack the vigor of the reds and seldom offset. They must be reproduced from seed, which is slow growing and doesn't always come true. Even rarer are orange-red types (variety *granataflora*). Like the pinks, they must be seed grown.

As beautiful and appealing as the pinks and oranges may seem to the mind's eye, they really have far less to offer gardens than the reds. It's not color that's at issue: It's strength and endurance that make these bulbs special in the first place. The ability to persist and survive counts a great deal. Our gardens are much richer for plants that happily blossom through adversity, like the old red oxblood lily.

The vigorous heirloom strain of *Rhodophiala* seems to be of true Southern origin, for it is unknown to gardeners in Argentina, where the bulbs are native. Although oxblood lilies are distributed widely through the South, they are especially common in the old Germanic communities of central Texas. Their concentration centers on Austin.

During the 1840s central Texas attracted immigrants from southern and western Germany, who came to the fledgling republic in search of political and intellectual freedom. Many were persons of romantic sensibility, with a love for nature and yearnings for an honest, agricultural life. They were captivated by the rugged, oak-covered hills and clear-flowing springs of the new land.

One among them, Peter Henry Oberwetter, took a special interest in the plants growing on his farm near Comfort, Texas. Oberwetter began collecting the wild rain lilies he found on the hills, and he sent them through the mail to gardeners around the world. During the Civil War, he moved south into Mexico (many German colonists sided with the North during this conflict, and left Texas to avoid persecution). While in Mexico Oberwetter continued to collect and export bulbs; when the war ended, he moved to Austin, where he lived until about 1915.

During this period Oberwetter introduced oxblood lilies to America, while he sent the native giant prairie lily, *Zephyranthes drummondii*, around the world. As he cultivated bulbs in Austin, he must have discovered and selected the vigorous *Rhodophiala* strain we now enjoy. His legacy lives on in the oxblood lilies flowering each autumn in countless dooryard gardens throughout the South.

❧ *Coconut Lilies*

One of the best bulbous plants of the fall is a curious native lily. If it were taller, it could pass for a foxtail lily (*Eremurus*), but even at its customary height of eighteen inches, it makes a bold upward thrust in the garden. This audacious plant is the coconut lily, *Schoenocaulon drummondii*. Its leaves look like graceful fountains of green grass, and its flowers resemble skinny bottlebrushes.

The almost unpronounceable botanical name comes from the Greek *schoinos kaulos*, or "rush stem," which describes the slender aspect of these flowers. *Schoenocaulon* has dispensed with petals altogether, so the bottlebrush effect comes from the feathery spikes of creamy stamens. These are tipped with fawn-colored anthers dusted in light yellow pollen, and the whole contraption smells delightfully of fresh coconut. This is a very unusual and pleasant fragrance emanating from a thoroughly hardy, unpretentious flower.

Coconut lilies are wildflowers of prairies in southern Texas and northern Mexico, where they appear during September or October, depending on rainfall. When moisture is sufficient, they keep their bright green foliage year-round. In droughty seasons the leaves die down during midsummer. *Schoenocaulon* thrives on sunny slopes and seems to accept almost any soil. Plantings quickly increase with offsets and self-sown seedlings. The grassy colonies blend nicely with other prairie perennials in a naturalized meadow.

The bulbs of the coconut lily are papery and thin, and they store poorly if allowed to become completely dry. As long as the roots can be replanted within a week or two after digging, *Schoenocaulon* transplants readily. The best time for division is early summer.

🐚 *Autumnal Onions*

One of the most charming of all the late bulbs is another native American, the prairie onion, *Allium stellatum*. Despite its pedestrian common name, these graceful flowers possess an air of sophistication. Globular clusters of starry, pink blooms are borne on six- to eight-inch stems, each with the sinuous curve of a swan's neck.

Through several weeks in October and November, orchid-tinted blooms gradually expand from the gently nodding buds into a bomb-burst of crowded, star-shaped flowers. The pearly blossoms are clear and bright in the crisp sunlight of Indian summer. They provide the ideal complement to falling drifts of tawny autumn leaves.

After blooming, the green, grassy foliage of the onion follows. The flowers usually ripen hard, black seeds, which may be planted straightaway. If the capsules are left to open on the stems, the tiny seedlings will sprout below to form a green winter lawn. Their foliage dies away with warm weather. In two or three seasons, they will begin to flower with their parent bulbs.

Prairie onions grow in moist grasslands from Texas north to Illinois and Minnesota. They perform admirably on heavy clay soils but also adapt to sandy ones. They seem indifferent to the heat and humidity of the South, since fair weather prevails by the time the bulbs begin to grow actively.

3

Winter Blooms

With the encouragement of September rains and open weather through the first weeks of autumn, December often sees blossoms from the paperwhites, *Narcissus tazetta* v. *papyraceus*. These are the delicate harbingers of a varied race of polyanthus narcissus to follow.

"Paperwhite" and *papyraceus* aptly describe the parchment quality and glistening whiteness of these flowers. The specific epithet, *tazetta*, originates from an Italian term for the "little cups," or coronas, of the blossoms, which are centered like expresso mugs in the elfin saucers formed by the surrounding petals. This species and its hybrids are popularly known as polyanthus narcissi for their multiple clusters of scented blossoms. These appear in groups of four to twenty, on top of hollow, sharp-edged stems.

Like the autumn-flowering *N. serotinus* and *N. elegans*, paperwhites are natives of the stony *terra-rossa* fields around the Mediterranean. As a gardener might apprehend from this, they thrive in mild, sunny regions but prove finicky in frosty areas. *Narcissus tazetta* v. *papyraceus* is most common in Spain, southern France, and Italy, where it has been cultivated since gardening began. The paperwhite appears to be an old selection, rather than a wild form. It may now be found naturalized throughout the warm regions of the world.

During the 1500s and 1600s, narcissi became great favorites of flower growers in England and Holland. Large numbers of bulbs were introduced to the south of France and the Channel Islands, where they were cultivated to provide winter blooms. In 1629 Parkinson listed ninety different sorts of *Narcissus*, the greater part of which were forms of *N. tazetta*. Many of these retained prominence well into the 1800s.

With the development of hardy hybrid

daffodils in the nineteenth century, the old multiflowered narcissi began to drop from growers's lists. Several cold winters combined with Holland's devastation during World War I to finally end the long reign of *Narcissus tazetta*. Except for the paperwhite and a few other types used for forcing, the group largely vanished from commercial trade.

It is in the warm regions of the world, in the South, California, New Zealand, and Australia, that the old *tazetta* varieties persist. Here they may be found adorning humble country dooryards and neglected cemeteries of the last century. Some are still passed along with their names intact from the 1600s, but more often these oldsters travel under affectionate bynames like "Pearl," "Twelve Apostles," or "Seventeen Sisters." Many are superb garden plants. For sheer bounty of color, reliable performance, grace, beauty, and longevity, these old tazettas remain unsurpassed.

❧ *Paperwhites*

The paperwhites usually begin their season in autumn. Between cold blasts from northers, they flower sporadically from late November through February. Temperatures below twenty degrees F occasionally damage these winter blooms, and if the mercury falls below ten, the silvery gray foliage may be nipped. Nevertheless, they seem to recover from these disasters, annually contributing plentiful flowers to gardens throughout the South.

Paperwhites are usually only fair in size, form, and substance, but their translucent cups issue a distinctive, penetrating fragrance. Maybe so musky and powerful as to be nauseating, it is nevertheless one of the scents whose very essence connotes winter. Even meager stems of paperwhites make fine flowers for cutting or garden adornment.

The major fault of these narcissi is a tendency to grow shallowly and to split and multiply to excess, thereby reducing bloom. Every few years the matted bulbs must be divided and reset at depths of four to six inches. This encourages the bulbs to enlarge and improves subsequent flowering.

The older strains of paperwhites have recently given way to newly bred selections developed in Israel, such as 'Ziva', 'Jerusalem', and 'Galilee'. The new types have superior size and substance but have not been in gardens long enough for sure reporting on their permanence. Their large bulbs probably will break into small ones after a few seasons, just as their old-fashioned relations do.

❧ *Chinese Sacred Lilies*

Hurricanes periodically collide with the maze of bays, lagoons, and barrier islands lining the Gulf and Atlantic coasts. The stormy tides inevitably crash over the dunes to tear at homes built foolishly near the waters. They often leave little but rows of wooden pilings projecting through the sand. Early in January the empty fields that once held houses fill with the sweet, exotic perfume of Chinese sacred lilies (*Narcissus tazetta* v. *orientalis*) persisting among the wreckage.

The Chinese sacred lily, or 'Grand Emperor', a first cousin of the paperwhite, is similarly valued for forcing. The fragrance of the blooms is distinctive; a heady aroma suggestive of spiced oranges. Although this narcissus occurs as a waif along the coasts of China and Japan, students of narcissi believe the variety originated in the Mediterranean. Presumably, Middle Eastern traders brought these bulbs to China centuries ago. They are held in high regard in the Orient, where the fragrant flowers are picked as decorations for winter festivals and the round bulbs are set with hooks as lures to capture octopus.

Everything about this narcissus conveys exuberance. Its sizeable blossoms appear in generous umbels of twelve to twenty. The broad, white petals are accented by substantial orange cups. Added to the distinctive blossoms are unusually lush, pale green leaves and the vigorous constitution of a true subtropical. Here is a narcissus suitable for underplanting a grove of palms.

The same coastal gardens housing the Chinese sacred lily often include its cousin, *N. tazetta* 'Romanus'. This ancient selection is better known by its English name, 'Double Roman', and also appears occasionally as 'Constantinople'. It looks exactly like the Chinese sacred lily in all characters, save the flowers, which are fully double and extraordinarily scented. In a contest of fragrance, 'Double Roman' outclasses all competition, for its many-petaled blooms carry a double dosage of sweet aroma.

These tender tazettas make fine garden subjects, but their January flowering season puts them at risk from cold. Only in regions where winter lows remain faithfully above twenty degrees F will the flowers appear dependably. In the South this limits them to gardens south of a line drawn from Austin, Texas, to Charleston, South Carolina. Elsewhere they may be grown in pots for indoor decoration.

As with all bulbs, the verdant foliage of these narcissi feeds flowers for the next season and must be left in place to yellow naturally in late April. Many other fading bulbs may be hidden under the leaves of later blooming perennials, but these rampant narcissi are not so easily disguised. It is, perhaps, a better course to make a feature of their yellowing foliage. It combines strikingly with vibrant April blooms like irises and mixes satisfactorily with the straw-toned blades of such ornamental grasses as needlegrass (*Stipa* spp.), weeping lovegrass (*Eragrostis curvula*), and Canada wild rye (*Elymus canadensis*).

Like their paperwhite allies, the single and double forms of the Chinese 'Grand Emperor' incline to overmultiplication. The miniature *N. tazetta* v. *lacticolor* ("Canaliculatus" of the trade) looks like a tiny Chinese sacred lily and is also notorious in this respect. The simplest solution for gardeners seems to be to divide and reset bulbs every two or three years. As a dividend, this provides a welcome opportunity to share offsets with other lovers of old flowers.

❧ The Golden Sun

The brilliant yellow, orange-cupped 'Soleil d'Or' is another narcissus that contributes glowing blooms and sweet fragrances each winter, just as it has for centuries. As with the old paperwhites and Chinese sacred lilies, the bulb trade still offers this antique cultivar for winter forcing. Few bulbous flowers could be more bright or cheerful.

'Soleil d'Or' resembles the Chinese sacred lily in its fruity fragrance, its light green foliage, and its deep orangey cups, or coronas. However, its starry petals are clear, lemony yellow. This gives the blossoms a special glow as they appear in early January.

'Soleil d'Or' suffers from the same frost-tenderness as its relations but, unfortunately, lacks their exotic vigor. Except in favored mild regions, these narcissi waste slowly away or, at best, hang on with little increase. A virus may be the culprit, for a number of the old narcissi show the telltale streakings in their foliage that indicate infection. Such diseases are seldom lethal, but they rob the strength and garden value of any plants infected.

The Israeli florists have been busy developing new tazettas, which may sidestep these problems. 'Bethlehem' ('Nony') and 'Nazareth' ('Yael') are selections with soft yellow petals and deeper golden cups. 'Israel' ('Omri') opens creamy yellow but fades to look more like the Chinese sacred lily. All of these flower in January and appear to need the same garden treatment as their older relations.

❧ *Monarques*

Along Mediterranean shorelines, paperwhites and Chinese sacred lilies often occur together. Although closely related, they maintain separate populations, because their genetic structure isolates them from one another. The paperwhite has a standard diploid (double) set of chromosomes. Its large cousin inherits a tetraploid (quadruple) complement. This accounts for the tremendous vigor of the Chinese sacred lily and also suggests that hybrids between the two varieties will be sterile mules with a triploid set of genes. As we have already seen, such plants often make fine garden flowers.

Tazetta crosses have in fact occurred, and several have been cultivated since the 1600s. These mules possess a number of distinctive characters making them unlike either parent. Instead of silvery gray leaves like paperwhites, or fountains of sage green foliage like Chinese sacred lilies, the hybrid bulbs often produce lush groups of dark green leaves. Their foliage and flowers usually emerge later and withstand more cold than their ancestors. These narcissi have proven hardy throughout the South, where they are among the most cherished garden heirlooms.

The first to bloom is a striking plant with slender white petals and small citron cups. If the winter is mild, as is often the case, dark green leaves emerge in November and bear flowering stems around the first of February. The effect of the starry, white blossoms with their cheerful yellow cups is charming, especially when the narcissi are growing around an old homestead nestled under pines.

In early literature this variety is called 'Minor Monarque', but those who prefer Latin often refer to it as *Narcissus tazetta* v. *italicus*. It's one of the most distinctive types, not likely to be confused with other hybrid tazettas.

Narcissus tazetta 'Avalanche'

Narcissus bulbocodium var. *conspicuus*

Narcissus tazetta 'Erlicheer'

Narcissus tazetta var. *orientalis*

Narcissus tazetta var. *papyraceus* 'Galilee'

Narcissus tazetta 'Grand Primo'

The confusion comes with a famous seventeenth-century cultivar known as 'Grand Monarque'. As with other horticultural antiques, it is nowadays impossible for anyone to say with certainty to which plant this old name belongs. That hasn't stopped people from trying.

Various plants pass under the name 'Grand Monarque' and have become the subjects of debate among narcissus fanciers. The experts (Californians, of course) are certain the bulbs Southerners know as 'Grand Monarque' are imposters. The "real" 'Grand Monarque', we are told, occurs only in old California gardens. Ours purportedly is another ancient selection called 'Grand Primo'. It is probably best to heed the advice of Hillaire Belloc:

> *Oh let us never, never doubt*
> *What nobody is sure about.*

❦ *Grand Primo (Grand Monarque)*

Certainly no finer flowering bulbs are available for Southerners than these old narcissi now known as 'Grand Primo'. They are by far the most vigorous, persistent, and floriferous members of their genus. Unlike their tender cousins, these oldsters continue flowering indefinitely, never requiring division or resetting. Since they emerge and bloom late in the season (usually the end of February or the first of March), they avoid the usual hazards of winter freezes.

'Grand Primo' is so extraordinarily tough that it thrives even on the heaviest clays. This narcissus also persists and increases in the dry climates of the Southwest. In Texas it is the most common of the old narcissi, and may be seen gracing many nineteenth-century gardens.

Although casual observers dismiss these old plantings as mere paperwhites, the leaves and flowers of 'Grand Primo' have several distinctive characters. The blossoms open with a cream color instead of white, and the bowl-shaped cups are light yellow. These colors are transitory and fade as the flowers age, so that white and yellowish blooms may appear on the same clump. Some plants seem to hold colors better than others, and it's likely that several different strains are lurking in gardens. French growers once listed a variant called 'Grand Primo Citroniere'.

The fragrance of these flowers is pleasantly sweet, with none of the overpowering muskiness of paperwhites. The creamy blooms appear in fat, rounded clusters of eleven to sixteen. These sit atop stiff, green stems, which display the blossoms to better advantage than in any other garden tazetta. The dark green foliage affords the perfect complement to the abundant groups of pearly flowers.

In contrast, the bulb Californians call 'Grand Monarque' is decidedly ungrand in the South, as it often fails to bloom. When it does flower, it may have as many as twenty-two blossoms to a stem. These differ from 'Grand Primo' in having more yellow in the coronas. The cups also have deeper rims and are less spreading than 'Grand Primo'. This so-called 'Grand Monarque' seldom persists in Southern gardens for more than a few seasons.

Other tazettas passing under names like 'Scilly White' and 'White Pearl' appear similar to 'Grand Primo' but tend to flower earlier. They also split and multiply excessively, so they are less desirable as garden plants.

🐚 'Erlicheer'

Although 'Grand Primo' is now rather unusual in the bulb trade, the double-flowered 'Erlicheer' has become common in recent years. This variety was discovered in New Zealand, where 'Grand Primo', 'White Pearl', and other old tazettas are still raised as cut flowers. 'Erlicheer' has the same vigor and good green foliage as 'Grand Primo', but it bears tightly clustered balls of double blooms. These are less showy in the landscape than 'Grand Primo', but appear to be equally permanent.

'Erlicheer' has become a standard item for Dutch growers, who market it as a novelty narcissus for summer bedding. They do this because Holland lacks sufficient heat to properly ripen these Mediterranean bulbs. The Dutch plant them out in the spring, then dig them in the fall and store them in warm, dry rooms over winter. This effectively simulates a summer baking, reversing the season for these narcissi. When these bulbs are planted in Southern gardens, they require several seasons of adjustment before blooming on schedule in early March.

🐚 Avalanche (*Compressus*)

One of the places where tazettas retain some of their former importance is a small group of islands off the southwest coast of England called the Isles of Scilly. Like the Channel Islands, the Isles of Scilly benefit from the warm waters of the Gulf Stream and have a perpetually mild climate. Since Elizabethan times they have been known as a haven for winter flowers.

Tresco is one of these isles, famous for its abbey and gardens. While walking the island one fortunate day, the manager of the estates, T.M. Dorrien Smith, discovered an old narcissus growing in a rocky crag along the seashore. The fields above had once been used to raise flowers, and it appeared that the old tazetta must have tumbled down the cliff toward the sea. Dorrien Smith retrieved the bulbs and registered this flower in 1955 under the name 'Avalanche'.

This is a fine narcissus with snowy petals and a wide lemony cup. It is probably one of the 300 different tazettas listed by Dutch nurseries during the nineteenth century. Which of them, it will never be known for sure. In old Southern gardens, there are similar flowers sometimes called 'Seventeen Sisters'. Narcissus fans have also tried to tag this clone as 'Compressus', another antique florist variety. It may be met under this name on some nursery lists.

For Southerners 'Avalanche' offers all the gaiety of the true 'Grand Monarque' on a much thriftier, more robust plant. The big groups of twenty flowers are borne on strong, eighteen-inch stems accompanied by good, green foliage. As with 'Grand Primo', flowering comes in late February or early March. One could hardly wish for a more pleasant harbinger of winter's demise.

❧ *Hoop Petticoats*

One of the real garden opportunities available to Southerners comes from an odd group of dwarf narcissi native to the hills and mountains of the western Mediterranean. These curiously designed flowers might be described as all cup and no petals, for that is the impression they give as they rise among their grassy winter foliage. The widely flaring blooms have been given the common name "hoop petticoats" for their resemblance to nineteenth-century hoop skirts. The petals of the impish flowers form narrow streamers, which fly out to form tiny stars. Their inflated cups reveal a projecting style and six stamens, inclined downward like a little *Habranthus*.

Although these elfin blooms hardly sound like the stuff of garden drama, hoop petticoats offer Southerners some of the most likely material for a scene worthy of an exclaiming Wordsworth. These miniatures flower over a tremendously long season and prosper mightily on acid sands or reddish clays. Although this "host of golden daffodils" is a tiny one, no other narcissi are so prolific in warm climates.

The varied hoop petticoats, or, as Haworth named them, *Corbularia*, differ widely in shape and size, and in color from white to deep gold. They seem to be a rapidly evolving section of genus *Narcissus*, with headquarters in Spain and across the Mediterranean in North Africa. Modern taxonomies group most of the yellow and gold forms under the principal species, *Narcissus bulbocodium*, with a few white or cream-colored types placed under *N. cantabricus*. In the South the yellowish forms may be expected to bloom from midwinter to spring, the whitish types in late fall or early winter.

In a normal Southern winter, if there is such a thing, periodic cold waves sweep over the countryside, with intermittent mild weather filling the days between northers. It takes sustained temperatures below 10 degrees F to damage the hoop petticoat blossoms, which emerge during the mild spells. It takes below-zero weather to damage their foliage.

The earliest blooming of these miniatures are forms of *N. cantabricus*. This transparent, pearly white blossom is native to both sides of the Strait of Gibraltar and occurs in several differing forms. Along with Barbary apes and other bits of regional natural history, this bulbous flower shows that Europe and Africa once joined together.

The most vigorous form of this species is *N. cantabricus foliosus*, the "leafy Cantabrian narcissus." Along with the pale yellowish *N. romieuxii*, this late fall bloomer has given rise to a series of quaint hybrids, the most famous of which are 'Jessamy', 'Taffeta', and 'Nylon'. In addition to named clones from this cross, nurseries often sell hybrid siblings together as a strain. All of these have creamy blooms and begin flowering in late November, often continuing until Christmas. Their sweetly fragrant, crepe-textured blooms appear among generous crops of green, threadlike leaves.

The pale yellow *N. bulbocodium* 'Tenuifolius' flowers during the same season as these pale hybrids. Although attractive and prolific, the small bulbs are less free-flowering than some later varieties. They should be reset periodically in fresh ground to keep them sized up and blooming.

In early January the gossamer yellow *N. romieuxii* comes to flower. This variety is sometimes placed as a variety of *N. bulbocodium,* but it differs in its sulfury blooms and exerted stamens and style. It comes from the Atlas Mountains in Morocco, where it grows in dry scrub under cedars and oaks. In the South these luminous, waxen blooms appear during the first warm spells of the new year. 'Julia Jane' is an attractive cultivar with a flat, ruffled corona.

With the arrival of spring in late February or March, these miniatures shade more and more toward gold. *N. bulbocodium* var. *citrinus* offers two-inch-long, primrose yellow blooms, with heavily fluted, flared cups. Some shelter from wind or rain will be appreciated by these oversized blossoms.

Next to flower is the distinctive *N. bulbocodium obesus,* the "portly" bulbocodium. Most *N. bulbocodium* variants offer copious tufts of slender foliage, true to their botanical name, which means "bulb wool." *Obesus* charts a different course with thick, prostrate rosettes, sprawled on the ground like little starfish. The lemony colored and scented blooms appear after the season of northers on fat spears, which rise between the leaves. In this variety there are often a few extra petals beyond the normal six, and each bears a slender, green stripe down its backside.

The most abundant and vigorous of all the hoop petticoats, *N. bulbocodium conspicuus* finishes the flowering season in late March or April. This showy type is a good doer and among the easiest to find on nursery lists. It is truly gold in color and makes a superb complement to the spreading blue mounds of Dalmatian bluebells (*Campanula portenschlagiana*).

This one has been in gardens for a long time and is probably the form Jefferson had at Monticello. There are several different stocks blooming at varying seasons, so it's a variety worth acquiring more than once. Like all the hoop petticoats, these tiny bulbs are remarkably tough and long-lived on dry, sandy ground.

❧ *Lent Lilies*

February in the South is a season of false promises. Unsuspecting blossoms are lured out during warm spells, only to be brutally reproached with the blue winds of northers. Strangely enough, there are certain plants whose peculiar demeanor suits them to this chancy weather. None is more welcome in gardens than the wild trumpet daffodil, or Lent lily, *Narcissus pseudonarcissus.*

These wildlings are the earliest flowering of their race, usually appearing at the beginning of February. Perhaps because of the coldness of the season, the stems never reach so high as the daffodils that follow. The entire plant generally stays only six or eight inches tall.

Despite this low stature, the blooms reach a respectable two to three inches in length. These proportions give the plants the charming aspect of Alpine miniatures. Pale yellow, dog-eared petals frame the deeper yellow trumpets.

The Lent lily is a wild European daffodil introduced to the South by early settlers. It has since spread far and wide in gardens, and has seeded and naturalized in fields and along roadsides. Although much like modern daffodils in construction, these wildflowers have a more relaxed appearance than their pedigreed descendents.

Daffodils are strangely built flowers, with a unique apparatus for attracting pollinators and protecting pollen and nectar. The value of this becomes immediately apparent with an early flower like the Lent lily. All you need do is stand for a moment in a cold February sleet storm to appreciate the advantage of the trumpet-shaped coronas, which provide shelter to the pollen and to the brave insects who venture out to visit the blossoms.

These wild daffodils are a less certain source of garden color than their large brethren, but they offer one of the surest paths to enchantment. If you wish to gaze into their small windblown trumpets, you must kneel down in their presence. If you want to smell their sweet fragrance on the frosty morning air, you must warm a blossom in your hands.

🐚 *Silver Bells*

Some of the old gardens in the South also include a beautiful cousin of the Lent lily with nodding milky blooms. By tradition, gardeners who have them call the graceful flowers "silver bells." Parkinson knew these bulbs as *N. pseudonarcissus* var. *moschatus*, "the lesser Spanish daffodil." Peter Barre listed them in his 1884 catalog as *N. cernuus*, the "drooping daffodil." They are supposed to have originally come from the Spanish Pyrenees.

These pale daffodils hang their heads the entire time they are in flower, with ghostly twisting petals swirling around the pearly trumpets. They usually flower early in February, in company with several erect, broad, gray leaves.

On poor, sandy soils, these elegant flowers are entirely permanent, but slow of increase. On heavy clays silver bells are apt to vanish, and they dislike heavy feeding. These bulbs are best left to their own devices on a patch of ground where the gardener will not meddle in their affairs.

Although hardly showstopping in size or quantity of bloom, the quietly beautiful flowers are great treasures. Since many of the modern white daffodils fare poorly in the South, heirlooms such as these are doubly valuable for early color. The bulbs of the silver bells are not common in the trade, but they may sometimes be had from generous gardeners or from dealers in the rarer old narcissi.

🐚 *Tommies*

Charm is a property of the crocus, and for many of the same reasons seen in the early daffodils. Miniature stature combines with oversized blossoms to invite us, and the bees, down for inspection. Sadly, it's real a challenge to find early crocuses that persist in the South for more than a season.

C. seiberi, *C. biflorus*, and cultivars and hybrids of *C. chrysanthus* can be successful in the middle and upper South, but neither lasts near the Gulf. These species come in many shades of yellow, gold, cream, and lavender and perform best if given raised positions with fast drainage.

The same range of adaptation applies to the old "cloth of gold" crocus, *C. angustifolius* (*C. susianus*), and the little crocuses called "gold bunch" by the trade (*Crocus ancyrensis*). Both bear thick clusters of brown-feathered, golden blossoms in early February.

The old 'Dutch Yellow' crocus commonly is planted in mixes with large purple and white forms of the Alpine *C. vernus*. This most popular of the yellows is an ancient, sterile hybrid between the cloth of gold crocus and the eastern Mediterranean *C. flavus* (*C. aureus*). It frequently persists in Southern gardens long after the purples and whites have failed.

Mediterranean species like *C. corsicus* would seem to be good bets, but they have not been widely reported in the South. The Italian crocus, *C. imperati*, has been a disappointment for those who have tried it. Despite its southerly pedigree, this species performs well in the northeastern United States, and any such accomplishment generally portends failure in warm climates.

The one early crocus regularly making itself at home in the South is *Crocus tomasinianus*, a species from the stony limestone hills of Serbia, Bosnia, and Dalmatia. Perhaps in rebellion to its tongue-twisting Latin name, gardeners have dubbed these little blossoms "Tommies."

It's a joy to know that at least this species finds Southern gardens congenial. Its amethyst flowers appear over a long season, from mid-January to early March. The reddish violet blooms, silver-gray in bud, make charming pools of color as they multiply in ever-widening patches. Silver stripes accent the grassy, green foliage that rises to accompany the blooms in early March.

The famous Carolina gardener Elizabeth Lawrence described the captivating movement of the Tommies in response to fickle Southern weather:

> *"The flickering color is delightful in the pale sunlight of late winter and early spring, and as soon as the sun stops shining the petals are furled again into thin silver spears."*

There are a few worthwhile color variations of *C. tomasinianus*, but only one improved cultivar, 'Ruby Giant', is widely available. It seems to offer all the vigor and adaptability of the species and has somewhat larger, more purplish blooms. 'Roseus' and 'Lilac Beauty' are selections with silvered rosy and pale lilac blooms, respectively. 'Albus' is a pure white variant of *C. tomasinianus*.

❦ *Algerian Iris*

The famous Algerian iris (*I. unguicularis*) is another flower beloved for its late-autumn or winter blossoms. This Mediterranean native requires a sheltered site and sandy soil to endure intemperate blasts of cold. It doesn't mind partial shade from deciduous trees like oaks, but it can be finicky about blooming in the South. *I. lazica*, a rare ally of *I. unguicularis* from the region around the Black Sea, might perform better here than its famous cousin, as it naturally receives more summer rainfall. It would be well worth seeking.

When coaxed to settle down, the tough rhizomes of these irises send up a steady succession of stems bearing frail, beardless blossoms. These sit down amid the narrow, strappy clumps of foliage and beg to be picked all winter. The delicate blooms are striped yellow at the haft and come in shades of purple, lavender, or white. These translucent irises are at their best when winter weather is all gloom and fog.

As they are true flowers of frost, Algerian irises receive universal praise from gardeners who succeed in blooming them. The rhizomes divide and establish most readily in early spring, when their wiry roots are white and active.

❦ *Roman Hyacinths*

The wild forms of the hyacinth are surprisingly graceful flowers compared to their highly bred, stiffly upright descendents. Most people wouldn't even recognize the old varieties as belonging to the same species. It's not until the sweet fragrance of the bell-shaped blossoms wafts through the air that the relationship becomes apparent.

The earliest and most abundant of the hyacinths in the South is the white French-Roman. A distinct form of the common hyacinth (*Hyacinthus orientalis*), modern botanists recognize it as variety *albulus*.

Although some sources say these flowers originated in Greece, their principal habitat today is southern France. In this region hyacinths have long played a role in the perfume industry and were formerly exported widely for winter forcing. In addition to the common white French-Roman, there are pink and blue selections, which became popular in the nineteenth century, known as Parisian hyacinths.

Several of these old flowers have found their way to Southern gardens. The white form, especially, offers blossoms during the bleakest weeks of winter. The small, globular bulbs grow shallowly and multiply into thrifty patches topped with waxy, bright green leaves. Around the first of January, slender spikes of pendant flowers begin to rise. The pristine white blossoms are scattered loosely around the stems and seem quite unlike the crowded, garishly colored mops of hybrid hyacinths.

What these graceful flowers lack in the bold form of their better known cousins, they make up for in generosity. Even small bulbs produce several spikes from between the whorled leaves. The spikes appear in succession for six weeks or more, so that most clumps remain in flower from January through March. It takes a really large planting to get much impact from the small blooms, but the combination of fresh green leaves and snowy blossoms offers some of the liveliest of winter scenery. Their sweet, spicy fragrance is unsurpassable.

In mid-February, as the white Roman hyacinths peak, their blue-flowered cousins are just beginning. These old garden plants have dusky violet flowers and rather dark green leaves. This makes them difficult to discern from a distance. It's quite conceivable to smell these fragrant flowers before you see them. They commonly naturalize in wide mats on the front lawns of old Southern homes.

Anemone coronaria 'De Caen'

Hyacinthus orientalis var. *albulus*

Anemone heterophylla

Crocus 'Dutch Yellow'

Ranunculus macranthus: large-flowered buttercups among spiderworts, bluebonnets, and daffodil foliage.

Crocus tomasinianus

Pink Roman hyacinths are more rare, but there is a double pink variety found in some parts. All of these are very old flowers. Gerard described both single and double hyacinths in his *Herbal* in 1596, reporting that the plants had been brought from the East. The Turks probably grew them for several centuries before Gerard made their acquaintance.

The single white French-Roman hyacinths are still popular in the bulb trade and command a good price, as Europeans value them for forcing even today. Blue and pink "Roman" hyacinths from commercial sources appear slightly different from the strains in old gardens, but they make worthwhile showings and seem permanent.

Some of the earlier-blooming Dutch hyacinths will also settle into garden life if offered an opportunity. Their blossoms soon revert and look much like the wild French-Roman types. Louise Bebe Wilder described this transition in her classic treatise *Adventures with Hardy Bulbs*:

> *"These stout fellows, when left in the ground for several years with
> no notice taken of them until their starched pride is somewhat
> subdued, acquire a slender grace and modesty that is most becoming
> to them, and may then take their place among other spring bulbs."*

❧ Blue Starflowers

The same benignly neglected lawns that afford homes for the antique hyacinths also hold small patches of grassy, gray foliage. After the new year, any brief spell of sunny weather will coax these leafy clumps into bloom. The flowers are a cheerful pale blue and resemble six-pointed stars. Once they begin to appear, the blossoms continue steadily onward through March.

These lovely blue flowers present a perennial mystery for gardeners who discover them in the grass. They seem to have created consternation for botanists as well. The usual questions are "What are they?" and "Where did they come from?" Everyone agrees the bulbs originated from Argentina and Uruguay, but that's as far as it goes.

Botanists have been shuffling these poor flowers back and forth for years. Their Latin names have included *Tritelia*, *Tristagma*, *Nothoscordum*, *Brodiaea*, *Milla*, *Beauverdia*, and *Leucocoryne*. Currently they are resting under the title *Ipheion uniflorum*.

Although their short stature gives these little plants a crocuslike personality, all one need do is lightly bruise the foliage to reveal their true affinity, garlic. *Ipheion* has the same acrid-smelling juice in its leaves as a wild onion. It's surprising that some botanist hasn't placed it in *Allium*.

Unlike *Allium* the inch-wide blooms of *Ipheion* appear singly, one to a stem. The bulbs multiply at an amazingly rapid pace by offsets, seed, and droopers (droopers are short runners that form bulbs at their ends). These South Americans readily naturalize on almost any soil.

Although *Ipheion* has no dislike of lime, on alkaline ground the bulbs should be planted where they will receive little summer water. This helps discourage rotting while the bulbs are dormant. On acid soils the natural chemistry discourages such problems, so they may be watered freely.

'Wisley Blue' is a supposedly improved *Ipheion* that seems hardly different from the old lilac types in Southern lawns. 'Froyle Mill' is more distinctive, with rich purplish-mauve blossoms. 'Violaceum' and 'Rolf Fielder' are good pale violet clones.

Jose Alberto Castillo of Buenos Aires, Argentina, has introduced several wild South American *Ipheion*, including a lovely large, white one ('Alba'). These snowy blossoms show much promise for Southern gardens. *Ipheion* provide exceptional companions to the rich violet of *C. tomasinianus* and the stunning gold of *Narcissus bulbocodium conspicuus*.

🌸 *Windflowers*

Like rain lilies, the little blooms of anemones have a long-standing association with the wind. Pliny remarked that they never opened, save when winter mistrals blew.

It's stirring to see a barren field dotted with these early blossoms. The pale, limpid blooms rest barely inches above the ground, so the earth itself appears to flower. They open and close in concert with the wintry shadows of each passing cloud. Although the grass remains cheerless and dun, the lively flowers offer vibrant, living mirrors to the alabaster and azure of the heavens.

Botanists recognize anemones as inefficient flowers with redundant structures of ancient design. Along with waterlilies, magnolias, and other primitive blossoms, these plants display blooms that center around a cone-shaped reproductive organ composed of many individual stamens and pistils. True petals are absent or greatly reduced in *Anemone;* the brightly colored sepals are what we see instead.

After pollination, the central mass of the flowers ripens into a compact dome of dry, feathery fruits. These achenes disperse with the winds that arrive in early summer. The feathery seed heads recall the powder puffs of virgin's bower (*Clematis*), which also belongs to this ancient, peculiar family.

The tubers of most anemones appear brown and misshapen. They look quite lifeless after drying out during storage. An overnight soak in fresh water before planting in autumn will restore plumpness and vitality. Even after this water treatment, it is often difficult to discern the top of the root from the bottom. Fortunately, there will be no setback to the plants if the tubers are accidentally placed upside down.

From Alabama westward into Texas, the most familiar native windflower is *Anemone heterophylla*. Its white, pink, or blue, daisy-shaped flowers appear singly above whorls of narrow, filigreed bracts. The parsleylike leaves are dark purple on their undersides and arise directly from the tubers. The foliage stands out prominently in dormant lawns. This dismays fanciers of manicured greenswards, but where allowed to naturalize on rockeries or in unmown buffalograss, these little wildflowers can be thoroughly charming. They thrive especially on heavy clay and limestone soils.

A. heterophylla yields a succession of blooms from each tuber and has a long flowering season, from February through April. Since the flowers come only one or two at a time, large groups of roots must be gathered and planted together in order to gain any effect. They look best in small groupings of a single color.

Anemone edwardsiana, a close cousin of *A. heterophylla*, bears two tiny blossoms on each stem. This is a localized central Texas species with a marked preference for woodland habitats and leafy, humus-rich soils.

Although neither of these native anemones is common in the bulb trade, the very similar Grecian windflower (*Anemone blanda*) is available in several color forms. In cooler sections of the South, this species naturalizes in leafy woodland wherever the winter sun shines to warm the soil. In warmer parts the tubers must be nestled in crevices between stones or placed in other situations guaranteeing a cool root run. Once established on well-drained soil with a bit of lime, the clumps spread steadily and increase in beauty each season. *A. appenina* is a similar, later-blooming relation from Italy.

More valuable than these on sandy, acid soils is another widespread native, the Carolina anemone (*A. caroliniana*). This species ranges through most of the South and Midwest, flowering in late winter. Its slender sepals run the usual gamut of white, pink, and blue colors, and its leaves are finely cut and unobtrusive.

In addition to their tubers, certain strains of *A. caroliniana* produce branching droopers that allow these beautiful flowers to creep gradually across an entire lawn. Each individual plant creates a pool of blue or white blooms, which can intermingle with colonial neighbors in an enchanting patchwork.

Another flower with a questing rhizome is the European wood anemone (*A. nemorosa*). This variety belongs to the section of the genus with poppylike blossoms. These are white in the common garden selection, 'Grandiflora'. The loosely double 'Bracteata' is an heirloom variety from the 1600s. Its blooms have numerous white and green, petal-like sepals. A few pink and lavender cultivars are also popular in Europe but are seldom grown in America.

These anemones are easy and permanent in Southern gardens if given woodsy soil with a bit of lime. They especially enjoy a shady patch of ground where their triparted leaves and woody rootstocks can ramble. Wood anemones can be delightfully wayward, with flowers appearing anytime from November to April. The snowy whiteness of these blossoms shows beautifully under Japanese maples (*Acer palmatum*), whose early spring leaves emerge with a delicate tinge of rose. The silky, nodding buds hover a few inches above the ground, then turn skyward as each opens in succession.

Another woodland flower, the rue anemone (*Anemonella thalictroides*) combines its tender white or pinkish blooms with thin, ferny, blue-green foliage. These little blossoms appear in clusters of three and have rounded sepals. Despite the delicate carriage of these plants, rue anemones seem surprisingly tough. Although they prefer moist woodland conditions, during drought they are capable of retreat to a clustered, tuberous rootstock.

The brightly colored poppy anemones of the Middle East, *Anemone coronaria* and *A. hortensis,* are so showy and pleasant, they are worth having even if they must be periodically replanted, which in much of South is an unfortunate necessity. Their tubers are readily available and inexpensive, and the flowers ask for little beyond a sunny spot sheltered from winter gales.

It's this winter shelter that often determines the permanence of these anemones. Their fresh, parsley green leaves emerge early in the fall and must successfully endure winter freezes if the plants are to prosper. In frosty parts of the South, they may be dug annually and replanted in December to delay emergence and thereby improve cold tolerance.

These Mediterranean windflowers reach nearly a foot in height in common hybrid strains and make excellent cut flowers. They descend from plants domesticated by the Turks during the Middle Ages. Their precise ancestry is now obscure, but most are listed as forms of *A. coronaria,* a native species of southern Europe. The vigorous, single De Caen strain and double St. Brigid group come in a wide range of colors, including white, crimson, pink, violet, and lavender.

The 'St. Bavo' hybrids are usually considered to be *A. hortensis* derivatives. With mostly lavender shades, they also vary to warm red. Their leaves are less finely divided, and their blooms have more petals, than *A. coronaria.*

More in the province of rock garden specialties are *Anemone biflora* and *A.* × *fulgens.* These have brilliant terra-cotta blossoms accented by black stamens. They enjoy dry summer bakings and gritty, lime-filled soil. Raised positions near the foot of a south-facing wall or boulder suit them well.

In addition to these tuberous species, there are many fibrous-rooted anemones worthy of cultivation in the South. Gardeners enchanted by the windflower tribe will certainly wish to grow the Japanese anemones (*A.* × *hybrida*), as well as several other species.

🐚 *Ranunculus*

First cousins of the anemones, and just as inclined to early bloom, are the various species of *Ranunculus.* These buttercups or marsh marigolds enjoy plenty of moisture during their spring blooming season, a characteristic alluded to by their Latin name, which means "little frogs."

Large-flowered buttercup (*Ranunculus macranthus*) is a Southwestern native that begins producing inch-wide, golden blooms in February and often continues into May. These waxy flowers are semi-double and appear in sizeable clusters. They have the reflective sheen typical of their race. These long-lived perennials self-sow and naturalize in grass. In summer they retreat to the distinctive clawlike cluster of tubers that characterize this genus.

Like the large-flowered anemones, the popular bedding strains of Persian buttercup (*Ranunculus asiaticus*) are a legacy of ancient Turkish ingenuity and were enormously popular flowers long ago. An English list from 1792 included over eight hundred named cultivars. Thomas Jefferson included both these and the poppy anemones in his spring bedding schemes at Monticello. With their feathery, green leaves and brightly colored and doubled blooms, these tuberous flowers bring a festive miscellany to early spring gardens.

Persian buttercups suffer in severe cold spells, usually failing to return in regions where hard frost occurs annually. Late planting overcomes tenderness, so gardeners often lift and replant ranunculus tubers in December to delay their emergence. They are inexpensive, and may be replaced annually, if necessary.

Of the several nontuberous *Ranunculus* species suited to the South, the European creeping buttercup (*R. repens*) and the native pine buttercup (*R. fascicularis*) are especially good performers. In March and April these vigorous species offer waxy gold and butter yellow blooms, respectively. They quickly spread over moist ground, like strawberries, on short surface runners. Although aggressive, they make good groundcovers for damp shade. Their three-parted evergreen leaves offer a pretty foil for the upward thrusting leaves of spider lilies, gingers, and other shade- and moisture-loving bulbs.

Jonquils and Kin

Around the first of March, winter begins offering obvious signs of its departure. Buds swell on the dendritic canopies of the elms. Grasses freshen perceptibly, and the low rosettes of annuals show progress by adding new rounds of leaves. The final signal comes when the gracefully inclined blooms of daffodils paint gold over the awakening landscape.

In the South nearly any yellow *Narcissus* may be affectionately pegged as a "jonquil," whether or not it deserves this title, for *Narcissus jonquilla* and its hybrids have long been the most prominent of their race. These daffodils show a special fondness for these quarters, revealed through brave persistence and steady increase. Gardeners reciprocate tender feelings, rightfully doting on these early treasures.

Narcissus jonquilla and its relations inherit tolerance to dampness, which suits them especially to the heavy cotton soils of the South, as well as to seasonally moist sandylands. Their native haunts center on Spain and Portugal but extend to southern France and across the Mediterranean to Morocco. In these sunny countries moist, cool spring seasons give way to long, warm summers, and all of these bulbs receive a good baking.

The true jonquil (*N. jonquilla*) is a tiny, golden flower that appears in scant clusters atop slender, jade stems. The powerfully scented blooms would seem out of scale if attached to the wide foliage of a common daffodil, but nature has wisely designed elegant, tapered greenery to accompany the endearing blossoms. The upright leaves, rounded in cross section, provide inspiration for the botanical name, *jonquilla*, which means "little rush." In the South (and, one supposes, in their native habitats), jonquils naturalize in bar ditches and other moist spots where their wild companions include true rushes (*Juncus* spp.). Perhaps the stiff, narrow leaves confer some disguise in this community that helps to protect them from browsing mammals or insects.

Another curious imitation of the jonquil is its blossom. Although designed along the same lines as *N. tazetta,* jonquil flowers have a different personality, which comes from their more casually disposed umbels, their brilliant gold-waxed petals, and their remarkably powerful fragrance. The redolent, honey-scented blossoms look and smell like the flowers of barberries (*Berberis* spp.), which appear at the same early season. Apparently, the spiny, shrubby barberry and the tiny jonquil are out to attract the same precocious insects.

Several strains of *N. jonquilla* appear in Southern gardens, differing primarily in blooming season. Early ones arrive in late February during a mild year but more often come in March. As soon as the little flower stems rise above ground, the buds begin to open. The scapes reach ten or twelve inches by the time all the blooms have expanded. At this modest elevation they strike an elegant pose amid the narrow leaves.

These early jonquils are particularly desirable for garden decoration, as the tiny blossoms can be enjoyed before the rush of spring flowers. They appear to be true heirlooms, unavailable in the Dutch trade but common along rural roadsides. In the South they form large colonies on the same acid sandylands that support loblolly pines and sassafras.

Later jonquils continue appearing into April, making fragrant additions for an intimate nook or bend along a sunny pathway. One of the most famous is the double *N. jonquilla* known as Queen Anne. These old flowers reside in some of the historic gardens of the South. Like most doubles, they tend more to green than gold, and tent to blast (fail to open properly) save in cool, moist springs. Nevertheless, the lemony, many-petaled blooms possess a special daintiness. They are greatly treasured by those who know them.

Commercial bulb suppliers often send out 'Baby Moon' in lieu of true species jonquils. This is a late-flowering hybrid between *N. jonquilla* and a close relation, *N. rupicola.* Looking like an overly precise version of its parents, its carefully fashioned blossoms stand stiffly, like small, lemon yellow wheels. 'Baby Moon' has dark green leaves sprawling more widely than typical *N. jonquilla.* It seldom exceeds six inches in height.

Rarer relatives of *N. jonquilla* include, in order of descending size, *N. fernande-sii, N. calcicola,* and *N. scaberulus.* These Iberian species succeed in the South and may sometimes be had from specialists. They are so small, though, that a great number would be needed to produce any effect in the garden. They make charming additions to a trough planting or a pot on a sunny patio.

The true jonquil fragrance empowers all of these flowers with romantic potency that goes beyond their midget proportions. The blossoms seem to speak directly, imploring gardeners to focus on the small, delicately fashioned blossoms. Jonquil voices may have spoken to Elizabeth Lawrence as she wrote of little daffodils:

*"When they are in bloom I feel as if I could not stop looking at them
for a moment, and when they are gone I am almost ashamed of the
sharpness of my regret."*

🌺 Campernelles

The larger "jonquils" common to the South are actually old hybrids between
N. jonquilla and other wild daffodils. The favorite of all is an antique called
the campernelle (*Narcissus × odorus* 'Campernelli'). It originates from southern
France, Spain, and Italy, where *N. jonquilla* overlaps and crosses with the Lent
lily (*N. pseudonarcissus*).

Campernelles provide more springtime gold in the South than any other
flowers, and they have done so since the earliest days of European settlement.
These richly colored blossoms flutter among groups of narrow, emerald green
leaves like troops of fragrant yellow butterflies. Their silhouettes always seem
graceful and unobtrusive. More delightful and suitable bulbs for naturalizing
could hardly be imagined.

The campernelle is another one of those gratifying old garden mules discovered by some alert plantsman or plantswoman of ages past. Clusius recorded
it in 1595, and Parkinson discussed this variety in his *Paradisus* along with the
single and double jonquils. The campernelle persists and thrives in our gardens
to this day, for it has that wonderful hybrid vigor (heterosis) common to many
sterile crosses. Like *N. jonquilla,* these daffodils have a special affinity for damp
conditions. They are the most successful of any narcissus on clay.

Campernelle flowers appear in clusters of two to five on top of twelve- to
fifteen-inch stems. They emanate the treasured jonquil perfume, though with
less intensity than their tiny parent. The blooms often show slight imperfections
and on close inspection may be curiously dog-eared or bereft, with only four
or five petals instead of the customary six. Although this keeps campernelles
off the show bench and bans them from plantings of daffodil connoisseurs, it
presents no barrier to their use in borders. If anything, this tattered appearance
adds to their charm.

These old-time flowers begin to show around the first of March, which is
early enough to make them welcome and late enough to avoid the most serious
freezes. The fragrant blooms appear for a fortnight, or longer if weather remains
mild. Their narrow foliage remains attractive after flowering is done, then draws
minimal attention as it fades in early summer.

In addition to the familiar garden campernelle, several other strains of
Narcissus × odorus may be encountered when ordering bulbs from abroad. Some
of these counterfeits are probably very old, for Haworth listed nine distinctly
different campernelles in his monograph of 1831. They must not be very enduring or free flowering in this country, for one seldom sees the other *N. × odorus*
cultivars in veteran plantings.

An exception, however, is the double form of the campernelle. These daffodils are just as fragrant, long-lived, and ready to flower as the singles. They
open a bit later, however, as their tightly packed buds require longer to expand.

Like other doubles in the South, these cabbagey blossoms run to green shades and usually blast or open poorly. Nevertheless, in certain springs mild weather stays long enough to permit flowering. In gratitude, these old flowers will then unfold like perfect, golden rosebuds.

❧ *Narcissus* × *intermedius*

In many old gardens there are strange-looking, sulfury jonquils that flower in April. Their homely, crimped blooms sit on short stems, which keeps the flowers hidden in the foliage. You have to get down on your knees and part the pale green leaves to see them properly. If you smell the frail-looking blossoms, their fragrance seems pungently sweet, with an aroma coming as much from Chinese sacred lily as jonquil.

These curious flowers belong to another ancient hybrid, a cross between *N. jonquilla* and *N. tazetta* known appropriately enough as *N.* × *intermedius*. Unlike campernelles, which are known only from man-made plantings, botanists have located *N.* × *intermedius* growing naturally in France, near Bayonne, in the foothills of the Pyrenees Mountains. Although still a wildflower in these regions, like other old jonquils *N.* × *intermedius* seems to have been grown in gardens from the start.

The most endearing characteristic of these daffodils is their unqualified toughness and persistence. They thrive equally on sand or clay and accept a wide range of Southern climate extremes. One often sees them happily flowering in vacant lots without any care whatsoever.

For best garden effect the rapidly multiplying clumps of *N.* × *intermedius* should be split and replanted every three years or so. This allows the bulbs to be spaced apart and keeps the overly generous foliage from crowding the blooms.

❧ *Montopolis*

On the sandy uplands of the old Montopolis district in Austin, Texas, several old gardens include what appears to be yet another jonquil hybrid. The flowers have distinctly rounded, creamy petals with sulfury cups, resembling small editions of *N. tazetta* 'Grand Primo'. Only the slender, dark green foliage gives away their jonquil ancestry.

These may be narcissi of true Southern origin, for they do not answer to the description of any well-known daffodils. Perhaps some industrious bee transferred the pollen of 'Grand Primo' onto a jonquil blossoming in an old Confederate garden. The resulting seed may have sprouted and bloomed for a lucky flower lover, who then shared bulbs with settlers moving west into Texas. These Montopolis daffodils may be among the first hybrid narcissi developed in the South.

❧ *Modern Jonquil Hybrids*

Unfortunately, precious little in the way of narcissus rearing has been attempted by Southerners. This is understandable, for our brief, uncertain springs offer a poor breeding environment for most daffodils. To find flowers for our borders, we have had to lean upon the work of gardeners in regions where spring is a more predictable season. The mild climates of Oregon, Ireland, and New Zealand seem to have attracted most of the breeders.

Even in these gentle districts hybridizing is a daunting prospect, for daffodil seedlings require six or seven years to mature and bloom, and longer before bulbs multiply to commercial numbers. These flowers demand a lifetime of devotion, and the folk who undertake to breed them do so for love, rather than for any hope of profit.

In the system of classification adopted by the American Daffodil Society, hybrids that inherit rushlike leaves or honey fragrance from *N. jonquilla* are grouped in Narcissus Division VII. Of all hybrid narcissi, these are the most fruitful for experimentation in the South. Nearly any Division VII daffodil will settle into garden life if offered ordinary care; most relish damp soils and summer heat.

Breeders have been active with the jonquils, and all the popular color combinations of white, pink, and yellow may now be secured for trial. The only general failing of this group is their tendency to bloom late in the season. This attribute is welcome in cool regions and has been actively developed by hybridizers. Although an asset in the North, in the fast-warming climate of the South, such late narcissi often fade prematurely. They may still be enjoyed but should be carefully positioned where they receive partial shade and shelter from hot winds.

There are, fortunately, several early- and midseason jonquil hybrids. All are excellent performers in the South and should be sought relentlessly. Of these, the preeminent variety is 'Trevithian', a 1927 introduction from P.D. Williams. This breathtaking flower is probably the best known of any Division VII hybrid. Its graceful foliage, gray-green and narrow, offers a perfect foil for the clustered blooms, which are precisely fashioned with round, golden petals surrounding a circular, butter yellow cup. The very picture of elegance, they make stunningly fragrant cut flowers.

It's surpassingly rare to discover a show-quality bloom with the garden vigor of 'Trevithian'. Around the Gulf local wisdom often portrays hybrid daffodils as mere annuals for winter bedding, but with 'Trevithian' gardeners have a perennial in the truest sense. These narcissi fill the role of refined, modern campernelles. They are now widely available and inexpensive, and so may be recommended for liberal planting. The clumps increase steadily, and a small investment in these bulbs will multiply tenfold in three or four years.

Other jonquil hybrids that have settled into Southern life include 'Sweetness', 'Lanarth', 'Golden Perfection', and 'Golden Sceptre'. They have mostly solitary blooms with wide, deep golden cups and petals. They look a bit like standard large-cupped daffodils, but with heavily textured petals, which are roughened and triangular in outline. This gives these flowers a starry appearance. They may be seen flowering faithfully in many gardens planted during the forties and fifties. They have since become scarce but may be acquired from a few specialists.

The bright yellow, orange-cupped 'Suzy' is a showstopping flower, usually with three blooms to a cluster. Although not permanent in all gardens, this bright flower is worth attempting. Other jonquil hybrids, such as 'Susan Pearson', have the same mix of reddish orange on yellow and should be tried, also. 'Golden Dawn' is a flashy orange and yellow bicolor, usually classed with the tazettas. It is completely at home in the South, rather like an improved *N.* × *intermedius*.

More recent jonquil hybrids from the Oregon breeder Grant Mitsch include a number charmingly named for wild birds. One of the most lovely is 'Quail', a rich yellow introduced in 1974. The cup of this variety is long and narrow, contrasting happily with the flat, radiating petals. The blossoms usually come in groups of three. They nod slightly, which gives them a hint of grace in spite of their rather boxy form. Even a modest clump of 'Quail' will provide a great deal of color and fragrance.

'Pipit' is a Mitsch introduction whose cups open light yellow, then fade slowly to cream. This eventually creates the avant-garde impression of a white cup against sulfur petals: in daffodil parlance, a reverse bicolor. Its pale, fragile-looking blooms nod gracefully and appear toward the end of April. 'Dickcissel', 'Hillstar', and 'New Day' have analogous forms and color schemes but possess darker, canary yellow petals behind their milky coronas. 'Pueblo' is all white, and 'Bell Song' is white with a pink cup.

These Mitsch varieties are treasures of form and color that seem entirely permanent. Several have been adopted by Dutch growers and are rapidly dropping in price as they increase in availability. Although these jonquils sometimes bloom late, they are lovely enough to warrant any small quotient of extra care.

🐚 *Modern Daffodils*

A number of gardeners in the South successfully cultivate large trumpets (Division I) as bedding flowers, but only a handful of these daffodils settle here with any permanence. During the Dutch narcissus embargo of the early twentieth century, American plantations raised thousands of bulbs of the best known trumpet, 'King Alfred', in the sandy soils of Louisiana and East Texas. This huge, golden variety and a few other early bloomers such as 'Golden Spur', 'Robert Syndenham', 'Emperor', and 'Empress', persist, and even thrive for some lucky folk, and may be seen in a few established gardens.

Bulbs offered in the trade as King Alfred today seldom fare so well, and may actually be substitutes of newer varieties, such as 'Dutch Master'. Although these inexpensive flowers grow magnificently the first year, they gradually give up blooming. After two or three seasons of dwindling performance, only gray foliage returns. The drab, flowerless clumps persist indefinitely as winter accents to neglected suburban yards.

🐚 *Incomparables*

Better garden value comes from the large-cupped narcissi (Division II), formerly classed among the primrose peerless, or incomparabilis, section. This varied

Narcissus 'Montopolis'

Narcissus 'Trevithian'

Leucojum aestivum

Narcissus 'Peeping Tom'

Narcissus 'Pipit'

Narcissus x *intermedius*

group descends from hybrids between *N. pseudonarcissus* varieties and various forms of the poet's narcissus (*N. poeticus*). The section offers the greatest range of colors and the most graceful, showy blooms among daffodils. Many are excellent for mass planting on loamy or sandy ground.

In a few old gardens, you may still see clumps of the starry-petaled 'Sir Watkin'. This famous flower is typical of many bicolors in this division, with buttery petals framing an orange-yellow cup. The corona is not so large as in the trumpet class but still makes a respectable show of itself. 'Sir Watkin' follows the early trumpets in bloom, usually appearing in March.

Another old hybrid, 'Lucifer', shows more poeticus influence. Its narrower primrose petals surround a shallow, chrome cup rimmed in orange. It's one of the few smaller cupped daffodils suited to the South. Occasionally, two blooms appear on the stalk instead of one.

Both of these incomparabilis hybrids are now hard to come by, but the brilliant orange-cupped, yellow-petaled 'Fortune' is just as well proven and may be readily obtained. This old variety is probably the best daffodil for a good bolt of springtime gold. 'Carbineer', 'Ceylon', and 'Rustom Pasha' are all fine, with orange-red on gold combinations, as well. 'Delibes' sets lemony petals around a large, flat cup banded in crimson. As an all-gold flower to substitute for yellow trumpets, 'Carlton' has long been a favored choice. All of these are early, putting in an appearance around the first of March.

Among the white varieties, 'Mount Hood' is reliable, as is the lemon-cupped, white-petaled 'Ice Follies'. None of the types with pink in the cup can really be called permanent in the South, although a few gardeners have modest luck with them. For this color it's usually better to return to the jonquil group.

🌸 *Angel's Tears*

Like many late jonquils, the Division V hybrids of *N. triandrus* often flower into April. This only lessens their value in a small way, however, for they have great substance in their thick petals, and they last better than other daffodils. They thrive in a variety of soils and prosper in partial shade. With their tilted blossoms, these are the most graceful of all the narcissi.

A wild form of *N. triandrus*, the variety *albus* has long been shared among gardeners under the charming name "angel's tears." The grassy, gray foliage of this familiar daffodil increases happily in the South, although the blooms do not appear freely in all gardens. When they come, they appear in groups of three, on six- to eight-inch stems. The individual florets nod like fuchsias and have shallow, rounded cups. They are a uniform creamy white, which gives them a ghostly paleness.

Many triandrus hybrids descend from a large, pale yellowish variety called *loiseleurii*, known only from the Isles of Glennan, off the southwestern coast of Brittany. A rare form and hard to obtain, it succeeds in the lower South and flowers more freely than the angel's tears.

The best known of the larger triandrus hybrids is 'Thalia', a creamy white, exquisitely proportioned blossom often nicknamed the "orchid narcissus." This is a very fine, fragrant, permanent flower, but, like many triandrus types, it is slow to increase. More recent whites include 'Ice Wings' and 'Petrel'. The latter is especially floriferous, with as many as five or six boxy blooms to a stem.

'Tuesday's Child' is a graceful, pendulous daffodil with white petals and a yellow cup. 'Liberty Bells' appears dressed all in soft yellow, like a sunny version of 'Thalia'. All of these appear toward the end of April.

'Hawera' is a miniature triandrus cross, whose other parent was a jonquil. This tiny daffodil inherits narrow foliage and a sweet fragrance. The starry rings of petals are a luminous, pale yellow, and the modest little blooms show a graceful inclination to nod.

Very different from this elf is the strong-growing 'Silver Chimes', a mighty descendent of *N. tazetta* 'Grand Primo'. This late-blooming flower is one of the best daffodils for heavy clay soils. Its tall, green foliage is much like its tazetta parent, but the clustered, milky blooms nod like good old 'Thalia'. It's one of the tried-and-true Southern daffodils, making a welcome April appearance in many gardens.

❦ *Reflexed Jonquils*

There is an odd little Portuguese daffodil with extraordinarily long trumpets and petals that turn back like a cyclamen blossom. Although the foliage accompanying the light, greenish gold bloom is flattened like a daffodil, it has the dark green slickness of a jonquil leaf. Gerard knew these miniatures as *"reflex junquilias."* Botanists call them *N. cyclamineus*.

These quaint little blooms need cooler, damper conditions than most of the South can offer, but they have sired a large race of hybrids that thrive on the acid sands of the Southeast. Many are early bloomers, so they are especially valuable in this climate. In gardens where the prevailing soil is a tight clay, they may be planted in raised beds of sand or decomposed granite. Under these conditions the cyclamineus hybrids (Division VI) will be long-lived and vigorous.

The most famous of this group are medium-sized bicolors, like the sulfur and yellow 'February Gold' and the white and yellow 'March Sunshine'. 'Auburn', 'Bartley', and 'Peeping Tom' are similar yellow types that may deputize for golden trumpets, although their petals sweep backward like those of their tiny ancestor.

In addition to these, there are many small or miniature cyclamineus hybrids. 'Tete a Tete' is a short, yellowish gold cross from *N. tazetta* 'Soliel d'Or'; it has become popular as a floristist blossom, forced in small pots for Valentine's Day. 'Jetfire' has similar, but larger, orange trumpets. 'Jack Snipe' combines a gold cup with near-white petals. 'Beryl' is a delicate, straw-colored descendent of *N. poeticus* with an orange-banded cup. These need more certain watering during growth than the larger cyclamineus hybrids but are otherwise hardy. They prosper in leafy soil with partial shade.

❦ *Poets*

Many later blooming poet and tazetta daffodils (Divisions VII and IX) perform poorly in the South, although a few of them have been in gardens for a long time. The old hybrid called April beauty or twin sisters is actually *N.* × *biflorus,* a natural cross of *N. poeticus* and *N. tazetta* cultivated since the sixteenth century. The whitish, orange-cupped blooms appear mostly in pairs, but sometimes singly or three together. They often close the daffodil season in late April.

Another old hybrid, the silver jonquil (*N.* × *tenuior* 'Gracilis') is descended from a cross between a poet and a jonquil and inherits the tall, slender foliage of the *N. jonquilla* group. The pale yellow, sweet scented blooms appear at the same late season as *N.* × *biflorus.* These old flowers are best in gardens of the middle and upper South.

Some of the older poetaz hybrids, such as the orange-cupped, white-petaled 'Geranium', do well, especially with partial shade from high-branching pines or pecans. 'Cragford', Matador', 'Martha Washington', and 'Mrs. Alfred Pearson' are all dependable.

🐚 *Double Daffodils*

The double 'Winston Churchill' is a newer poetaz variety that appeared spontaneously among a stock of singles. Although certain to succeed here as a plant, it needs an unfailing supply of moisture to keep from blasting.

The unpredictable springs of the South try the patience of many double daffodils. Few open properly, even when the plants grow well. The same is true for many of the strange split-corona daffodils, in which the cups divide to form an extra row of petals.

An exception among doubles is the ancient incomparabilis selection 'Orange Phoenix', known in the South as "eggs and bacon." These oddities are in many old gardens and, although ragged and tattered, offer an annual curiosity with their jumbled, yellow and orange blossoms.

Should the general failure of double daffodils and other bizarre types bring disappointment, Southerners may console themselves with the words C.L. Allen penned in 1915:

> *As flowers begin to be appreciated for their intrinsic worth, when*
> *we look into them rather than at them, when we see all their parts*
> *and their wonderful adaptation to each other, the beautiful necessity*
> *there is for each, our respect for double forms will be lost in our*
> *admiration for the single flower, perfect in all its parts as it was*
> *when it first beautified the earth, and there was none to admire it*
> *than the Power that gave it.*

🐚 *Snowdrops and Snowflakes*

Southerners receiving bulb catalogs in early summer go through a perennial moment of consternation when deciding whether to order snowdrops (*Galanthus* spp.) or snowflakes (*Leucojum* spp.). These similar-looking allies of the daffodils carry pendant, white blossoms marked with green, and their common names are similar enough that may people feel comfortable in interchanging them.

Except in the damper, cooler parts of the South, though, this confusion soon resolves itself, for *Galanthus* rarely persist more than a season. The robust flowers merrily chiming out spring in every Southern dooryard are those of the summer snowflake (*Leucojum aestivum*).

There are a few *Galanthus* from drier, sunnier regions that might prosper in the South, but most come from soggy alpine meadows. Without melting snow to feed their succulent, early growth, they can hardly be expected to thrive. Any kind of prolonged drought means doom to these flowers, and knowledgeable nurseries never sell the bulbs in a desiccated condition. These little plants are best moved "in the green," with a good bit of moist soil surrounding the roots.

The most likely snowdrop to succeed in the South is *Galanthus byzantinus*, a vigorous flower native to western Turkey, where the bulbs inhabit mountain forests in heavy soil. This is one of the species with grayish foliage. *G. elwesii* is similar and easy to bloom the first season, but it seldom establishes in gardens. Both of these flower anytime from Christmas onward.

The common snowdrop (G. nivalis) comes in several forms, all with lush, green foliage and snowy, pendant blooms. Such vigorous selections as 'Scharlockii' and 'Sam Arnott' are the most likely to succeed. They should be offered positions with shade and rich soil and should never want for moisture. Flowers may be expected in February or earlier.

The spring snowflake (*Leucojum vernum*) is as ill-suited to Southern conditions as most *Galanthus*, but this failure is of little consequence. Although the species often appears on the lists of importers, they invariably ship the similar summer snowflake (*L. aestivum*) in its stead. This one positively thrives in the South, and you could hardly ask for a more appealing spring flower.

The name *Leucojum*, an old one used by Theophrastus, translates as "white violet." These tiny, pure white, bell-shaped blooms have a subtle, sweet fragrance and appear in drooping clusters of two to six. They rise on twelve-inch stems directly from the robust, clustered bulbs. The six snowy petals are marked with unique thickened, green spots at the tips, and these give the fairy-sized blooms an air of unreality.

This is somewhat overcome by the tremendous bunches of lush green leaves rising from the round, narcissuslike bulbs. This excess of foliage is needed to set off the tiny sprays of bloom, and it does a fine job if the bulbs are planted together in clumps of at least six. 'Gravetye Giant' is a select large-flowered form that originated in the garden of the famous English horticulturist William Robinson. It is worth seeking out.

In their homes around the Mediterranean these bulbs grow in mucky soils along streams. In such a situation they prosper on a surplus of spring moisture and a long summer baking. This prepares the flowers especially for the heavy cotton soils of the South, and they also perform well on moist sand.

It seems hard to believe that summer snowflakes, so common and prolific in old Southern gardens, have become endangered in their home countries, but this appears to be the case. Overcollection for the bulb trade is one culprit, but widespread habitat destruction is another cause of decline. When purchasing bulbs, it is prudent to look for nursery-propagated stock. In your own yard, you can help these lovely, old-fashioned flowers by generous division and exchange with other interested gardeners.

Spring Treasures

Early bulbs like jonquils, irises, and tulips possess an extravagance of beauty that attracts all eyes. Smaller, more delicate flowers charm us with their frail countenances. A goodly measure of our delight comes from mixing the pallid, demure blooms with their bolder cohorts. Through several months each spring, Southerners may revel in a diversity of bulbous flowers and combine them in an endless array.

🌸 *Alliums*

The wild onions (*Allium* spp.) include both bold and shy flowers with a great role to play in Southern gardens. Although the genus is best known for its pungently odorous edible members (onions, leeks, chives, and garlics), it includes a wide assortment of showy flowering types. All the members of the tribe inherit the onion smell in their bulbs and foliage, and all hold blossoms in rounded clusters, or umbels. Beyond these common parameters, they achieve surprising diversity.

As a rule, hardy bulbs take several years to go from seed to flower, but many *Allium* grow rampantly, and seedlings frequently bloom only a season or two after planting. The tiny, black seeds may be scattered directly in the garden where bulbs are desired. This offers an inexpensive way to naturalize mass displays, which would be difficult to achieve through bulb planting alone.

🌸 *March Snow*

Even in this land where snows come rarely and tarry only for unpredictable instants, we may blanket the ground in pristine purity. All we must do is introduce a few round bulbs or seeds of the Naples onion (*Allium neapolitanum*). Set in an untended bed beneath

75

a grove of high-branching trees, they form a lush green understory. During the first days of March, swarms of loosely clustered blossoms rise to dance above the tapered foliage. Even while still closed tightly in bud, the clear white blooms reflect all light.

Although a small bulb, the Naples onion increases rapidly on any soil and soon extends in impressive patches. If it were not so well mannered about departing after its season, it might even be regarded as a weed. The profuse, titanium white flowers silence any such concerns. These early flecks of snow afford one of the telling moments of Southern springs. Scarcely any other blooms seem so fresh and alive at this tender season.

The very earliness of these blossoms puts them at some risk from northers, which can nip the precocious buds. In most gardens the Naples onion benefits from a position near a south wall or beneath the protective canopy of a tree. Beyond this shelter, these bulbs ask only for restraint of the lawn mower prior to May, when the rosettes of long, tapered leaves yellow and die away for summer.

Like other ornamental garlics, the foliage of this Mediterranean bulb emits a pungent scent when bruised. Although some might object to the odor, this subtracts in no way from the beauty of the flowers. The blooms themselves are sweet scented, sometimes called daffodil garlic in reference to their fragrance. Florists in Europe often set them in dye to color them.

The Naples onion has become well established in the Dutch bulb trade, despite its less than hardy inclinations. 'Grandiflorum' is a selection reputed to have large flowers. Also rather sizeable is a bulb sold as *Allium cowanii;* this name belongs to a variant that botanists now include under *A. neapolitanum.* *Allium subhirsutum* is a related species with slightly hairy leaves. All of these look so similar that no one would want them together in the same garden, but each seems well adapted to the South.

❦ Drummond's Onion

One of the most charming of the small onions is *Allium drummondi.* It's hard to understand why this sprightly native of Texas, Mexico, and the Great Plains has not been used more often in gardens. It's hardy everywhere, and the little bulbs seem to accept anything from thin, rocky ground to damp bottomland. The dainty clumps multiply swiftly, naturalizing if allowed to mature their narrow, gray leaves. The blooms come in cheerful tones of rosy-purple, pink, or glistening white, arriving usefully in March, in time to join the displays of daffodils and hyacinths.

These wildflowers radiate a potpourri of spicy fragrances much like the scent of old-fashioned sweet William (*Dianthus barbatus*). This seems a bit out of place on a little member of the garlic clan but adds greatly to their charm. The interestingly detailed blossoms also attract attention for their color variations, for each petal darkens in tone on the keel while paling toward the edge.

Even the bulbs of this onion have a surprising daintiness. They surround themselves in tawny, netlike coats that botanists term *reticula.* These fibrous covers help the little bulbs survive the dry months of summer on their native

Allium drummondi

Allium neapolitanum

Allium texanum

Allium coryi

Allium fraseri

Allium 'Margaret Kane'

prairies. As the plants grow, they multiply by dividing in half. If you peel back the reticulations, you often discover that the bulb in your hand is really two bulbs held tightly together by these protective coats.

Allium drummondi is one of the wild onions that lend themselves to naturalizing by seed. The tiny bulbs can be tedious to plant over large areas, yet seed can be readily sown anywhere. The young onions will flower the second spring after planting. *Allium drummondi* makes a wonderful early show when included in a buffalograss meadow along with other prairie flowers. This kind of semiwild garden can be successful anywhere in the South.

Since both bulbs and seeds of this variety are hard to come by in the trade, gardeners may wish to mark a native stand during the blooming season and return to harvest seed in late April or May. Once you've got a patch blooming in your yard, it's a simple matter to collect seed each season and spread the bulbs further.

🌿 *The Only Yellow Allium in North America*

The arid mesas and rugged basaltic mountains of west Texas are home to a surpassingly lovely garlic, *A. coryi*. The leaves and bulbs of these little flowers resemble those of *A. drummondi*, but their blooms are a rich, waxy yellow. Scattered among the dark volcanic rocks of their homeland, the tiny blossoms look like carpets of sunlight. One could never have too many of these glowing treasures, the only golden garlics in North America.

There are two or three yellow alliums native to the Old World, the most famous of which is the lily leek of southern Europe, *A. moly*. This variety, showy and well loved in gardens elsewhere, fares poorly in the warm climate of the South. The Mediterranean *A. flavum* does better, but it blooms in June or July. By this time, temperatures have climbed too high for its meager, primrose flowers to last.

Of honestly golden alliums, only *A. coryi* accepts Southern hospitality. This species increases rapidly through self-sown seed and bulb splitting. The one occasional pitfall seems to be rot during summer rains. This is particularly a problem in gardens with alkaline soils, which accelerate the activity of bacteria and fungi. The best remedy is usually a raised bed filled with acid sand or decomposed granite. The bed can be left to dry out in summer, or the bulbs may be dug and stored for replanting when cool weather returns.

In the wild, *A. coryi* usually blooms in April, but in gardens it flowers a month earlier, along with *A. drummondi*. If both species are planted together (a delightful plan), they will hybridize. The offspring of this cross are pale straw, with pink tints on the keels of the petals. When viewed with sunlight shining through them, the colors suffuse and blend to warm apricot.

🌿 *Canada Onions*

There are many native alliums that would make excellent garden bulbs, yet most seem to have been intentionally ignored by gardeners. This is perhaps the fault of the notorious Canada onion (*Allium canadense*). The frightful weediness of this widespread bulb makes poor public relations for all of our wild garlics.

This species produces tiny bulbils (miniature bulbs) in place of, or among, its chalky flowers. In some strains the bulbils take on reddish casts and can be fairly attractive. Nevertheless, any show offered hardly apologizes for the bad habits of this species. When the bulbils ripen, they fall to the ground like hundreds of rice grains, and nearly everyone sprouts. Even in a wild, naturalistic garden, this onion soon makes a pest of itself by crowding less aggressive neighbors. The best revenge is to take these prolific herbs into the kitchen, where they may be pressed as garlic and sent straight into the pot.

Inexcusably, taxonomists have attached the tainted reputation of these onions to a number of potentially useful garden flowers listed as varieties of *A. canadense*. This is an extreme case of what is known in botanical jargon as "lumping." Several distinct pink-, rose-, and white-flowered alliums, entirely lacking the treacherous bulbils, have been corralled and dumped into the same pile with a horrendous weed. One can only recall the couplet:

> *His is not to reason why;*
> *His is but to classify.*

One of the "varieties" included in this morass is *A. hyacinthoides*. This is a distinctive flower from north Texas and southern Oklahoma. The sweet, hyacinth-scented blossoms, held in small clusters, are shaped like miniature Grecian urns. They appear in early March, coming in strong shades of pink, old rose, or lavender. The gray-green leaves of *A. hyacinthoides* emerge wide at their bases, but taper quickly to narrow points. This is a hardy, fragrant allium, well suited to the middle and upper South. In the wild it grows in sun or shade, occuring on both sand and clay.

Near the Gulf, the April-flowering *A. ecristatum* offers similar charms on plants especially suited to damp conditions. Like *A. hyacinthoides*, this onion has rosy blooms cupped upward like little bells or pots. The flowers, which smell like carnations or pinks, are accompanied by green, tapered foliage. They often bloom in standing water in their soggy native habitat on the Texas coastal plain.

This species relishes heavy clay soils and multiplies quickly on damp ground. Although *A. ecristatum* needs an unfailing supply of water during the spring growing season, it appears indifferent to drought during summer. The intriguing bulbs are covered in wide, thick reticulations, which look like miniature lattice work. They multiply by splitting in half.

A. mobilense (*A. canadense* v. *mobilense*) is the common flowering onion in most of the South, with a range extending from Georgia west to Missouri. Its delicate lavender flowers appear in April on top of thin, twelve-inch stems. The petals spread out star fashion around the pale green ovaries. Although these individual florets are small, they mass together into attention-grabbing umbels. These lilac globes seem to float in the air as they perch above the slender leaves.

Through most of its range, this species occurs on loamy prairies that stay moist in spring and become dry in summer. In gardens *A. mobilense* responds to damp conditions and acid soil. The bulbs multiply swiftly from offsets appearing around the base. For best effect these pale blooms should be used in large groups. They may be posed before a dark groundcover of bronze ajuga to highlight their pallid translucence.

The deep sand ridges of central Texas provide the home for an aristocratic cousin of *A. mobilense*. The big, lilac spheres of this onion, rising above sparse, stiff leaves, sit atop stems that may achieve an extravagant eighteen inches. This elegant species was once given the queenly name of *Allium zenobiae* by botanists who knew it as a friend, but current taxonomic opinion discards this flower in the same pile with *A. canadense*. J.N. Giridlian glowingly described *A. zenobiae* in the 1954 catalog of Oakhurst Gardens:

> *"A recent discovery from Texas, and to our way of thinking the finest of the alliums both for garden and for cutting. The large umbels consist of over 150 florets of satiny white tinged pink."*

These orphaned flowers deserve to have homes in Southern gardens, despite questions over their botanical pedigree. They make a lovely spring combination with drummond phlox and are excellent for sandy sites. Many gardens with poor, dry soil would profit from their inclusion.

Allium fraseri blooms on the prairies and oak savannahs of Texas during April, and later as it follows spring northward to South Dakota. Its blooms are an alabaster white, like *A. canadense*, but the umbels lack the telltale bulbils of that species. *A. fraseri* also prefers drier, better drained soils than the Canada onion.

This variety is an easy-growing spring flower that can be massed as a foil to vibrant blooms like byzantine glads or irises. They seem to accept almost any soil. The stems reach eighteen inches or more when well grown.

Even larger and better is the "white king" (*A. texanum*). This is a robust upland species from the hills of Texas and Oklahoma. Its blooms are chalk white like *A. fraseri*, but its wide, strappy leaves are silver-blue. The flowers assemble in big, dome-shaped umbels that expand near the end of spring, usually during the first weeks of May. White kings provide fine companions for early daylilies.

❧ Leeks

Every country person knows how a thriving row of leeks dresses up the vegetable plot. The stunning, tall foliage and big orbs of pinkish green blooms recommend these perennials for flower gardens, too, though they have seldom been invited to such places. Northerners may plead lack of room, but Southerners have no good reason to exclude leeks (*A. porrum*) from their plantings: The other big alliums (*A. giganteum*, *A. christophii*, *A. aflatunense*) perform dismally in this climate.

Leeks are bold, architectural vegetables that seem to thrive in all regions. In many parts of the South, their wild ancestor, *A. ampeloprasum*, has escaped from old farms and run wild through the countryside. These old-fashioned flowers look much like traditional culinary leeks, but they make smaller stems.

Multiplying at an extraordinary pace, leeks may be seen colonizing old fields and rough woods.

Elephant garlic, another variant of the *A. ampeloprasum* group, resembles an enormous version of its namesake. Its toe-sized cloves have garnered a considerable following and may be found in many supermarkets. One may debate their culinary value as compared to traditional garlic (*A. sativum*), but there can be little question as to superior productivity. Each clove swiftly multiplies into a leek-sized clump in the garden.

Gray-green, sheathing leaves, overlapping like on a stalk of corn, give the leek and its allies character, whether they are in flower or not. It's this leafy, edible stem that has brought them fame as vegetables. These noble potherbs have thereby earned their place in heraldry, for the leek is the emblem of Wales.

All of the *A. ampeloprasum* variants grow easily and thrive even on poor soils. They are gratifyingly "perpetual" in Southern gardens, readily reproducing by offsets. The perfectly round clusters of flowers appear in May and last for a month in the garden, where they make a handsome focal point or tall backdrop. The blossoms may also be picked and put in a vase without water, where they will last indefinitely.

🐚 *Egyptian Onions*

Another culinary allium that may be put to service in flower gardens is the old multiplying type known in the South as the Egyptian onion. This variation of the common table onion (*A. cepa*) shares its distinctive, hollow leaves. It differs by having replaced its blooms with fat heads of edible bulbils. These are often shared by gardeners over the fence.

Egyptian onions belong to the readily propagated proliferum group of onions. The true bulbs never get large, and for culinary purposes they are generally harvested and chopped green as scallions. They may be left in the ground over summer, unlike traditional onions, which easily rot away in warm climates.

As with the leek, the value of these bulbs for ornamental gardens is in their unique architectural line. The Egyptian onion produces several hollow leaves in a small cluster. These reach upward like pale green kelps around a medusa head of pinkish green bulbils. The whole assemblage looks as if some exotic sea creature had crept into the garden one early day in May.

🐚 *Chinese Chives*

The common chive (*A. schoenoprasum*) is popular in herb gardens for its flavorful leaves, which are hollow, like those of table onions in miniature. Their charming domes of lavender, appearing in early spring, make a good showing as a border or low edging. During the protracted months of summer, however, these Alpine herbs decline. There is often little left to revive in the fall.

For this reason the chive of choice in most of the South is a very different bulb from Asia, *A. tuberosum*. This plant has been fondly nicknamed the "Chinese chive" or "garlic chive" in reference to its aromatic, strappy foliage. This is a common herb in Oriental cookery. Its garlic-scented leaves are used in soups, salads, and other dishes for the same oniony effects as European chives, but always added fresh, since cooking destroys their flavor.

The Chinese chive is a handsome plant and one that takes happily to garden life. The bright green leaves are accompanied by flat umbels of white, starry blooms. These flowers are modest and unpredictable in their season, often beginning as early as May and continuing as late as November. Although entirely ordinary in appearance, the blossoms appear faithfully, last well when cut, and complement a variety of other flowers, both in arrangements and in the garden. In many ways they are among the most valuable of Southern garden blooms.

Unlike the strictly bulbous alliums described above, *A. tuberosum* has developed a novel creeping rhizome from which individual bulbs sprout at close intervals. This allows these perennials to clump like dense, green grasses. They multiply swiftly and may be divided and replanted at almost any time of year. The leaves die away briefly in winter but are otherwise continuous. This is a reversal of the seasons observed by most alliums.

🦪 *Drumsticks*

Other than the Naples onion, only a few European species seem happy in the South, and most are both dowdy and uncommon in the bulb trade. One that is rather attractive and available is *A. sphaerocephalum*. The tongue-twisting bit of Latin used to name this species translates as "round-headed." Although vaguely descriptive, such a comment offers little distinction in this genus of orb-topped herbs. The common name seems more definitive (and pronounce-able): "drumsticks."

The conical, wine-purple buds of *A. sphaerocephalum* elongate slightly as the flowers open. This slowly warps the ball of blooms into a pear shape, so that the expanding umbel appears not unlike the tip of a drumstick in gross outline. The uniquely shaped clusters are one-and-a-half to two inches across. They sit atop stems reaching twelve to eighteen inches in height.

The flowers of the drumstick onion arrive late for Southerners, in mid-June, so they benefit from partial shade to prolong their display and prevent scorching. Otherwise, these alliums are easy and rapid of increase. The erect, blue-green leaves are so sparse and slender as to be invisible. The wispy plants may be mixed among shrubs and perennials without fear of intruding on the design. The rich purple blooms show well among gray artemisias or santolinas.

🦪 *Society Garlic*

A pretty South African ally of the alliums, *Tulbaghia violacea* is known as wild garlic or *wilde knoflook* in its homeland, and as society garlic in America. This is a marvelous bulb for Southern gardens, with a flowering season lasting the whole summer. The rich lavender-pink blooms, with tiny crests in the center of the petals, grow together in tight umbels on stems a foot high. The more or less evergreen leaves clump prolifically, like Chinese chives.

Society garlic has a wide range, from the Cape Province north to Rhodesia and the Transvaal, and therefore adapts to varied soils and climates. It would make a fine cut flower if not for the rank juice in its stems and leaves. This slimy fluid smells like a mixture of onion and turnip, causing one to wonder in what kind of "society" these garlics would be appropriate.

In the garden, *T. violacea* is tough and enduring, readily recovering from drought and from temperatures as low as 15 degrees F. Gardeners will be rewarded with better, more prolific bloom, however, if they give regular moisture through summer and modest shelter from frost during winter. This advice goes double for the beautiful, white-variegated selection, 'Silver Lace'. Society garlics thrive best on a rich, well-prepared loam. They prove equally happy in open sun or part shade.

The "pink agapanthus," or sweet garlic, *T. fragrans*, is larger and more beautiful in most respects than *T. violacea*, but its winter flowering season prohibits use north of the lower South. Where frost is severe, these bulbs may be enjoyed in tubs on the patio. This species has very wide, gray foliage, which grows lavishly in summer but may flag and die away somewhat in winter. The dormant, leafless bulbs send up long-stemmed umbels of fragrant, pink blooms. Appearing from November to April, they will last a week or more in a vase.

🦪 Crow Poison

In early March, before most other other native flowers have awakened from winter sleep, roadsides and lawns begin to brighten with the small, creamy flowers and glossy, green leaves of crow poison (*Nothoscordum bivalve*). These tiny, yellow-centered blooms could be overlooked, if not for their welcome earliness and pleasant fragrance, which is sweet and spicy like old-fashioned carnations. On damp, protected banks near streams, the little blossoms appear in company with lush green winter grasses and blue, purple, and wine-pink spiderworts. In such situations these precocious wildlings show their cheery blooms long before spring begins elsewhere.

The crow poison is a common native of the South, growing also in Mexico and in South America, where it has several relations. The members of the genus *Nothoscordum*, or "false onions," all have an onionlike build, but they lack the pungent odor of true alliums. They bear fewer blossoms in their umbels, and the bulbs are white coated, with a peculiar spongy texture unlike the hard skins of an onion. All of the varieties flower over a long season in spring and early summer and thrive under ordinary care. Many, including *N. bivalve*, return to flower with fall rains. Although seldom showy, these small blooms are welcome.

The spreading tendencies of *N. bivalve* offer little threat, but the same cannot be said of its weedy cousin, *N. inodorum* (*N. fragrans*). This Argentinian variety produces larger, more fragrant blooms than *N. bivalve*, but also forms myriad bulblets. In only a week's time, a dried bulb set in a paper bag might produce fifty offsets, each prepared to rain down on the ground and begin to grow.

Allium ampeloprasum

Androstephium coeruleum

Allium drummondi

Triteleia laxa 'Queen Fabiola'

Erythronium albidum

Allium tuberosum: Chinese chives flowering with wild bergamot

Unless gardeners are wary, entire yards may be swallowed in the dirty white blooms and gray foliage of this aggressive species.

Although *N. odorum* should be avoided at all costs, there are several other South American *Nothoscordum* of merit. *N. nocturnum* has long, grayish leaves and nice-sized, whitish blooms marked with purplish keels. These flowers remain partially closed in the daytime but open at dusk to emit a sweet, musky perfume. Although *N. montevidense* is small, it sends up a succession of bright golden blooms that would be an asset to any garden. *N. arenarium* contributes starry umbels of pure white blooms in spring and fall.

🌺 *Blossoms of the Harvest*

As a rule, most things Californian fare poorly when brought to the South. The languid atmosphere here sets a different pace for life than the sunny breezes of the west. Still, there are a handful of onionlike westerners that persist, so long as they are offered spots where they may bask. In nature these flowers bloom at the onset of summer drought. On rolling hillsides dotted with evergreen oaks, they occur mixed among masses of ripening grass. When the hay is harvested, the blooms may be cut and baled.

In early classifications these papery flowers were grouped together in the large genus *Brodiaea,* but now they may also be met under such names as *Triteleia* and *Dichelostemma.* Their six-petaled blossoms appear in sparse clusters that superficially favor alliums. The meager, unscented leaves are angular in cross section and rise from corms instead of bulbs. In California these plants are sometimes called fool's onions.

During the years between 1893 and 1950, an unusually capable plantsman, Carl Purdy, brought several of these western flowers into wide cultivation. Only a precious few of his introductions remain in commerce. Those which may be had are permanent but slow to increase in Southern gardens. They may be raised from seed more rapidly than from offsets.

One of the most widespread of the old brodiaeas is the blue-dicks (*Dichelostemma pulchellum*). Its natural range extends from Baja California to Oregon and inland to New Mexico. In mid-March the washy, lilac blooms rise in tight clusters on twelve-inch stems. The individual florets have tiny crests like blooms of society garlic. They last almost a month, while the leaves simultaneously yellow and wither.

Other bulbs in this western group mostly flower in May and hold their cupped blooms in loose umbels like crowds of tiny shuttlecocks. One of the best of these later types is the wild hyacinth (*Triteleia hyacinthina*). Its blooms, usually with milky petals with green keels, occasionally shade to pale lavender. The flowers are sweetly fragrant and may be cut and dried for long-lasting winter arrangements. In the wild this species occurs from British Columbia to California. Unlike most of its kin, this brodiaea does well in low, moist areas.

Ithuriel's spear (*Triteleia laxa*) has more typical preferences. In nature it grows in areas of adobe soil. It doesn't mind waterlogged sites in the garden during winter, but when summer arrives it expects to be thoroughly dried and ripened.

These one-inch flowers awaken May gardens with an explosive charge of gentian blue lined in dark green. Such rich hues are rarely available to gardeners in the South, so these blossoms may be forgiven for their sparse, yellowing foliage at bloom time. If planted among waving winter grasses, as in their native California and Oregon hills, the tattered leaves will disappear from view, and the deep violet flowers will shine like sapphires set in gold. Canada wild rye (*Elymus canadensis*) and needle grass (*Stipa* spp.) turn to ripe straw in late April and make suitable companions in the South.

In addition to the common strains, an improved selection, 'Queen Fabiola', is also widely available. *Triteleia* × *tubergenii* is a hybrid between the Ithuriel's spear and a related species, *T. peduncularis*. It looks like a lilac edition of *T. laxa*.

❧ *Spring Stars*

A diminutive ally of the brodiaeas, *Androstephium coeruleum* grows on undisturbed prairies from central Texas to Oklahoma and northward. Those who know this short, early flower sometimes call it blue funnel lily, but most people have never even seen it. The pale lavender blooms appear in March before the grass greens up, and it takes an observant eye to spot them hovering above the drab ground. Once discovered, they will not be forgotten, for the slender, starry petals have a succulent, transparent beauty. When numerous, they resemble fields of celestial anemones.

These little flowers favor gravelly areas with thin soil and fast drainage. In gardens they are useful for rockeries or troughs, where their small stature will not be overpowered by taller, more aggressive flowers. They have never entered the regular bulb trade but may sometimes be had from rock garden specialists. As with brodiaeas, *Androstephium* multiplies most quickly from seed.

❧ *Woodlanders*

For a magical few weeks, certain Southern woodlands fill with carpets of spotted leaves. In February the delicate, marbled foliage unfurls into the frosty air and lays close against the earth. March brings ephemeral nodding blooms to join the dappled greenery. As April thunderstorms arrive, everything yellows and retreats into the ground to await another season.

This is the fleeting life cycle of *Erythronium albidum*, the trout lily, one of the well-loved forest flowers of America. The picturesque common name recalls the spotted skin of the brook trout, which resembles the mottled, elliptical leaves. "Fawn lily" and "adder's tongue" also refer to this foliage. "Dog-tooth violet" is a quaint title inherited from the European *E. dens-canis*, whose long, pointed corm suggests a canine fang.

These small wildlings, because they nod and face the earth like tiny tiger lilies, can only be viewed properly with close inspection. Despite their unimposing proportions, the subtly colored flowers provoke delight in all who see them.

The little blooms bespeak secret charm, as if they knew hidden groves where the forest fairies dance on moonlit nights.

Trout lilies are mostly native to places where spring is a longer, milder season than in the South. In consequence of this, their period of growth and flowering in the South has been curtailed to a few brief weeks of spring. Only those who walk the woods on a regular basis know these flowers intimately.

The white- to lavender-flowered *E. albidum* ranges through the middle and upper South, where the small corms grow on loamy terrace soils along watercourses. This is the easiest of our natives to bring into gardens, as it withstands drought and heavy soil. The yellow-flowered *E. rostratum* is also common in some parts of the South, but only in rich woodlands. It is a variation of the widespread yellow dog-tooth violet of the North, *E. americanum*. Its corms, resembling the true bulbs of tulips, grow deeply in leafy, moist ground. They must have similar soil conditions in gardens if they are to persist.

Both of these wildflowers have reputations as shy bloomers. This diffidence usually is blamed on their tendency to multiply by underground stolons, so that the plants develop into big patches of undersized bulbs, each with a solitary leaf. Only bulbs that mature and make two or three leaves will flower. Nestling these plants against rocks or trees will often encourage them to size up and bloom.

🌸 *Wake Robins*

As with erythroniums, wake robins (*Trillium* spp.) are flowers of cool, moist forests. They put in an ephemeral spring appearance before leafy canopies fill in to block the summer sun. Although they might seem out of place in company with palmettos and magnolias, several species are native to loamy, neutral soils in Southern woodlands. They grow readily enough in shaded gardens to recommend their use even in the warmest parts of the South. Their creeping rhizomes slowly develop into good clumps, which may be divided and reset in any shaded position.

The most prolific and drought-tolerant wake robin in the South is *Trillium gracile* (*T. ludovicianum*), an ally of the more widespread eastern toadshade, *T. sessile*. Although less glamorous than some of the northern trilliums, this species shows this genus' typical redundant pattern of three. The attractive mottled foliage rises in early winter, expanding in a whorl of three triangular leaves. A greenish, three-petaled bud, sitting firmly in the center, persists in a closed position until late February, when it opens to reveal a dark maroon interior and three brownish red, upright inner petals. The somber color scheme is complemented by an unusual fragrance reminiscent of morel mushrooms.

T. gracile has a pale greenish yellow form (var. *luteum*), as well as the typical dark purple-red. In addition to these, the purple trillium, or bloody butcher (*T. recurvatum*), also with dappled leaves and purplish blooms, and the pink-tinged, green-leafed *T. pusillum* may be met in Southern woodlands. These are the easiest types near the Gulf, but several rarer, showier species would be worth trying in the upper South. Elizabeth Lawrence gave a tantalizing discussion of a few successful types for the Carolinas in *The Little Bulbs*.

All native trilliums are well worth acquiring for shady gardens. However, the delicate tubers should be moved from the wild with reluctance. Several specialist nurseries propagate these wildflowers, and a variety of lovely species may be had in good conscience and at nominal cost.

❧ *Solomon's Seals*

The Solomon's seals (*Polygonatum* spp.) are leafy lilies whose associations are with the coolest, most boreal forests. They seem poor choices for warm climates like the South, yet a handful survive here and prove amazingly tough, thriving even on poor ground. The elegant, leafy arcs of foliage and tiny, drooping, bell-like flowers have much to offer any shady garden.

These hardy perennials spring from an elongated, horizontal rhizome with annular rings like the roots of a bamboo. This is the source of the old Greek name of these herbs, *polygonaton*, which means "many knees." This characteristic also explains the common name: Each year a new ring appears on the roots after the leaves and flowers wither, and this is vaguely suggestive of a rounded seal.

The great Solomon's seal (*Polygonatum biflorum*) is the most common type in native woodlands. This handsome variety is sometimes listed as *P. giganteum* in catalogs. It's an excellent grower, achieving three feet on rich, moist soil. It ranges through the South and down into the forested mountains of Nuevo Leon, Mexico. The delicate, greenish flowers of these plants make do with quiet beauty instead of loud color. When well treated, they ripen to purplish berries.

P. falcatum (*P. japonicum*) is usually cultivated in its choice variegated form. This variety ('Variegata') develops creamy edges on the leaves, beautifully accented by purplish colors on the stems. This tough native of Japan and Korea does surprisingly well in the warm climate of the South, returning faithfully each spring, even if subjected to scorching drought in summer. The rhizomes require several years to settle in before offering much bloom, but the lovely foliage offers a show from the outset. This combines happily with leafy banks of ferns or other woodland perennials. 'Variegata' may be had in warm gardens where other variegated subjects, such as hostas, swiftly melt away.

❧ *Tulips*

Tulips have long been features in the same gardens where the formal cult of azaleas and camelias holds court. These tall, majestic flowers are annually bedded in wide rows before glittering green shrubs, or may be massed in deep beds to bloom with dogwoods, redbuds, and wisteria. Less lively flowers would expose the artifice of these orchestrations, but the ravishing loveliness and rich color of tulips invariably bring off a grand show. In the South warm temperatures may advance and threaten their flowering season, but spring would be less magnificent if we did not at least try to grow these flowers.

Beyond these annually renewed displays, however, very few Southern gardeners give these blooms a second thought. Tulips are hardly ever advanced for use as perennials. The hybrid bedding varieties are casually selected by

Trillium gracile

Tulipa clusiana var. *chrysantha*

Scilla hyacinthoides

Tulipa sylvestris

Polygonatum falcatum 'Variegata'

Leopoldia comosum 'Plumosum'

color, with little thought of their potential for long-term survival. While it is true that most tulip varieties are ill suited to Southern latitudes, a few are satisfactory, and more might be discovered or developed if gardeners made an effort to explore the genus instead of replacing bulbs each fall.

The first garden tulip, like the first anemone, hyacinth, and ranunculus, was the pet flower of some ancient Eastern sultan. Turkish horticulturists are often credited with their domestication, but Persians had tulips at an early date and also participated in their development. In both countries warm, dry summers follow spring. The old tulips grew in a much balmier climate than Holland, where our modern types have been bred.

Twelfth-century Persian poets praised the beauty of "multicolored tulips"; some historians have taken this as the first evidence of these flowers in gardens. Authorities disagree on the origin of the tulip but consider *Tulipa gesnerana*, a scarlet species from Asia Minor, as the most likely progenitor. The first domestic derivatives were introduced to Europe from Turkey in the late sixteenth century. Our modern hybrids are descended from this initial oriental infusion.

🦪 *The Lady Tulip*

It is possible that the old poems refer not to the hybrid tulip, but to what Parkinson and other early botanists called the Persian tulip (*T. clusiana*). Modern gardeners know this pink and white species as lady tulip or candy tulip. These cheery blooms rate among the most useful and permanent types in the South. They may also be the oldest of their race in gardens.

Like many bulbs that excel in warm climates, *T. clusiana* is blessed with an added arsenal of DNA. Technically, the species is a pentaploid, with five sets of chromosomes. Despite this anomalous condition, it sets viable seed and has naturalized in several countries around the Mediterranean. The vigorous bulbs also multiply by droopers (stolons) and, in some strains, by offsets or buds from the base.

Carolus Clusius (Charles d'Ecluse), author of *Rariorum Plantarum Historia* (A History of Rare Plants) and the man remembered in this flower's name, reported the introduction of *T. clusiana* to the gardens of Florence in 1606. The original home of the lady tulip seems to have stretched from the mountains of Iran to Kashmir, but it has been cultivated for so long that the limit of this distribution is now unclear.

This history would mean little today if it concerned a drab, ordinary flower, but the lady tulip ranks as one of the prettiest species of its genus. The cheerfully marked blooms reach a respectable size yet always appear nimble and lithe. The twelve- to fourteen-inch stems carry a few slender, gray leaves with reddish margins. The upper two-thirds of the flower stalk remains bare, so as to show off the bright red and white blossom. Long stems may be cut without removing foliage, and buds may be guiltlessly harvested for indoor arrangements.

Vibrant cherry splashes appear over *T. clusiana*'s outer petals. Only their margins show a bit of white, so the flowers appear entirely red when closed. Milky inner petals become visible as the bloom opens. When the long buds fully expand, they reveal a cream-colored interior with a central blotch of carmine and six purple stamens.

One of the delights of the lady tulip and other members of this genus is their daily ritual of movement. Tulips show their love for the spring sun by tracking the heavens each day. In the cool of the morning, the buds nod to the east and slowly open wider as the day progresses. By noon they are spread flat and looking skyward; at four o'clock they lean toward the setting sun and begin to shut for the evening. In a clump of a dozen bulbs, this lively activity may repeat daily for a fortnight as each flower matures and runs its course.

In the South the lady tulip may be planted in large groups among clumps of summer snowflakes (*Leucojum aestivum*) and *Narcissus* 'Trevithian'. These three bulbs bloom reliably at the same season, usually in mid-April. Their slender grace complements one another, and they will all return and increase without need for disturbance. Bluebonnets (*Lupinus texensis*) and wild foxglove (*Penstemon cobaea*) are other good companions.

Lady tulips have an undemanding nature, but they prosper best when offered well-drained, limy soils like those of their homeland. The small, brown-skinned bulbs bear a tuft of hair at the tip. This is part of a silky tunic surrounding the bulbs and preserving them through the arid summers of Persia. Gardeners should take a hint from this natural device and offer these flowers a good summer baking. Beds filled with gritty, perfectly drained compost will be welcomed. This ensures the continuance of these Mideastern flowers for many seasons.

A form of the lady tulip from Afghanistan and Kashmir, var. *stellata* differs in having narrow petals and a yellow central blotch. Another relation, *T. clusiana* var. *chrysantha* originates from India and has blooms with a bright yellow ground marked red. 'Cynthia' is a hybrid with sulfur- and red-flamed blooms. The Dutch firm Van Tubergen developed this flower by crossing var. *chrysantha* with ordinary *T. clusiana*. All these enjoy similar treatment to common lady tulips. They stay shorter, usually six to eight inches, and may bloom slightly later.

❧ More Tulip Species

The Cretan tulip (*T. saxatilis*) has a reputation for shy flowering, since some strains multiply to excess. All too often, only blind, undersized bulbs are produced. The lush, glossy foliage tells the tale when it comes up in December and makes its green sheet across the rockery. Nothing could frustrate a gardener more than the sight of a forest of solitary leaves, for this is a sure sign the bulbs will be too small to flower.

Like many species tulips, *T. saxatilis* naturally propagates with droopers. Although nurseries have offered bulbs with these multiplicative habits in the past, recent selection efforts have sought to eliminate such traits. The improved *T. saxatilis* offset instead of running. Nurseries sometimes list them under the old synonym *T. bakeri* or under the variety name 'Lilac Wonder'. Under any title these modern editions of *T. saxatilis* are improvements, offering bigger bulbs and surer flowering.

This is a very happy turn of events for gardeners, since the blooms of *T. saxatilis* are colored a delicious mixture of pink-lilac around a yellow center. The flowers are short but open into wide bowls. When well grown, they arrive three to a stem. The bulbs resemble those of *T. clusiana* and seem equally permanent. As the name *saxatilis* ("rock dwelling") suggests, these Mediterranean flowers prefer a gritty, well-drained compost with plenty of lime.

In more moist aspects of the garden, the species to try is the Florentine tulip (*T. sylvestris*). Although the Latin epithet seems to imply a preference for woodland, this early flower is more often a denizen of fields and meadows. Its native range extends over Persia and Europe, where it is common in old pastures and vineyards. It has also escaped from gardens to run wild in the middle Atlantic states of the United States. Thomas Jefferson reportedly had both this and *T. clusiana* in his garden at Monticello.

T. sylvestris has a slender, lithe appearance and a modest, twelve-inch stature. The medium-sized bulbs are covered with silky tunics that glow with the warm orange tone of sandalwood. There are two or three flowers to a stem, with several thick, gray leaves near the base of the stalks. The pale lemon buds are suffused with green and nod gracefully prior to opening. In mid-March they turn upward and expand into fragrant, yellow goblets. The pleasant scent of these blooms, vaguely resembling that of sweet violets, inspired the fulsome title of a previous era, *Tulipa florentina odorata*.

T. sylvestris is yet another tulip with a well-known spreading tendency. This may cause some loss of bloom, but if the soil is deep and rich, the bulbs should establish and yield enough flowers to justify the colonies of leaves. A selection from Iran called 'Tabris' and another called 'Major' are supposedly larger, more free flowering, and less colonial. *T. sylvestris* var. *australis* is a Mediterranean variant with slightly smaller blooms.

Another curious cultivar sometimes included on nursery lists is the horned tulip, *T. acuminata*. No one seems sure about the origin of this plant. The extraordinary, skinny flowers showed up in gardens about 1816, reportedly as imports from the Levant. Their long, undulating petals are orange-red and long lasting, but their thinness makes the flowers more odd than attractive.

Somewhat similar to the horned tulip, an old cultivar called *T. retroflexa* was used to breed the modern lily-flowered varieties. These late-blooming tulips were developed from crosses with Darwin tulips. They were once included among the cottage tulips, a race of perennial types rediscovered and collected from old gardens during the nineteenth century. The lily-flowered tulips inherit graceful, vase-shaped blooms and strong, upright stems. Some, such as the orange-flowered 'Ballerina', show their legacy of antique breeding with a sweet fragrance.

Lily-flowered tulips have no need of winter chilling. In the South vigorous selections, such as the glowing red-and-yellow 'Queen of Sheba', will perpetuate so long as they are kept dry over summer. This may be accomplished with a raised bed of sand or by lifting and storing the bulbs over summer. Since the lily-flowered cultivars are among the tallest tulips, deep planting is preferred to prevent rocking about in windy spring weather. Six to eight inches is standard.

❧ The Red Ones

The gaudy red *Tulipa eichleri* is another variety that endures in the South if sheltered from summer dampness. Although a natural species, its brilliant flowers compete in showiness with any hybrid. The magnificent blooms nestle between broad, gray leaves. Shiny black, yellow-edged blotches gleam back from the center of the flowers. The plants don't always achieve their full twelve-inch height in unsteady spring weather, but this species is as reliable for early color as any tulip and longer lasting than most. The native haunts of *T. eichleri* are in Turkestan and Iran, where the bulbs inhabit dry hillsides and fallow cornfields.

The showy *T. linifolia* also provides its red flowers without need for winter chill. This black-eyed miniature hails from Uzbekistan in central Asia and is ideally suited to rock gardens. The narrow leaves spread out like little, gray starfishes. Eye-popping silky, red blossoms appear between the foliage in April. Several showy hybrids between *T. linifolia* and the soft yellow *T. batalanii*, with bronze, scarlet, or apricot flowers, may be had as well. If protected from summer wet, all of these types will return for several seasons.

❧ Blue Bottles

One of the first flowers met by any child growing up in the South is the little blue muscari, known fondly as the blue bottle or grape hyacinth. These modest yet bright blossoms are in all the old lawns. They spread quickly by bulblets and seed and have naturalized in all sorts of places. The dark green, wiry leaves come up in the fall, so the clumps make an obvious green tuft all winter. In early March the bulbs send up sweet-scented, violet-blue spikes. This is when children discover them and gather the blooms in tight handfuls to inhale their fruity perfume.

These old flowers have made themselves at home in our country and may be seen growing on many soils and exposures. They are the first spring bulbs that come to mind when anyone speaks about naturalizing. It's often taken for granted that any grape hyacinth will settle down and spread, just like the ones populating wayside gardens. In truth, the standard muscari of commerce seldom naturalize in the South, although nearly all flower well for a season or two.

The authentic dark blue bottles so widespread in old gardens belong to a European species that has never been common in the bulb trade. It is known by tradition as the starch hyacinth. Parkinson may have initiated this title when he described the fragrance of the small violet blooms as "like unto starch when it is hot and new."

The confusing botany of the muscari presents difficulty even for experts, and the dust has yet to settle on any listing which might be regarded as final. However, the old grape hyacinth of the South displays characteristics readily distinguishing it from other varieties. Its globular, blackish blue flowers congregate in spikes, or racemes, with up to thirty downward-drooping blossoms. These sit on six- to eight-inch stems among the overly lush clumps of foliage. The lowest blossoms open first, revealing a rim of white teeth as they expand. At the top of the spike, a group of sterile florets shades to azure. The old-fashioned grape hyacinths have been called *Muscari racemosum* or *M. atlanticum* by past authors but are better known today as *M. neglectum*. This seems an appropriate title for a bulb so common about abandoned homesteads and untended meadows.

The muscari imported from Holland are mostly forms of *M. armeniacum*. This species is similar to the starch hyacinth in size and form but has showier azure or purplish blue flowers. The Italian grape hyacinth (*M. botryoides*) is also close to these. This type is commonly grown in its white variety, 'Album', which has the appealing nickname "Pearls of Spain." The beautiful, sky blue *M. tubergenianum* is another look-alike grape hyacinth. It reportedly originates from the mountains of Iran. These commercial varieties may be coaxed to persist in the South if planted in raised beds of sand, but otherwise they are likely to dwindle away and require replacing every few years.

❧ *Feather Hyacinths*

Gardeners love a curiosity, as surely is testified by the prevalence of the plume hyacinth in old Southern gardens. Other than *M. neglectum*, this novelty is the only grape hyacinth likely to be met in a naturalized condition. Thomas Jefferson recorded their bloom at Monticello on April 25, 1767.

These singular flowers, already well known in Parkinson's time, were probably introduced by the same ingenious Turks who developed the tulip and other Near Eastern bulbs. Botanists generally regard the plume, or feather, hyacinth as a sterile form of the tassel hyacinth (*Muscari comosum*). In its ordinary dress the species appears as a drab, loose, olive green spike garnished with a topknot of dark purple.

The feather hyacinth hardly resembles this wild form. Instead of the bell-shaped blooms of the ordinary muscari, its intriguing spike has transformed into an amethyst filigree. The branched, feathery tassels have a delicate translucence, which makes them seem glassy when lit by the April sun. They rise eight to ten inches above the curling, succulent, gray-green leaves.

Feather hyacinths bloom after the big rush of spring flowers, toward the end of April or first of May. Since the blossoms last for several weeks, they provide a useful accent at this transitional moment, when so many early flowers are finishing and the blooms of summer have yet to begin. Their delicate lavender combines happily with broad, gray foliage, such as lamb's ears (*Stachys byzantina*). The shallow bulbs do well in either sun or partial shade, so long as they are provided reasonably well-drained soil. They multiply swiftly and may be divided and reset every two or three years.

There is a move on among botanists to transfer the feather hyacinth, the tassel hyacinth, and a handful of other odd muscari into a separate genus, *Leopoldia*. If this view is followed, then *Muscari comosum* becomes *Leopoldia como-*

sum, and the feather hyacinth should properly be *L. comosum* 'Plumosum'. Most nurseries continue to list these old flowers simply as *Muscari plumosum.*

🌺 Nutmeg Hyacinths

Another odd flower sometimes segregated from the herd of muscari is the nutmeg hyacinth, listed either as *Muscari* or *Muscarimia ambrosiacum.* This pale lavender and white flower is thought to be an old garden form of musk hyacinth (*Muscarimia moshatum*). Tiny spikes of barrel-shaped blooms rise above its thick-rooted bulbs toward the end of March. These flowers can hardly be considered showy, but they are worth planting for their sweet fragrance. Gerard explained in 1597:

> *They are kept and maintained in gardens for the pleasant smell of their floures, but not for their beauty. For that, many stinking field floures do in beautie farre surpasse them.*

These old Turkish bulbs flower readily in the South, persisting if planted in raised beds of sand so they may remain dry during summer. Their flowers and foliage are so small and meager, however, that most landscape companions are likely to overpower them. An attractive niche of stones and a top dressing of crushed gravel may be positioned to show off the blooms and shelter the bulbs from aggressive neighbors.

🌺 Hyacinth Squills

In old gardens, you may often see dark green rosettes marking winter beds like rows of lush, glossy starfishes. If you dig up the clumps, they reveal substantial, white, fleshy bulbs with large, visible scales. In many instances, these leafy perennials disappear mysteriously in early summer without ever having offered a bloom, and gardeners are left to wonder for another season what curious flower belongs with this robust foliage.

Sometimes the solution to the puzzle is met along a nearby creek. These same bulbs escape cultivation to naturalize on the loamy terrace soils on moist riversides. Here they receive enough spring moisture to complete flowering. The big bulbs do not disappoint, for in late April they send up impressive, three-foot spikes of starry, lavender flowers. Arranged in loose, pyramidal racemes that open from the base, swarms of hazy lilac blooms and similarly colored flower stems expand below a tight spear of pale green and lavender buds.

This original and dramatic bulbous flower is known as the hyacinth squill (*Scilla hyacinthoides*). It's a Mediterranean native that persists indefinitely in Southern gardens but rarely blooms without coaxing. To encourage regular flowering, it's best to lift bulbs annually as the foliage yellows in early June. They may be replanted in autumn in rich, well-prepared ground. If irrigated generously through April, flowering will be ensured.

This obscure yet traditional flower is often confused with a similar blue squill from South Africa, *Scilla natalensis.* Although the two species are remarkably alike in flower, *S. natalensis* has fewer, wider leaves and normally grows with its succulent bulbs protruding from the ground. This subtropical is a summer grower, flowering in July. It would be worth trying in warmer parts of the South.

The meadow squill (*Scilla litardieri*) is a slender relation of *S. hyacinthoides*, with similar flowers grouped in a more modest, eight- to fifteen-inch raceme. This hardy Dalmatian bulb was formerly known as *S. pratensis* and *S. amethystinus* and will still be met under these names on nursery lists. Although native among limestone rocks, in the South it also grows and increases well on sandy soils.

❧ Cuban Lilies

Another large squill successful in Southern gardens also carries an air of mystery, although not from shy flowering. At some point in history it acquired the curious common names "Peruvian lily" and "Cuban lily" and the Latin name *S. peruviana*. Since this plant grows naturally in hot, dry countries along the western Mediterranean, there seems little explanation for these titles. An old Spanish tradition holds that this exotic-looking bulb originated in South America; this, presumably, is the source of confusion. Similar bits of country wisdom in the South sometimes attribute native wildflowers to the activities of the lost tribes of Israel.

In gardens *S. peruviana* sends up bright green leaves to form winter rosettes like *S. hyacinthoides*. In a sunny exposure on poor, stony ground, this foliage remains hardened and resistant to frost. In too generous a spot, however, the leaves elongate and may be damaged with any serious cold. In late February dome-shaped clusters of buds begin to show in the midst of the leaves. At the first warm spell, the eight- to ten-inch stems bolt upward and expand into a bee swarm of indigo blue stars.

This prolific squill multiplies rapidly, usually needing dividing every two or three years. Although *S. peruviana* has a reputation as a tender bulb, its foliage stands plenty of cold while still in a tight rosette. Cuban lilies may be grown anywhere in the South if they are planted on exposed positions to discourage dangerous early growth and bloom. A rare white form of *S. peruviana*, 'Alba', is also worth having.

❧ Spanish Bluebells

The flower that comes to mind for most Southerners when "squill" is mentioned is the Spanish bluebell or wood hyacinth. Although long known in garden literature as *Scilla campanulata*, botanists have shuffled these poor flowers about in recent years, first to the genus *Endymion*, then to an uncomfortable resting place with the alliterative appellation *Hyacinthoides hispanica*.

None of these names do justice to the stately spikes of wisteria blue that blossom in April gardens. The unscented, bell-shaped flowers of the Spanish bluebell hang down from twelve- to sixteen-inch stalks. Their thrifty bulbs soon seed and multiply in lavish pools, which spread out under the trees. This old Southern favorite is one of the finest spring bulbs for naturalizing deciduous woodland. The round, white bulbs are happy anywhere they receive ample

Ornithogalum narbonense

Schoenocaulon texanum

Ornithogalum umbellatum

Scilla peruviana

Zigadenus nutallii

Camassia scilloides

spring moisture. They have been popular since Elizabethan times and came to the South with the earliest settlers.

In addition to the common blue strains, there are several fine selections of Spanish bluebells with darker violet, pink, or white flowers. Nurseries often offer these bulbs in a mix, but such combinations are best avoided or quickly separated following bloom, as the various colors combine in a gaudy pattern. Sometimes, a mixed portion of newly planted bulbs mysteriously fails to return the following spring. Those that do come back seem as permanent as iron and will steadily multiply to replace any failures. The related English bluebell (*Hyacinthoides non-scripta*) is a less robust flower that needs cooler, damper conditions than the South can provide.

🐚 Star of Bethlehem

Matted leaves of grape hyacinths often mix with the low winter foliage of star of Bethlehem (*Ornithogalum umbellatum*) on the same old Southern lawns. These bulbs' foliage would be difficult to separate, if not for telltale silvery streaks marking the leaves of *O. umbellatum*. This is sort of a reverse color scheme of the flowers, which, as in all *Ornithogalum*, are white stars marked down the back with green keels.

Dioscorides receives credit for the curious botanical name of this genus, which translates as "bird's milk." The little, round bulbs of common star of Bethlehem are theorized, also, to be the biblical "dove's dung" sold during the Babylonian siege of Jerusalem. Other common names, such as "sleepy Dick" and "nap at noon," refer to the daily openings and closings observed by these flowers in response to the spring sun. In France they are called *belle d'onze heures*, "beauty of the eleventh hour."

Many gardeners regard *O. umbellatum* as weedy; in truth, the green and white clusters of starry blooms are only modestly showy, at best. Nevertheless, these small Mediterranean bulbs have proven faithful in adversity, and they disappear after spring flowering with little fuss. This is one of the few early flowers suited to naturalizing in lawns. It makes a fine companion for *Allium drummondi*, *Crocus tomasinianus*, *Anemone caroliniana*, *Ranunculus macranthus*, and other low-growing, hardy flowers.

Showier, but less common in Southern gardens is the drooping star of Bethlehem (*O. nutans*), known to Parkinson as the "Starre-flower of Naples." The satiny flowers of this variety appear on six- to ten-inch spikes among four or five straplike leaves. These graceful blooms are strung upward along one side and open from the bottom up, like small, flaring bells. Moist, shady positions suit these European natives better that most plants, and they grow well in borders of deciduous shrubs. In the upper South these bulbs occasionally run wild in rough grass and woodland, although with less passion than shown by *O. umbellatum*.

The greenish black ovaries of *O. arabicum* stand out like shiny beads against the pearly flowers, giving this star of Bethlehem a personality entirely distinct from *O. umbellatum*. Like the Cuban lily, this Mediterranean bulb is often regarded as tender, but it will stand cold if planted on a sunny, exposed position in gravelly soil. Its flattened, gray leaves spread flat against the ground over winter, then send up a two-foot stem in April. This carries a compact grouping of creamy, round buds, which open gradually from the outside. These pleasant blossoms have a sweet fragrance and last well when cut.

Although *O. arabicum* is widely available and commonly planted, colonies seldom establish in the South. This failure is probably the fault of gardeners who are too generous to these desert flowers. They thrive on the most barren sands and rocky soils, kept dry over summer. They would be an excellent choice for seaside gardens.

The graceful, upright wands of *O. narbonense* rise fifteen to twenty inches and open into loose spikes, like a milky white version of *Scilla hyacinthoides*. The gray foliage is flattened and sparse like *O. arabicum* but always stands erect. The brittle, long-necked bulbs of *O. narbonense* thrive even on the heaviest clay soils and may be found about older gardens in the middle South. This bulb has been in gardens for many years, but it is seldom listed today. When it is mentioned at all, it is often called *O. pyramidale*, a synonym alluding to its tall, pyramidal spike of blooms. In their homeland of southern France, these flowers are known as "the Virgin's spray."

These blooms perform the same daily openings and closings seen in others of this group, but they still make fine cut flowers or good focal points for a herbaceous border. Wine pink *Penstemon triflorus* is a fine April companion, and the coral pink, asparaguslike buds of *Hesperaloe parviflora* rise and mix with these flowers while they are at their peak. Colonies increase well from self-sown seed and soon cover large areas.

🌿 *Wild Hyacinths*

Remarkably similar to *O. narbonense* in general build are the American camas lilies, or wild hyacinths (*Camassia scilloides*). In the South they may be found on prairies and rich grasslands from Georgia to central Texas. These native bulbs vary in color from lead white to violet but most often appear in light lavender tones. Such pale colorings require skill to properly show off in the garden but carry with them some of the wild beauty of Southern meadows. The tender lavender stars of the wild hyacinth make an elegant complement to April tulips and are worthwhile in any bedding scheme, if used in good clumps. They have a delicate, sweet fragrance.

Other camassias available in the trade, such as *C. quamash* and *C. leichtlinii*, are universal failures in warm parts of the South but might be tried in cool, damp places along the Mason-Dixon line. These natives of western North America are famous for their edible bulbs, which fed the army of Chief Joseph and the Nez Perce tribe in their war with the United States. The name *Camassia* derives from the Nootka Chinook name for the edible bulbs, "quamash."

🌿 *White Camas*

The South has several creamy, lilylike flowers with vague similarity to the wild hyacinth. These blossoms are known as wand lilies, white camas lilies, zygadenes, or by the more treacherous name "death camas." This last is due to the poisonous alkaloids found in the leaves and bulbs of several varieties. The odd botanical name, *Zigadenus*, Greek for "yoke gland," refers to the floral glands found at the base of the crimped, starry flowers, which have something of the appearance of camassias. Their fragrance, however, is heavy and cloying, like privet or wild plum.

Since these wildflowers carry suspicious reputations for toxicity and come mostly in drab off-white tones, they attract less attention from gardeners than some other native bulbs. These are poor excuses for neglect, since the white camas lilies are among the most graceful of our native lilies. They adapt well to cultivation, so long as their thin-skinned bulbs or tubers are returned to the ground promptly after division, so as not to dry out.

The large-flowered zygadene (*Zigadenus glabberrimus*) grows from a blackish, creeping rhizome and occurs in coastal savannahs, bogs, and damp pinelands through the Southeast. Its whitish yellow flowers have purple spots in the centers and appear from June to September in loose, pyramidal clusters. These summer growers thrive on abundant moisture and rich, acid soils. *Z. leimanthoides* is similar, but it bears smaller flowers on a more widely branched inflorescence.

Earlier blooming and better suited to dry situations is *Zigadenus nutallii*. This rugged uplander grows from a true bulb, rather than a horizontal rhizome. It does well on neutral or alkaline soils and enjoys mucky, black clays. The bright green, grassy leaves rise in three ranks in early spring, and are as valuable in the garden as the flowers. The blooms follow in late April, packed in dense spires on two-foot stalks. These ragged, milky blossoms, with the texture of crumpled tissue, display yellow blotches at the base of each petal. This quaint color scheme inspired the charming name "merryhearts," which is certainly preferable to "death camas."

Fly poison (*Amianthium muscaetoxicum*), bunchflower (*Melanthium virginicum*), and featherbells (*Stenanthium gramineum*) are three allies of the zygadenes native to the acid sandylands of the South. Their four-foot spikes of porcelain white bloom appear from May to July and would make fine additions to the back of a damp border. The white-flowered false asphodel (*Tolfieldia racemosa*) and the apricot yellow sunny-bells (*Schoenolirion croceum*) are smaller Southern natives suitable for foreground plantings. Like their relatives, some of these lilies are considered to be toxic. Early settlers crushed the bulbs of *Amianthium* and mixed them with sugar to attract and destroy houseflies.

🌸 The Green Lily

For drier gardens the green lily (*Schoenocaulon texanum*) offers an interesting April accent. Like the fall-flowering coconut lily (*S. drummondii*), this central Texas native throws feathery, pinkish green wands above its evergreen clumps of foliage. These unscented blooms lack true petals and produce the same bottlebrush effect as the coconut lily.

With their mounding, grassy leaves, these hardy bulbs look good at the top of a stone ledge. The spires of clustered stamens provide a sort of miniature fireworks display in the spring border, and the leaves remain attractive all year. The brownish, spindle-shaped bulbs endure any amount of drought, seeming to thrive on the poorest soils. As with many other neglected natives, the carefree vigor of these graceful Southern lilies recommends them for wider use.

Irises, Gladioli, and Shellflowers

Southerners love the elegant iris, or fleur-de-lis, as much as gardeners in any part of the world, but the peculiarities of the territory emphasize a unique range of blooms. The tall bearded hybrids popular in other sections of the country do not wholly adapt to the South, requiring careful placement in this warm, humid climate. They take second place to races whose affinity for warmer gardens makes for real opportunity, if only Southerners resolve to seize it. Instead of lamenting the failure of some of the tall bearded irises, gardeners may bravely delve among the neglected subtropical beauties of this genus: Louisiana hybrids, spurias, Spanish and Dutch irises, historic bearded irises, remontant irises, and many others.

❦ When Old Is Better Than New

In spite of their obvious merit elsewhere, many newer iris creations remain suspect in the South. This warm climate promotes bacterial soft rot (*Erwinia carotovora*) and other pathogens that threaten the starchy tubers borne by these perennials. The disease causes a basal rot of the rhizomes, and whole plants often seem to melt away in the middle of the summer. Bacterial rots become progressively worse as one goes south, so that while many bearded irises thrive along the Mason-Dixon line, few endure in the climate of the Gulf Coast. Avoiding heavy fertilizers and keeping flower beds dry and well drained through the summer reduces afflictions, but only up to a point.

A few exceptional irises have proven themselves less susceptible to bacterial rots: these are the types best suited to gardens in most of the South. Many originate from regions surrounding the

Mediterranean. Like other flowers from these territories, they perform best on mellow soils with a measure of lime but will give faithful service if offered less. These irises endure even on the poorest, driest soils.

The usual way to acquire these resistant varieties is as divisions shared by other gardeners or collected from old, abandoned homesteads or cemeteries. Many lovely types lurk in neglected corners of the South and are worth seeking out. Although the old irises lack the size, substance, and color range of modern hybrids, they make up for this in vigor, tenacity, and historical value. Several varieties common in the South have had a presence in gardens dating to the Middle Ages.

🐚 *White Flags*

The first perennial irises to bloom in spring are several antique bearded types of dwarfish stature. Because their height is modest, they are usually included in the median iris group (*Iris* Barbata-Media) in modern classifications. The beards of these species are formed by long rows of feathery stamens, which mark the centers of the three outer petals, or falls. The inner petals, or standards, curve upward and inward to create the familiar fleur-de-lis seen as a motif in historic art and architecture.

Like all bearded irises, these heirloom varieties grow from fat, starchy rhizomes. The tubers creep along close to the soil's surface and multiply swiftly with side branches and by forking. The plants may be easily divided for increase at any season but customarily are separated in fall or immediately after spring bloom. To ensure flowering, at least one good-sized fan of leaves should accompany each division.

The most familiar of the historic irises in the South is the old white flag (*Iris albicans*). The Latin name, which translates as "off-white," was given to plants found growing in Spain during the mid-1800s. Although these irises are common waifs in many warm countries today, their original homeland appears to be on the Arabian Peninsula. Tradition holds that the Moors carried this iris wherever they traveled in conquest, planting the flowers as memorials on the graves of fallen Muslim soldiers. When Spanish colonists came to Florida and Mexico, they brought this Mediterranean flower with them and continued the Moorish tradition of planting them in cemeteries. These are now the most common irises in the South.

The leaden flowers and gray, sword-shaped leaves of *I. albicans* line paths and fill graveyards and vacant fields in March. They are often accompanied by the "early blue flags," thought to be variants of the same species. On some occasions a blue flower may be seen sporting from the side of an old clump of white *I. albicans*. In all respects save color, these two forms appear identical. Officially, the blue flags may be called by their cultivar name, 'Madonna.' They supposedly originate from Yemen.

For as long as *I. albicans* has been in gardens, it has suffered confusion with a near relation, the pale white Florentine iris (*I. florentina*). This famous variety is the preferred source of orris, a fixative used in the perfume industry. The rhizomes are harvested, dried, and grated or distilled to release a fragrance resembling sweet violets. This iris is still raised for this purpose in Tuscany and has been grown for its aromatic roots since Gerard's time. In previous centuries many irises were valued as much for their supposed herbal or medicinal virtues as for their showy flowers.

The Florentine iris differs from *I. albicans* in its taller, more open spikes of bloom. These spikes carry papery bracts, which often dry and turn brown by the time the flowers open. Although the blossoms are larger than those of *I. albicans*, they open sparsely and are less effective in the garden.

Early garden writers described *I. florentina* as a natural species, but botanists now regard it as an ancient hybrid. Like *I. albicans*, it has a blue variant. Although less common and prolific in Southern gardens than the early flags, *I. florentina* tolerates the climate better than many modern bearded irises. It appears occasionally in old gardens and may be seen blooming in April, several weeks after *I. albicans* finishes for the season.

❧ Italian Irises

Even if the Southern climate defeated all varieties save the red-purple Italian iris (*I. kochii*), gardens here would be rich and enviable. Like *I. florentina*, this tenacious flower is another old pseudospecies inherited from the gardens of antiquity. Tradition holds that the first plants were found growing on hills above Lake Como. These lovely blooms are now widely distributed and may be seen in mild-climate gardens all over the world.

The compact, fragrant blooms of *I. kochii* glow with a warm reddish violet and are striped creamy yellow by the short, dainty beards. The vibrant flowers display that rare intensity of color that mixes happily with almost any hue. Blossoms appear in earnest during March, along with the white and blue flags, and just as the early campernelles and other narcissi are fading. Italian irises may also give a reprise performance in autumn, and in mild years they sputter in bloom right through winter.

No more beautiful flower grows than these short-statured irises. Their Tyrian purple vibrance is unmatched, and it can be telling if mixed among bright orange California poppies (*Eschscholzia californica*) or wallflowers (*Erysimum* spp.). Coppery wild columbines (*Aquilegia canadensis*) and waxy, yellow buttercups (*Ranunculus macranthus*) make other worthwhile companions. These irises always look good in combination with gray foliage or white blooms, like those of ornithogalums or alliums. On a raised rockery, they might join the bright red and yellow goblets of *Tulipa clusiana* var. *chrysantha*.

❧ German Irises

Nurseries formerly grouped several of the old garden irises as varieties under *I. germanica*, the German bearded iris. These plants were not strictly of German origin, but during the Middle Ages they were commonly cultivated in northern Europe and naturalized along stone walls surrounding castles. Botanists now understand that these irises, too, arose as early garden hybrids, rather than as

Iris germanica 'Nepalensis'

Iris 'Ambassadeur'

Iris kochii: Italian iris with wild columbine

Iris albicans 'Madonna'

Iris pallida 'Dalmatica'

Iris 'Madame Chereau'

natural species. Like *albicans*, *kochii*, and *florentina*, they are sterile horticultural mules with abnormal complements of forty-four chromosomes, rather than the customary numbers of forty or forty-eight.

The most prominent of these border stalwarts is an early-flowering iris with tall stems and rich violet-purple blooms. In old catalogs it was listed as 'Atropurpurea' or 'Purple King'. During the 1800s collectors discovered the same variety in the gardens of Katmandu and introduced it under the name 'Nepalensis'.

These old purple flags bloom a little after *I. kochii*, and along with *I. florentina*. They have taller, better branched stems than the earlier irises, and the flowers achieve better size and proportion. The deep mulberry falls and upright signals reflex entirely, so the flowers present the greatest possible surface to the viewer. This shows off the pale beards, which shade from yellow at the throat to creamy white in the center of the petals.

These rich, succulent blooms emit a heavy, honey-sweet fragrance, attracting a steady procession of large, black and yellow bumblebees. Their appearance signals the arrival of high spring in the South, and coincides with the blooms of double bridal wreath (*Spiraea prunifolia*), dogwoods, wisteria, and the first flushes of the red and pink China roses. 'Nepalensis' may be seen in nearly all the old gardens, and in many modern ones as well. Gardeners still share these prolific plants with one another, as they have for centuries.

❧ Dalmatian Irises

The fine broad foliage and tall, lightly branched stems of *I. pallida* give this old garden species a more graceful aspect than is typical among bearded irises. The common strain in the South, which many know as 'Dalmatica', seems all the more elegant for its delicate amethyst, white-throated blooms. These appear in April, a little later than the purple *germanica*. Erect stems hold the blossoms above the pointed leaves and bear short bracts, which dry to a silvery translucence at bloom time. Blue-gray foliage, opalescent petals, white beard, and yellow pollen all harmonize in an extraordinary way.

Although resident in gardens for as long as *I. germanica*, the Dalmatian iris appears little changed from its wild form. The species is common on the southern foothills of the Alps and ranges eastward as far as the Crimea. In Italy it is raised to produce orris in the same way as *I. florentina*.

In addition to the old pinkish purple 'Dalmatica', nurseries offer a beautiful, cream-striped *pallida* with pale blue flowers. This selection, dating from 1901, is aptly called 'Variegata'. The showy foliage makes it one of the most valuable of border plants, although it is shy with its porcelain blue flowers. 'Variegata' seems more prone to bacterial rots than the pinkish 'Dalmatica', but is worth attempting for the sake of its milk-streaked swords.

❧ More Intermediates

The good foliage, large flowers, and noble deportment of *I. pallida* may be seen in many of its descendants. This species and *I. variegata*, a central European species with yellow standards and brown-stippled falls, are believed to have been the principal forerunners of garden irises. The early crosses between them developed mixed purplish or bicolored blooms. In the Victorian catalogs of the English nurseryman Peter Barre, these were listed in various "species" classes based on the patterns of their flowers. Lavender to violet blooms such as the old variety 'Princess Beatrice' were grouped with the *pallidas* while yellows and maroons fell among the *variegatas*. *Iris amoena,* a strain with white standards and purple falls, was nicknamed the "agreeable iris" for its pleasant mix of colors. The *plicatas* bore white blooms frilled with edgings of lavender or purple, as did the elderberry-scented *I. sambucina*. The indescribable *squalens* group included bronze varieties and fantastic yellow-purple blends and combinations.

So many hybrids have been made among these old sections that it is impossible now to find one's way with these antique names. In humble country gardens, one still sees irises that look no different from those painted by Redouté, as they grew for the Empress Josephine at Malmaison. 'Madame Chereau', a nineteenth-century *plicata,* may still be seen in the South. An assiduous search through April gardens and countrysides will reassemble several of these old varieties, as well as many more recent hybrids of value.

During the first half of the twentieth century, intermediate strains of irises received serious attention from breeders for the first time. Several irises from this period are now common denizens of Southern gardens.

A yellow hybrid often seen in the South is 'Shekinah'. This favorite shows a light brown thumbprint at the throat but is otherwise a rich buttery tone. A famous old bronze, 'Ambassadeur', blooms with these, along with the early, lemon yellow daylilies. This vigorous hybrid was introduced by the Vilmorins, who bred irises near Paris before World War I. They regarded 'Ambassadeur' as their masterpiece. Its translucent lavender standards combine with yellow beards and deep plum falls, which are striped and penciled white and purple at the throat.

❧ *Remontants*

Several of the intermediate iris hybrids descend in part from *I. kochii* and inherit its inclination to fall and winter flowering. This ability to bloom again in autumn is one of the most desirable traits an iris may possess in the South. Brief, erratic springs sometime play havoc with early flowers, but the mild weather of autumn generally encourages long-lasting blossoms. In favorable years these reblooming irises offer a succession of blooms through the entire winter.

The old yellow 'Golden Cataract' is a compact-growing variety gracing many established gardens. Its warmly colored blooms often put in an appearance on Christmas Day. One of the few true dwarfs worth attempting in the South, the old yellow bicolor 'Jean Siret' is another late fall rebloomer. 'Crimson King' and 'Eleanor Roosevelt' bear deep red-purple blooms like their ancestor, *I. kochii,* but are even more regular in fall bloom. 'Black Magic' offers an autumn reprise of its dark blackish purple blossoms. In certain favorable years, the old purple *germanica* will throw a few November spikes of bloom, as well.

One of the most valuable of all the rebloomers is an old selection called 'Pink Classic'. In cold springs this variety begins flowering with *albicans* and *germanica,* but in a forward season it may appear even before these early types. With favorable weather, the spikes of bloom continue intermittently through the entire year, with concentrations in fall and early spring. The clear pink flowers, with their lively, tangerine beards, offer one of the best sources of these warm colors. 'Pink Classic' displays its sizeable, well-formed blooms on tall, symmetrically branched stems.

In addition to these proven rebloomers, many newer irises may be tried for fall flowers. Hybridizers have recently married the fall-flowering habits of the intermediate race with the modern forms and colors seen in the tall bearded. One may now choose among hundreds of rebloomers with all the qualities of modern breeding. Few of these have been tested for resistance to bacterial soft rot, but they seem the most promising of modern irises for the South.

During the years before World War II, breeders strove to develop tall bearded irises with pendant falls and erect standards like those in the old purple *germanica.* This style of blossom gives a great deal of color in gardens but makes the blooms appear coarse and cabbagey in outline. More recent efforts have focused on enlarging individual flowers and bringing up falls toward a horizontal plane. This upright carriage and the many new color patterns available combine to give modern hybrids a decidedly different appearance from previous varieties. Both old and new irises make lovely garden scenes, but, as with antique and modern roses, they are more effective when kept with their own kind.

The orchidlike quality of bearded irises comes into its own when mixed in a sizeable collection. One, two, or three colors blooming together seems mundane, but a dozen multicolored irises together in a patch looks as if a flock of gigantic butterflies had descended. If a liberal sprinkling of blue cornflowers, crimson poppies, and violet larkspurs can be seeded among the rhizomes in early fall, they will join the irises in April to complete this charming garden scene.

❧ *Aril-breds*

The strange mourning iris (*I. susiana*) is another bearded type that has been in gardens for several centuries. Its globular blooms bear heavily veined and stippled patterns. The background color of the rounded falls is a light cream, but the markings themselves are a dark brownish purple. The beard and standards verge on black.

These somber characteristics show that these blooms belong to the oncocyclus or aril group of irises. The members of this curious section come from parts of the Middle East where winters are mild and damp and summers are rainless. They have always been difficult to grow in humid climates such as the South, but the odd markings of the flowers are so extraordinary that devotees maintain collections by lifting the rhizomes over summer and storing them in dry sand for replanting in autumn.

Breeders have been active with this section and have made several crosses between these Middle Eastern irises and the more moisture-tolerant tall bearded irises. The hybrids, known as aril-breds, show more vigor than the aril species. Few of them have been widely tested in the South, but it seems likely that some will eventually prove permanent. Their unusual patterns and mysterious colors are reason enough to try.

❧ Spuria Irises

During the first weeks of May, many older gardens boast clumps of narrow, dark green leaves topped with tall, white and yellow irises. These are the old Turkish salt marsh irises (*I. orientalis*), well known to a previous generation of gardeners under the name *I. ochroleucus giganteus*. In the South these enduring perennials flower just as the tall bearded varieties fade, in concert with the old, fragrant, red-flecked white peony 'Festiva Maxima'. Their vanilla-scented blossoms have a slender elegance, which makes them ideal for cutting.

I. orientalis and its relations comprise an expanding group known popularly as spurias. These Near Eastern plants seem particularly successful in the South, ranking among the most adaptable irises for all warm climates. Less common, but also to be seen in old yards, are some allies of *I. orientalis*, the dark golden *I. crocea* (*I. aurea*) and the pure, bright yellow *I. monnieri*. This last variety has been known as the iris of Rhodes, but seems to be an early French sport or hybrid from *I. orientalis*, rather than a native of the eastern Mediterranean. Lemmonier grew it at Versailles, and it is his name that is commemorated in the Latin title of this flower.

The white *orientalis*, yellow *monnieri*, and violet-blue *I. spuria* have combined in a wide range of hybrids. Many of the first crosses made in this group had narrow petals and pale colors, but the shapely yellow hybrid 'Wadi Zem Zem' has since given rise to fine varieties with deeper hues and better formed blossoms. All seem to thrive in the South, and gardeners may have their pick among the latest, most beautiful spuria creations.

One old species spuria is worth retaining for its dwarfness. The plum-scented iris (*I. graminea*) is a short central European native with narrow leaves. Its violet-purple blooms are marked with yellowish streaks. They rest down amongst the grassy foliage, so gardeners must stand near to appreciate them. These favorite flowers appear two to a spike in early May and smell delightfully of ripe plums.

If your garden includes roses as well as irises, by the time the spuria hybrids come to bloom, you may well have a thriving population of fig beetles (*Cotinus* sp.). These large, greenish insects love to bury themselves among freshly opened flowers, especially soft-petaled blooms of old roses and irises. This usually ruins blossoms just as they reach their peak.

In a small garden these beetles can be controlled by hand picking, but if your collection is large, you will need to treat the ground around the roses to rid the soil of overwintering grubs. Milky spore, a natural fungus enemy of these insects, may offer some control. If you plan to use your irises mainly as cut flowers, they may be harvested while in tight bud to prevent entry of the beetles, solving your problem, also.

All spurias are easy to grow from divisions, and most will bloom in three or four years from fresh-planted seed. Unlike bearded irises, spurias enjoy a covering of two or three inches of soil over their rhizomes and may be mulched freely with leaves or compost. The clumps dislike frequent division; they may be separated for increase every five to seven years.

When the big bunches of spuria leaves die down in late summer, they leave sizeable holes in the garden. It is good idea to have nearby perennial or annual flowers to fill their places during the July and August interregnum. With fall rains the beautiful leaves return to add their bold upward sweep to the garden melee.

❧ Short-Stemmed Iris

There is another beardless iris common to Southern gardens with tall, narrow foliage just like the spurias. Unless the plants are in bloom, it's nearly impossible to tell them apart, but the late April to May flowers tell the story. These are a ravishing blue marked with bright yellow eyes, and they have a flattened fullness unlike any spuria.

The dark green leaves of these irises are particularly attractive; this plant was once named for them as *I. foliosa*. It is properly known today as *I. brevicaulis*, or "short-stemmed iris," because the blooms sit on ten- to twelve-inch zigzagged stalks set down amongst the leaves.

This flower is one of the South's most beautiful garden irises—and one of the most valuable, as it tolerates shade. Average garden soils suit them perfectly, and they will thrive under all but the most arid conditions. The clumps will even continue flowering in an aggressive matted groundcover like English ivy. This is something few perennials of any kind can promise.

Apart from its place in older Southern gardens, *I. brevicaulis* is best known to iris lovers as one of the parents of the Louisiana hybrids. Although not a true water iris like others of this group, *I. brevicaulis* is closely related and crosses freely among them.

❧ Water Irises

When J.K. Small published his *Manual of the Southeastern Flora* in 1933, he listed dozens of different irises as natives of the bayous and swamplands of the lower Mississippi delta. Most of these plants have since been identified as natural hybrids, and more recent botanists have reduced Small's original number of species down to only four or five. Although taxonomists no longer recognize many of these varieties, the Louisiana irises are gaining wider recognition in gardens every day. In only a few decades, flower lovers have generated an entire garden race from these beautiful Southern wildlings.

These indigenous blossoms grow well under ordinary damp garden conditions as well as in bogs, and they now come in a wide range of colors, including the most vivid reds seen among *Iris*. They vary in size from elegant three- or four-inch miniatures, such as the old wild *I. fulva*, to gargantuan blossoms seven to eight inches across, like the monstrous 'Godzilla'. The velvety petals may droop or flair, remain separate or overlap, and, in the best types, show ruffling or bicolor effects. All the Louisiana hybrids have lovely, narrow, green foliage to complement their April blooms. With tall, slender stems, many make choice cut flowers.

In addition to modern forms, several of the original species may be seen in older Southern gardens and are still worthwhile. The copper iris (*I. fulva*) is the most famous for its unique, warm red blossoms. This species occurs as a wildling from the Gulf north to southern Illinois. Although the flowers are on the small side and the petals droop as if they were sad, blooms of the copper iris make an effective, relaxed display. These irises also thrive in damp shade, which makes them doubly valuable.

Very similar but much larger is *I. nelsonii*, a robust species known to collectors as the Abbeville red. This iris, ranging from crimson to yellow in various wild forms, has been used extensively in breeding. Many of its descendents show good vigor and broad, overlapping petals.

The dark blue, purple, to cream or white *I. giganticaerulea* is an early-blooming species with especially lush, blue-green foliage. This is a common flower in the marshes of the central Gulf Coast. It seems less hardy to cold than some of the other Louisiana irises, but it is one of the most vigorous types. Along with *I. brevicaulis*, it is the source of blue and purple pigments seen in many hybrids.

In addition to these wild forms, a rich violet cultivar, 'Dorothea K. Williamson', is common in many old gardens. This tough, hardy hybrid from *I. fulva* and *I. brevicaulis* was introduced in 1918. It thrives on damp, heavy ground, rapidly propagating by vigorous rhizomes.

The roots of most Louisiana hybrids run about incessantly, and it is futile to try to separate varieties in the garden if they are planted near each other. After a good season of growth, many types will travel as much as three feet from their original location. Any collection quickly becomes confused, with the labels left in the dirt far from the young fans that will flower the next spring.

All the Louisianas thrive as bog or aquatic plants, so one way to keep varieties separated is to plant each one in an individual plastic or stainless steel tub. These may be sunk in the ground or disguised with leafy perennials, so as to blend in the garden. Under these conditions culture is simple: All the flowers require is an occasional topping up with water from the hose.

Any gardener who develops a serious interest in the Louisiana irises should consult Marie Caillet and Joseph K. Mertzweiller's monograph, *The Louisiana Iris*. This gives an up-to-date overview of the many hybrids available in this section. Several nurseries specialize in these Southern irises, and their catalogs contain valuable information as well.

In addition to the species used to breed the Louisiana hybrids, the South has two other native aquatics of value. Both have attractive blue, beardless flowers marked with small spots of yellow at the haft. The prairie blue flag

Iris orientalis

A spuria iris hybrid

Iris brevicaulis

Iris virginica

An Aril-bred iris flowering in a bed of Louisiana phlox.

Foreground: *Iris siberica* 'Caesar's Brother'; rear: *Iris* spuria hybrid

(*I. hexagona*) grows around the Gulf of Mexico to Florida, and north to South Carolina. Found in flooded ditches and bogs in sun or shade, it needs a moist, acid soil to prosper.

The Virginia iris (*I. virginica*) grows in swamps, moist meadows, and salt marshes throughout the Southeast. Although these habitats usually have acid soils, some forms tolerate alkaline conditions, if given plenty of moisture. In addition to the common blue *I. virginica,* there are also white and pink selections. 'Socastee Strain No. 1' appears to be a hybrid of this species with either *I. tripetala* or *I. versicolor.* The young spring fans and flower stems emerge dark purple. Flowers appear in April, along with the Louisiana hybrids.

The yellow water iris (*I. pseudacorus*) is a European species often seen as an escape on the sides of streams and ponds in the South. It produces absolutely enormous masses of upright foliage like big clumps of cattail, reaching four to six feet or better. The yellow blooms, topping the leaves in April, have a flounced, orchidlike appearance. Nurseries offer an old, heirloom double and a showstopping variegated form of this species, also. All need abundant water to thrive but are otherwise easy and tolerant of limy or acid conditions. Thomas Jefferson had these irises at Monticello, where he knew them as "flower-de-luces."

The Japanese irises (*I. ensata*) are the glamorous cousins of *I. virginica* and *I. pseudacorus.* They have been widely hybridized in the Orient and include many magnificent varieties. Unfortunately, they are not so easy of growth as other water irises. They demand partial shade and acid, damp conditions. They quickly fail if subjected to drought.

In the lower South these irises usually sulk in summer heat unless immersed in the cool waters of a garden pond. The most satisfactory varieties for general use are old, tested hybrids, such as the white 'Gold Bound', and purplish 'Mahogany'. These flower after the Louisianas, extending the water iris season.

❧ Siberian Irises

The title "Siberian iris" is something of a misnomer, for *I. siberica* has a much wider range in Europe and Asia than the frostbitten region for which it is named. Several color forms and hybrids with white and purple blooms may be had from perennial dealers, but only an old, dark violet sort is common in the South.

These are moisture-loving irises, best suited to heavy soil and low ground. They may be grown in water-filled tubs or at the edge of ponds, like Louisianas. Most of the whites and blues tolerate slight alkalinity, but the red-purple strains need acid soils. The Siberians resemble spurias but reach only half their height and size. They are especially valuable for positions in partial shade, flowering happily under tall pines.

❧ Piedmont Iris

The miniature, blue *I. verna* is a delicate woodlander native to the hills and mountains of the Southeast. Although fussy about receiving a moist, acid soil, it is worth having for its dainty, sweetly fragrant flowers. These are beardless, coming in lilac-blue marked with wide blotches of orange. The entire plant, blooms and all, remains under a foot. The very early flowers appear in March, so these understory plants can complete growth before trees leaf out for summer.

❧ *Gladwyn Irises*

Another type valuable for shade is the Gladwyn iris (*I. foetidissimma*). This variety is a native of limy soils in Mediterranean countries and in western Europe. The unflattering botanical name translates as "stinking," but this seems a bit harsh, as the flowers are not unpleasant, and the leaves and stems produce an odor only if crushed. The blossoms of this iris are small, marked only in quiet tones of fawn and washy lilac. It is the lustrous evergreen leaves that make the plants an asset in the garden.

Another show comes in autumn, when the capsules ripen and split to reveal the orange-red seeds. Looking like small, bright marbles, they last well in the garden or in a vase for winter decoration. A slow-growing variegated type ('Variegata'), a yellow selection ('Lutea'), and blue and white variants are available from specialists.

❧ *Crested Irises*

The crested irises entirely lack the thickened rhizomes, bulbs, corms, or other means of storage common to *Iris*. They get along, instead, on wiry, running roots and evergreen fans of foliage. The flowers bear slightly elevated crests intermediate between a bearded and a beardless condition. All the members of this group enjoy leafy, humus-rich soil. Although they stand some drought, their appearance is better with regular watering. In the South they perform best with partial shade.

The Japanese roof iris (*I. tectorum*) is famous in its native country as a flower for planting on sod roofs, just as houseleeks are used on cottage roofs of France. In gardens the silky, green fans of leaves form large patches, making fine subjects for the foreground of a shady border. In April the ruffled, orchidlike blooms appear among the handsome leaves. In common forms these are a rich, mottled blue, with white crests. Even more lovely are the white, yellow-crested blooms of *I. tectorum alba*.

The native dwarf crested iris of the Great Smoky Mountains (*I. cristata*) looks much like *I. tectorum* but is less vigorous in Southern gardens. It needs a thoroughly cool, shady position and must never be allowed to suffer drought.

More in the vein of subtropical flowers are some of the crested irises of the Far East. *I. japonica* produces branching stalks of pale lavender blooms flecked with deeper lavender and orange spots. These appear above the glossy, green fans in April. 'Uwodu' is a select improved form; *I. japonica* also comes in two stunning variegated strains, 'Variegata' and 'Kamayana'. This species multiplies vigorously from slender stolons, which run just under the surface of the ground. Although fairly frost-tolerant, the attractive fans of foliage benefit from a mulch of pine straw when temperatures dip below twenty degrees F.

Such care will also be appreciated by 'Nada', a hybrid of *I. japonica* developed by California plantsman J.N. Giridlian. The other parent of 'Nada' is an obscure iris from Sichuan and Yunnan called *I. confusa*. 'Nada', a tremendous grower in the lower South, sends up tall sprays of ruffled, white blooms marked with orange speckles. Where frost is severe, the early-rising flower spikes may be nipped, but this spectacular iris is otherwise easy to grow in a shady bed. 'Darjeeling' is a second-generation child of 'Nada', with larger, more lavender-toned blossoms. 'Fairyland' is a delicate hybrid of *I. japonica* 'Uwodu' and *I. confusa*.

🌺 *Bulbous Irises*

Perhaps because Dutch and Spanish irises are so common in the windows of flower shops, these honestly bulbous types are less appreciated in gardens than they might be. The florist industry forces these beautiful flowers by the thousands, so they may be had cheaply and in variety year-round. They offer gardeners one of the best bargains among bulbs adapted to the South. The narrow-petaled blooms, with the same elegant proportions as spurias, come in several good colors, especially rich blues, strong yellows, and warm bronzes.

Gerard and Parkinson knew the Spanish iris as the "onion-rooted fleur de luce" or "Barbary fleur de luce," and these bulbs have played a role in gardens since at least the late 1500s. Botanically, these bulbous irises belong to *Iris xiphium* (*Xiphium vulgare*) and its allies, which are native to Spain and surrounding countries. The Latin comes from the Greek *xiphos*, or "sword," which refers to the slender foliage of these irises. The translucent, grayish leaves of xiphiums reflex gracefully, making the plants look like diminutive leeks when they are not in flower.

The modern Dutch hybrids (*I.* × *hollandica*) are derived mostly from the yellow, white, or blue Spanish iris (*I. xiphium*) and the deep blue Moroccan *I. tingitiana*. Both species grow naturally in seasonally wet areas on granite or limestone. They enjoy plenty of water while in growth during fall and winter, and they value a long summer baking afterward. Both clay and sandy soils suit them. The similar but leafier English irises (*I. latifolia*) were derived originally from moist, cool meadows high in the Pyrenees. They sulk in Southern heat, flowering poorly, if at all.

Strong-growing Dutch iris varieties, such as the ultra-gentian blue 'Prof. Blau', will naturalize and may be seen in many older gardens in April. Paler blues, like 'Wedgwood', are descended from *I. tingitiana* and usually flower several weeks earlier. The older, seldom offered strains of "Spanish iris" are similar to the Dutch hybrids but bloom later and have more delicate appearances. The most common ones in gardens are narrow, small-flowered yellows. A wide collection of these bulbous irises will provide bloom through a period of two months.

Both the Dutch and Spanish varieties make foliage early in the season, so bulbs should be planted in fall as soon as they can be obtained. The slightly built leaves and stems are inadequate foils for the jewel-like flowers, so these slender irises may be planted in groups against backgrounds of hardy shrubs or perennials, or mixed in winter bedding schemes of violas and dianthus.

Since the bulbs do not mind compacted earth, they offer an excellent solution for winter borders where large clumps of subtropical crinums disappear after frost. The irises may be set nearby to fill in during the cool season. They will bloom and disappear happily under the emerging leaves of the crinums in late spring.

Junos, Hermodactylus, and Reticulatas

I. persica is a frail, translucent flower in the mysterious Juno group of irises. With its slate-colored petals appearing above very short leaves early in the season, it is one of several old flowers sharing the nickname "fair maids of February." Parkinson grew this small, fragrant iris four hundred years ago, and it has been shared among gardeners in America since colonial days. Thomas Jefferson planted it at Monticello in 1812.

Although fairly well suited to the upper South, *I. persica* seldom persists near the Gulf. In its Middle Eastern home, this species grows in dry oak scrub where the plants receive little rainfall in summer. In the South these bulbs prosper when planted under the eaves of houses or against sunny walls, where they may bake dry over summer.

Another iris with similar wants is *Hermodactylus tuberosus* (*Iris tuberosa*) the widow or snake's head iris. The somber blossoms of this Mediterranean species, with black falls and olive green signals, appear in the midst of long, sparse, four-cornered, gray leaves. The weird roots creep about and resemble long, white worms. The name *Hermodactylus,* translated as "Hermes' finger," refers to these tubers. Although they are closely related to other bulbous irises, botanists usually give these flowers a genus of their own.

The snake's head iris establishes readily and can be very free of increase with its long, spiky foliage. Flowering is unpredictable, however, unless the bulbs are well ripened over summer. Raised beds of sand, decomposed granite, oystershell, or lime rubble will provide the fast drainage necessary, with an arid summer, to prepare flower buds for the following spring. The gardener's reward will be a bouquet of sinister, gray-green blooms in early February.

The miniature reticulata irises (*I. reticulata*), coming from the cold, dry uplands of Turkey, are reliable perennials only in the upper South. They return and bloom easily, however, if dug and stored dry over summer; a raised bed of gravelly soil may harden and preserve the bulbs in the same way. They are worth any minor trouble, for the tiny, violet-scented blooms are valuable at their early February blooming season.

There are several color forms of *I. reticulata* in shades of violet, lavender, and blue, all marked with a bright yellow eye. Another commonly offered iris in this group, *I. danfordiae,* has clear golden blossoms. It is less reliable in its flowering than *I. reticulata,* and the bulbs split into multitudes too small to bloom after their first year.

I. vartanii is a related dwarf iris from Israel, where it is especially abundant around the city of Nazareth. The pale blue or white blossoms are striped with light yellow and customarily appear in December. Only the white variety, 'Alba',

Iris foetidissima

Iris foetidissima (in seed)   *Iris* x *hollandica*

Iris reticulata

Iris tectorum   *Iris pseudacorus*

is in the trade, but it is the most vigorous form of the species and the best variety to establish on a sunny bank.

❧ Spanish Nuts

The little blue irises called Spanish nuts belong to a group of cormous irids native mostly to Africa's Cape of Good Hope. The sole Mediterranean representative of the section is the only species suited to the South. Formerly classed under *Iris*, it now is known as *Gynandriris sisrynchium*. The species name is from an old Greek word for iris, and perhaps this is same flower that the ancients knew.

If planted in the fall, the brown-coated corms send up several narrow, channeled leaves over winter. In April and May the pale or deep blue flowers follow on slender stems set among the leaves. The ephemeral blossoms bear creamy blotches, and several open in succession from each spike. These short-lived blooms expand in the afternoon and fade by midnight.

The Spanish nut comes from regions with shallow, rocky soil and little summer rain. Raised beds or dry, sunny positions under the eaves of the house are best. Winter cold is no trouble for them.

❧ Butterfly Irises, Cape Tulips, and Fortnight Lilies

In the mildest parts of the South, a few of the butterfly irises, or Natal lilies (*Moraea* spp.), may be tried, although only the most vigorous will establish and return. The true moraeas develop corms and, like the Spanish nut, were once included in *Iris*. All the members of this group are South African, and most operate on a winter growing schedule. For this reason they are hardy only where frosts are light.

The most successful variety is *Moraea polystachya*. In fall and winter it sends up sparse, linear leaves and two-foot, branched stalks dotted with handsome, lilac blooms. These resemble miniature irises with orange eyes in the middle of the outer segments. In mild climates of California and the Southwest, this variety seeds itself into great patches, but in most of the South, it is slow to increase, if at all. These corms prosper with gritty or sandy soil and a dry summer rest.

Homeria is a related African genus that may flower in the South after a mild winter. The muted salmon and yellow blooms of the commonly offered *Homeria breyniana* (*H. collina*), fragrant and enchanting, warrant an attempt, even at the risk of failure from unseasonable cold. If set in sandy soil, each corm sends up a single, wiry leaf in fall, with the crocuslike flowers following on branched stalks in March and April. In their South African homeland, these little blooms are known as Cape tulips or *rooitulps*. The flowers close at night and during cloudy weather, but they appear over a period of four or five weeks in spring.

Gardeners often apply the name "moraea" to the summer-growing fortnight lilies, now placed in the genus *Dietes*. These clumping irises are more at home in the humid South than their corm-bearing relations, but they still run some risk of damage during cold winters. The swordlike, evergreen leaves rise from a sturdy, creeping rhizome and arrange themselves in slender fans like spuria or Louisiana irises. This exceptionally handsome foliage makes the *Dietes* popular landscape specimens in mild climates.

In their South African homeland, the fortnight lilies often grow along margins of ponds. Although tolerant of drought, they are more regular and generous bloomers if fed and watered. The individual flowers last only a day, but they appear over a long season from spring through fall. Intermittent crops of bloom come in bursts separated by two-week periods, hence the name "fortnight lily."

There are two *Dietes* species common in gardens along the Gulf Coast. *Dietes vegeta* (*Moraea iridioides*), the one more often seen, bears distinctively broad, rich green, three-foot leaves. Glistening white or light lavender, iris-shaped blooms appear in small groups against the dark foliage. 'Lemon Drops' and 'Orange Drops' are hybrids with creamy blossoms and bright blotches of yellow and orange.

The yellow African iris (*D. bicolor*) has narrower, paler green foliage and light yellow flowers marked with maroon spots. Its elegantly slender foliage combines strikingly in a variety of settings. Bright orange *Zinnia angustifolia* and rich purple *Setcreasea pallida* may be planted around it in a large pot for an exotic, subtropical display on a sunny patio.

🌺 Cape Bulbs

The Cape of Good Hope has one of the richest floras in the world. The iris family, in particular, has undergone an explosion in diversity there. Many South African irids have fantastic blossoms marked with brilliant colors and iridescent spots like the feathers of peacocks.

Most of these flowers come from mild, winter-rainfall regions, so they usually balk at the South's hot, damp summer and frosty, unsteady winter. Along the Gulf, *Freesia, Sparaxis, Tritonia,* and *Ixia* may flower successfully after a favorable winter, but they are unlikely to establish or return. The corms of these small, exotic irids are available and inexpensive, so they may be replaced annually, if desired.

Better suited to most of the South are plants from tropical Africa and Transvaal and Natal provinces, where summer rains predominate. In American gardens such plants complete their growth and bloom during the subtropical months of summer, then retreat below ground to wait out periods of winter frost.

🌺 Painted Petals

One dainty, warmly colored irid that especially thrives in the South is called painted petals in its African home. The bright scarlet flowers have darker reddish spots at the base, which account for the charming appellation. Botanists call this species *Lapeirousia laxa* (*Anomatheca cruenta*).

The flowers of painted petals appear in loose, one-sided spikes up to a foot or two in height. They usually arrive in spring but may come at almost any season, depending on when the corms break dormancy. Some start into growth in fall, others in early summer, so a succession of flowers may be secured;

furthermore, no weather disaster will befall all of the colony at one time. The small, light green fans of foliage remain attractive even without bloom.

Around Johannesburg the little corms of painted petals grow in rich woodland. They thrive in leafy shade in the South. Sun will not harm them as long as they receive plenty of moisture while in growth. The corms usually enter dormancy in late summer, after the flowers swell into oval pods. The hard, round seeds that form inside may be planted in pots or left to naturalize in the garden, where they will germinate in the coming spring. Corms multiply in this fashion into thriving patches.

In addition to the shrimp red of the common painted petals, there is a good white form, 'Alba'. Although not as vigorous as the scarlet, it comes true from seed.

🐚 *Montbretias*

"Montbretia" commemorates Antoine Francois Ernest Conquebert de Montbret, a botanist who accompanied Napoleon on his invasion of Egypt in 1798. Gardeners still attach his name to a lovely, old hybrid that is now classed as *Crocosmia*, although for a while it was placed under *Tritonia*. The present title means "crocus, or saffron, scented"; the colorful blooms, if dried and placed in water, develop a strong smell of saffron.

The old montbretia of Southern gardens ranks as a first-class border flower, thoroughly hardy and undemanding in rich, moist soil. Its bright green sheaves of flattened, grassy leaves send up a succession of brilliant, nodding, lilylike flowers held in graceful sprays. They are orange-red on the exterior but glow with yellow from the inside, where their throats are marked with reddish brown streaks. The corms multiply rapidly in good neutral or acid soil, so there are always plenty to share or move about.

This vigorous exotic descends from an 1882 cross made by the famous French nurseryman Victor Lemoine, of Nancy. The parents of the hybrid were the orange *Crocosmia aurea* and the rich crimson *C. pottsii*. When Lemoine introduced his creation, botanists gave it the confusing name *Crocosmia* × *crocosmiiflora*, the "crocosmia-flowered crocosmia." This certainly offered sufficient excuse for gardeners to continue using "montbretia."

A great number of *Crocosmia* hybrids have been created since, and several different ones may be had in a range of colors through cream, yellow, orange, and crimson. 'Solfatere' is a famous turn-of-the-century hybrid with apricot-yellow blooms and bronze-tinted foliage. It's one of the most beautiful types suited to the South.

The golden swan montbretia (*C. masoniorum*) is sometimes offered by nurseries, also. This species has vermillion flowers that look upward from its arching stems. 'Lucifer' is a flaming orange-red hybrid between this and a close relation of *Crocosmia*, the pleated-leafed *Waaierlelie* (*Curtonus paniculatus*). The foliage of 'Lucifer' is lush, bronzy green and reaches three feet, with the showy blooms extending above.

All of these will succeed on rich soil, but none can match the vigor of the

Neomarica caerulea

Iris fulva

Iris florentina

Gladiolus natalensis (G. psittacinus)

Crocosmia x 'Lucifer'

original montbretia, and Lemoine's hybrid still takes pride of place for garden use in the South. The brilliant midsummer flowers last four weeks. Color schemes of summery blue Cape plumbagos, buttery cannas, and tall white phlox mix vibrantly with these glowing orange torches. Hummingbirds swarm around them.

❧ Gladioli

The gladiolus, or sword lily, is the best known of all the African irids. It has been a popular bedding flower since the middle of the nineteenth century, when florists bred the first tall varieties suited for cutting. All the members of this large genus bear sword-shaped foliage; *Gladiolus* translates as "little sword" in Latin.

The modest requirements of the modern gladioli include rich, moist soil and early planting. In the South it is customary to set out fresh, blooming-size corms at biweekly intervals from mid-January until mid-March. This assures a succession of bloom extending through early May. Later plantings are usually futile, since thriving populations of thrips and sweltering heat do these flowers in during the summer. For autumn bloom a few corms may be retained in refrigeration for planting in June or July. If flowers are cut for the table, at least four or five leaves should be left to feed the large, flattened corms. With good care, these plants easily multiply from tiny offsets called cormels.

Although many hybrid gladioli are perfectly hardy in the South, most deteriorate and cease bloom without annual replanting in fresh, prepared soil. A few old species exhibit sufficient vigor to consider as true perennials. All are choice and among the most desirable of garden flowers.

One of the old varieties seen in the South is the parrot gladiolus, or Natal lily (*G. natalensis*), formerly known as *G. psittacinus*. This is one of the principal species used to breed the modern hybrid gladiolus, and its stiff, veined leaves and tall stature have a familiar appearance. The brilliant orange, hooded blooms are very showy, and they appear on three- to four-foot spikes in early May. Each flower has three upper segments forming the orange hood, while the lower three petals reflex and glow with a buttery yellow tone. Four or five blooms open at any one time.

These robust plants fend for themselves on the poorest soils, but their beauty increases dramatically with generous feeding and watering. The large corms soon multiply into attractive stands, and they may be set in groups of five or six to punctuate the rear of an early summer border. Either sun or part shade is satisfactory, but it is well to keep in mind that the one-sided flower spikes face south and will be most attractive if placed to the north of viewers. Setting the corms at least four inches down in the soil will overcome any need for staking.

❧ The Maid of the Mist

Around the turn of the century an engineer named F.S. Thompson was engaged to build a bridge over the Zambesi River below the Victoria Falls in Zimbabwe.

On the rocky slopes below the waterfall, he spied a clump of clear yellow gladioli. They had graceful blossoms with the upper petals bent over to form hoods. Thompson noticed that these specialized blooms protected the flowers' reproductive organs from the continuous spray of the waterfall. Excited collectors soon gathered and introduced corms of this new variety, dubbed the maid of the mist (*G. primulinus*), nearly exterminating it in the wild in their enthusiasm.

When bred to various large-flowered hybrids, this yellow species sired a race of extraordinary, graceful blooms. The delicate colorings of the hooded blossoms ranged from pale yellow through apricot, salmon, saffron, and orange-red. Flowers of "primulinus" hybrids also spaced themselves farther apart on the stem than other gladioli.

These orchidlike flowers have tremendous vigor, and their lighter, airier appearance and graceful, arching stems make them especially beautiful in gardens. They make lovely, permanent additions to a May border. Modern butterfly gladioli descend from the original primulinus hybrids. Their frilled, satiny flowers have vivid markings of red or rose in the throat.

❧ *Acidanthera*

The fragrant Abysinnian gladiolus (*Gladiolus callianthus*) has long been known to gardeners as *Acidanthera bicolor*. Long-tubed, creamy blooms give this nocturnal flower a distinctive appearance. In its native east African home, this summer grower inhabits rich, marshy ground. Since the blooms open in the evening, they escape the heat stress experienced by day-flowering gladioli.

These fragrant flowers thrive in damp borders, and rooted corms may even be immersed in shallow water, where they will revel in the abundance of food and moisture. The sweet, primrose-scented blooms open one at a time over several weeks. The strain sold as *Acidanthera bicolor* has creamy blooms marked with chocolate brown spots. *Murielae* is taller, with purplish markings. The robust 'Zwanenburg' flowers early, with handsome dark blotches.

Along the Gulf Coast, the Abyssinian gladioli may be expected to return, if they have been well fed and watered. In the upper South, they may be dug and stored over winter. *G. callianthus* is a delightful, fragrant companion for summer phlox, rudbeckia, and other moisture-loving perennials.

❧ *Corn Flags*

Although most gladioli are African, there are a few hardy species scattered around Europe and the Mediterranean, the most famous of which is the old-fashioned Byzantine gladiolus (*Gladiolus byzantinus*). The magenta spires of this invaluable flower appear at the same time as bearded irises, reaching above the deep green clumps of swordlike leaves. Each claret-cerise blossom curves beautifully and fits tightly into a showy spike. Creamy flashes mark the lowest three petals.

These tough, old flowers, thriving on heavy clay soils, may be seen in many gardens in the South, where they persist indefinitely without attention. They are often set in large rows to edge paths or borders of roses, but they also look good in informal borders, where they flower along with the yellow, blue, or white false indigos (*Baptisia* spp.) Byzantine gladioli have been cultivated since ancient times in Europe. Dioscorides began the tradition of calling them corn flags, and they may often be seen growing in fallow cornfields around the Mediterranean.

The corms of *G. byzantinus* should be planted in the fall, if they are to bloom on schedule. Tiny cormels may be set out along with blooming-size corms to add foliage, or they may be grown on in rich soil, where they will flower after three years. The frost-hardy foliage usually shows above ground in January, with blossoms following in April. The papery leaves, ripening toward the end of May, may be disguised among leafy perennials or allowed to develop their natural straw tones in a grassy meadow.

The true strain of *G. byzantinus* is a robust, upright plant with dark-colored flowers. Nurseries sometimes offer this heirloom but may also send out smaller, paler flowers under the same name. These are usually related, inferior species, such as *G. communis*. These counterfeits may establish in Southern gardens, but they fail to provide the impact of the proper form. Other allied gladioli, such as *G. imbricatus* and *G. segetum,* may be had from specialists and would be worthy of trial.

'Alba', a delightful white sport of the true *G. byzantinus,* is found in some older gardens in the South. Although slow in growth, it is permanent and ideal for planting designs in which the magenta of the common form would be overly harsh. In Europe this lovely gladiolus is raised for the cut flower trade.

In addition to these denizens of old gardens, a variety of modern "hardy glads" will perennate in the South, although some bloom too late in the season to be of much value. The "baby glads" (*G.* × *colvillei*) are descended from the yellow marsh Afrikander (*G. tristis*) and the waterfall gladiolus (*G. cardinalis*), hardy miniatures from Natal and the mountains of the southwestern Cape. They do well in rich soil, if planted in time to flower before the onset of summer heat.

The numerous cultivars have pink, rose, peach, or white blooms, charmingly flashed with darker spots. They bear such enchanting, descriptive names as 'Blushing Bride', 'Peach Blossom', and 'Charm'. These small, slightly fragrant flowers appear six to a stem on wiry, graceful plants.

More recent hybrids from Israel marketed as "Orchidiola" gladiolus have distinctive blooms in shades of red, mauve, primrose, and lavender, with soft greenish yellow markings at the throat. Along with their thin foliage, this color scheme suggests they may descend from *G. papilio,* a hardy yellow and lilac native of Natal. Since these new gladioli flower seventy to eighty days after planting, they may prosper in the early-warming spring of the South.

🌸 Shellflowers

When Gerard wrote his *Herbal* in 1596, he related the tale of a fantastical flower, "a kinde of Dragons not seene by any that have written thereof." He doubted the existence of this bloom, "the floure of Tigris," but described it for his readers to expose the fraud:

*The root (saith my Author) is bulbous or Onion fashion, outwardly
blacke; from the which spring up long leaves, sharpe, pointed,
narrow, and of a fresh greene colour: in the middest of which leaves
rise up naked or bare stalkes, at the top whereof groweth a pleasant
yellow floure, stained with many small red spots here and there cast
abroad: and in the middest of the floure thrusteth forth a long red
tongue or stile, which in time groweth to be the cod or seed-vessel,
crooked and wreathed, wherein is the seed. The vertues and
temperament are not to be spoken of, considering that we assuredly
persuade ourselves that there are no such plants, but meere fictions
and devices, as we terme them, to give his friend a gudgeon.*

Having seen a *Tigridia* in actual blossom, a gardener can well imagine how
difficult it must have been for Gerard to believe such a flower could be real.
The bulb is ordinary enough, but the foliage is strangely pleated, like the seedling
leaves of a palmetto. The wiry stalk holds up gaudy, carmine, reddish orange,
yellow, pink, or white, triangular blossoms. With a glowing, silky texture, like
the pearly interior of a conch, the blossoms carry an indescribable pattern of
yellow and purple dots and blotches. These are distributed about the bases of
the three largest petals and entirely cover the three smaller ones, which form a
depressed cup. From the midst of this dazzling display rises the long, three-
pronged staminal tube, with the stigma protruding like some exotic antenna
reaching out to the stars.

The Mexican shellflower, or tiger flower (*Tigridia pavonia*), is one of the
marvels of the plant kingdom. These gorgeous iris relations once grew in the
ancient gardens of the Aztecs, who cultivated them not only for their beauty,
but also for their edible bulbs. Their name in the Aztec tongue, *oceloxochitl*,
means "ocelot flower" and seems to be the direct antecedent of both the English
common name "tiger flower" and the Latin *Tigridia*. Since the blooms are spotted
and not striped, the Aztec comparison to the ocelot seems more apt.

"Shellflower" refers to the delicate, shell-like appearance of these blossoms,
which belong to a large group of American irids. All of these tigridioids share
pleated foliage and true bulbs covered in papery, brownish coats. Their beautiful,
spotted flowers last only for a day, but they continue to open in succession over
several weeks through the summer.

The common strains of *Tigridia pavonia* available in the trade descend from
the original stocks developed by the Aztecs in the high, eternally fresh climate
of the Valley of Mexico. In Southern gardens they are unhappy in the heat of
summer and must be given rich, well-watered soil to see them through. Partial
shade is welcome, and the bulbs should be set at least four or five inches deep
to assure a cool root run. If treated generously, *Tigridia* may return as a perennial,
but it is customary to lift the bulbs, gladiolus-fashion, and store them in a dry
place over winter. After frost they may be tied in bunches and suspended in
the air to prevent predation from hungry mice.

There are many lovely species of *Tigridia* scattered over Mexico. Although most are high-elevation plants suited to cool climates, a few, including some strains of the showy *T. pavonia*, grow at lower altitudes. Available in limited numbers from collectors, they one day may be developed into a race better suited to the warmth of the South. These flowers are so lovely they deserve all efforts necessary to cultivate them.

In addition to the common up-facing, iris-shaped *Tigridia*, some species bear nodding, bell-shaped flowers. Such types often come in brownish tones and checkered with spots so as to resemble the European *Fritillaria meleagris*. *T. ehrenbergii*, one suited to the warmth of the South, produces attractive yellowish buff bells from July through September. It comes from the oak-covered Sierra Madre Oriental in northeastern Mexico.

🌸 The Pine Woods Lily

The South has a native tiger flower with blooms inclined to one side, sort of halfway between a nod and an upright stance. This displays the rich, purple glory of the pine woods lily (*Alophia purpurea*) to perfection. The larger violet petals surround a shimmering cup flecked with warm brown spots. Three yellow and white eyes sit at the tips of the smaller petals.

This exotic color scheme must have special meaning for the pollinators of this flower. Botanists believe tigridias actually mimic insect appearance with their blooms. This strategy is also pursued by some orchids, usually to entice male wasps, who fertilize the blossoms as they attempt to "mate."

In the rich, sandy soils of eastern Texas and Louisiana, and south along the Gulf into Mexico, these vigorous irids may be seen flowering in damp places among grass or under pines. Depending on rains, they may flower over the entire summer. The blooms open freshly each morning, lasting until noon, or later if the weather is overcast. The pleated leaves die down for winter but emerge early in spring. Pine woods lilies, growing readily from seed, naturalize in sun or part shade. The slender foliage is never obtrusive, and the blooms are always astounding.

In addition to the rich purple of the common Southern form, there are additional species from Mexico that seem equally permanent. *A. veracruzana* is a vigorous type with lovely, pale lilac-blue flowers. The drought-tolerant *Eleutherine plicata*, a Mexican ally of *Alophia*, has fragrant, white blooms opening in early evening. Botanists once included the pine woods lily in the genus *Eustylis*, and these flowers may still be seen in some references under this name.

🌸 Celestials

A blue shellflower worthy of a favored place in any garden is the celestial (*Nemastylis acuta*). These crocuslike Southern natives have forsaken the irregular form and spots of their allies, but they retain the the pleated, grassy foliage and deep-rooted bulbs typical of other tigridioids. The hardy leaves rise during late winter, with the ephemeral, sky blue flowers following in April and May.

Celestials, looking best when planted in large groups, grow well in partial shade as well as sun. The bright yellow anthers give the delicate blue of the petals an extra zest, setting them apart from more ordinary blooms. Although seldom offered for sale, celestials may be marked in fields and roadsides during May, so that gardeners can return to harvest seed in June. The seed should be held for fall planting in pots. Although the hard, round seeds are slow to germinate, *Nemastylis* grow rapidly with good treatment.

In addition to the blue-flowered *N. acuta* (*N. geminiflora*), the violet, white-eyed *N. floridana* of northeastern Florida would be worth acquiring. The purple *N. tenuis*, a summer grower from the Southwest, may also be expected to prove hardy. The yellow, starlike *N. revoluta* of western Mexico would be worthy of trial.

🌑 *Prairie Nymphs*

Many gardeners along the Gulf discover the April blooms of the prairie nymph (*Herbertia lahue*) appearing spontaneously in their lawns. These tiny, exotically spotted, blue irises grow in the heavy coastal clays where sod is raised; they often pirate their way into gardens along with St. Augustine grass. Since their narrow foliage comes in winter, they are at little risk from lawn mowers. The up-facing blooms scarcely top six inches but make up for their small size in mottled glamour. As with all of these American iris relations, the blossoms open freshly each morning and close up promptly each afternoon.

Herbertia pulchella is a nearly identical relation from South America, where many small tigridioids grow on the subtropical savannahs. Most are suitable to the South, but they are rare and hard to obtain. The orange-gold *Cypella herbertii*, one that may sometimes be had, is hardy and reliable on acid clay or sand. The flower is exotically spotted like *Tigridia*, but it appears more orchid shaped and a good deal smaller. *C. plumbea* sends up fleeting, three-inch, gunmetal blue blossoms marked yellow at the bases. The Mexican *C. rosei* has incurved white or purple blooms with blue and yellow markings.

Other unusual bulbous irids worth growing in the South include *Rigidella*, with orange-scarlet blossoms reflexed like shooting stars, and *Cipura paludosa*, with tiny, glistening white blooms like a miniature gladiolus. *Herbertia amatorum*, *Kelissa*, *Calydorea*, *Gelasine*, and *Catila* are South American rarities with miniature flowers like tiny, lavender orchids. All of these prosper in summer on damp, acid soil.

🌑 *Bartram's Ixia*

Among the rarest of all the little irids is a Southern native from a small, curious region west of Jacksonville, Florida. The ephemeral flowers are known to locals as violets and to botanists as Bartram's ixia (*Sphenostigma coelestinum*). They occur in a sort of refuge area for unusual North American plants. Their closest relatives are Mexican and South American.

The tiny, autumn blossoms of these irids resemble *Cipura*, but they are violet toned, with white eyes. Only early risers may appreciate them, for the flowers open with the sunrise and close by eight A.M. These rare, fleeting beauties were first discovered and reported around 1730 by John Bartram of Philadelphia.

Gladiolus byzantinus

Nemastylis acuta

Tigridia pavonia

Eleutherine plicata

Alophia purpurea

Herbertia lahue

This intrepid gentleman, America's first native botanist, discovered and introduced an amazing number of Southern rarities. His son William gave an especially romantic account of their explorations. After sleeping in a bed of soft Spanish moss at their lakeside camp, they awoke to "behold the azure fields of caerulean Ixea!"

❧ *Walking Irises*

Much easier to obtain are several walking irises (*Neomarica* spp.) of the American tropics. They grow from clumping, perennial rootstocks instead of bulbs, but they show relation to tigridias in their ephemeral, spotted blossoms. After flowering, the flattened scapes sprout leafy plantlets. As the stems bend over, these form roots and "walk" about the garden. Since these flowers propagate themselves, they are often shared. The evergreen foliage of walking irises is tender, but the rootstocks will usually recover from freezes if the plants are well mulched.

The white and blue flowered *Neomarica gracilis* is easy and popular, not only for its blooms but also for its glossy fans of leaves, like those of *Iris japonica*. The apostle plant (*N. northiana*) sends up similar white, violet-stained blooms with a sweet fragrance. The three-foot *marica*, or Brazilian walking iris (*Neomarica caerulea*), prefers good, acid soil. Its pale green, leaflike stems produce a succession of rich, blue-spotted blossoms, barred with yellow-brown, and equal to the most lovely tigridias.

The yellow walking iris (*Trimezia martinicensis*), the most drought tolerant of the group, stands hot sun as well as part shade. It also endures alkaline soils and seems indifferent to heavy clays. The crimped, three-quarter-inch, orange-yellow blossoms resemble *Cypella*.

❧ *Blue-Eyed Grass*

The blue-eyed grasses (*Sisyrinchium* spp.) are miniature interpretations of the walking iris theme, with grassy clumps of foliage and tiny, short-lived, blue, white, or yellow blossoms. They are wholly American in distribution, with ninety species distributed from Canada to Tierra del Fuego. Although several attractive, blue-flowered natives occur in the South, these little flowers are largely overlooked in regional garden making. There is no good reason for their neglect, as all make good dwarf plants for April and May bloom.

The most common varieties on nursery lists are selections of *Sisyrinchium bellum*, either the common blue or the white, 'Album', and the yellow *S. californicum*. These species usually prove temporary in the South, but are not difficult during the cool part of the year. The Patagonian *S. striatum* is also available and sends up two-foot spikes of pale straw, purple-keeled flowers. 'Aunt May' is a showy variegated form of this.

A South African ally of the blue-eyed grasses, *Aristea ecklonii*, makes leafy fans of foliage dotted with rich blue April blooms. It grows quickly from seed and makes a good border plant in the subtropical lower South. Rich soil and partial shade are preferred.

🦪 *Blackberry Lilies*

There is a speckled Asian irid which offers something of an analogue to the American tigridias. The old botanical name for the plant is *Pardanthus*, or "leopard flower." In the South these rich orange, purple-spotted blossoms have long been familiar as blackberry lilies, for the round, black seeds, which persist clustered like blackberries after the fat pods open. Modern botanists call these perennials *Belamcanda chinensis*, from a Latinized version of their Asian name, *balamtandam*, and their home country, China.

This flower was once common in gardens but is now more often seen as an escape, growing on damp, acid soil. Like many other deserving plants, this easy-growing irid has yielded its place to more obvious blooms. Jefferson had it at Monticello, where he knew the colorful blossoms as Chinese ixia.

The ephemeral flowers of *Belamcanda*, appearing on slender stems above short fans of irislike foliage, continue over a long summer season. After the pretty flowers fade, the capsules enlarge to form the handsome "blackberries," which persist over winter and as cut decorations for autumn vases. The fleshy roots develop offsets which may be divided for increase, and the seeds, when sown, often flower the first season.

In addition to the common purple and orange of the wild *B. chinensis*, nurseries provide a strain of blackberry lily hybrids descended from the Mongolian *Pardanthopsis dichotoma*. Usually sold as "pardancandas" or "candy lilies," they come in a wide range of exotic, warm-colored pastels. All grow readily on damp ground and make easy, showy, but short-lived perennials. They grow quickly from seed and mix cheerfully in borders of white phlox, yellow daylilies, and blue mistflowers (*Eupatorium coelestinum*).

Crinums and Spider Lilies

At some point in May, the freshness of spring finally gives way to the steady warmth of summer. There can be no further pretense about gardening in a temperate clime. The subtropical season has arrived, and the South hereafter takes on an exotic ambience. The heat of the day sends gardeners cowering under porches or hiding beneath their hats. At dusk this uncomfortable warmth yields gradually to a pleasant humidity. A palpably thick atmosphere pervades the evening, seeming as if it were specially created for the sweet fragrances of jasmine, gardenia, and magnolia. If you walk among the borders at nightfall, you may spy the expanding buds of the most wondrous flowers of Southern summers, the powerfully fragrant blossoms of a freshly opened crinum or the delicate, fringed cups and dangling petals of a spider lily.

Of all the bulbs cultivated in the South, none seems more "Southern" than these, and none is more important to regional gardens. Both *Crinum* and spider lilies (*Hymenocallis* spp.) display special affinity for this region, and their lavish foliage marks many gardens. The sword-shaped leaves of spider lilies appear in two opposite ranks, like those of *Amaryllis*. Crinum foliage is distinctively whorled in lush rosettes.

❧ *Crinums*

The flowing fountains of crinum leaves are a hallmark of traditional plantings. Their sweet-scented flowers, cherished since colonial times, have been shared, bred and improved by enthusiastic Southerners up to the present day. Old clumps of *Crinum* embellish antebellum estates and sharecropper's hovels with equal abandon. Often the deep-rooted bulbs have

131

outlived their associated architecture, and they may be seen marking sites of old homes, plantations, and cemeteries. Through their robust habits, enduring vigor, and showy, fragrant blooms, these virtuous bulbs have carved a niche in regional landscapes like no other flowers.

Crinums are noteworthy not only for their incomparable, exotic blossoms, but also for their amazing ability to perform in the poor soils and erratic climate of the South. Seemingly intractable heavy clays and nutrient-poor sandy soils grow fabulous *Crinum*. In nature the bulbs are often found in seasonally flooded depressions, swamps, arid sandylands, or among coastal dunes. Their growth cycles respond to the irregular supplies of moisture they receive in these difficult habitats. Many *Crinum* species behave as true opportunists, producing leaves and flowers following each downpour. After blooming and making seed, they rest until the next shower. Like giant-size rain lilies, these bulbs bloom many times over the year in response to precipitation. Few flowers contribute so much and ask so little.

When summer downpours moisten the ground, awakening their enormous bulbs, crinums respond by erupting in lush fountains of straplike foliage. Leaves are quickly joined by thick flower stalks, which appear at the sides of the bulbs, then rise above the foliage. About ten days after the rains, the first buds open atop the tall scapes. Blooms may number fifteen to twenty or more in an umbel, so plants remain in flower for several days as blossoms open on successive evenings. If cut and set in a vase, the thick scapes will continue to open new flowers each night, just as if they were in the garden.

In the border these plants perform services more akin to peonies than to lilies. Their vast clumps of foliage provide an important focal point or anchor, whether the bulbs are in bloom or not. Like peonies, crinums dislike unnecessary disturbance and should be treated as long-lived perennials, rather than bedding flowers. They develop an enduring system of fleshy roots, which spreads as much as six feet in all directions. For this reason, crinums flower more prolifically and continuously when left in the ground for several years. When well treated they develop large clumps with numerous flowering-size bulbs together.

Crinums benefit from good soil preparation and should be set deeply, at least twelve to eighteen inches down. The plantings may then receive a thorough mulching, giving them a moist, cool root run in summer and protecting them from penetrating frost during the winter. Mulching and deep planting also encourage the bulbs to size up, rather than offset, so individual plants flower more freely.

Like other subtropicals, crinums respond with dramatically larger, more abundant blooms if dressed with rich compost or manure. The practice of making manure tea or liquid manure is also beneficial. It's a tradition in the South to take a brew of manure or grass clippings steeped with water and pour it over the leaves of crinums so nutrients may be absorbed as a tonic. This not only feeds the plants but also stimulates them to throw up bloom spikes.

Many crinums grow well as partial aquatics, and potted bulbs may be set in pans of standing water through the entire growing season. Slow-release

Crinum moorei var. *Schmidtii*

Crinum macowanii

Crinum bulbispermum 'Sacramento'

Crinum asiaticum

Crinum americanum

Crinum scabrum

fertilizers or water-soluble plant foods will encourage prodigious growth on bulbs receiving this "bog culture." Most crinums also thrive if planted near the margin of a garden pond.

When dividing an established clump, it is best to dig a trench around the entire group before attempting to undercut the deep-rooted bulbs. It is a good plan, also, to lift and separate all of the bulbs, rather than risk slicing them to pieces by digging off the sides one at a time. The largest two or three bulbs may then be returned to the hole and replanted to make a quick show, while the offsets can be planted elsewhere or shared with friends. Dividing these big perennials requires considerable effort and a sharp, sturdy spade. The plants usually take a year or two to reestablish and resume full flowering, so this is a task best performed infrequently; once every three to five years is often enough.

🌺 *Methuselah*

Part of the allure of crinums stems from their mysterious, antediluvian origins. Many gardeners in the South maintain large collections of these border stalwarts, but even the most meticulous record keepers face a challenge telling names of bulbs in their charge. More often than not, these sturdy plants have been inherited as heirlooms, obtained from a kindly neighbor, or liberated from a vacant field or cemetery. They may have persisted unnoticed, unrecognized, and with little or no attention for decades.

The origins of several garden crinums lie shrouded in the mists of nineteenth-century horticulture. Quite a few appear to be products of casual backyard hybridization, and such ignominious births may never have received proper christenings. Nurserymen and inventive flower lovers have provided their own titles for these bulbs, and names like "lily of the dawn" or "snow white angel" will be met in the lists and market bulletins offered by the farm ladies of the South.

The history of crinums as garden plants is a long one, and *Crinum* species were among the first flowers to be deliberately crossed by early breeders. The Hon. and Rev. William Herbert, Dean of Manchester, compiled a listing of hybrids in 1837. This tally included nearly thirty varieties, many of which probably remain in cultivation today, although their identities have been lost. These early hybrids were widely distributed by sailors who carried the bulbs home on their ships. Their continued presence in gardens is a living testament to the movement of peoples through the warm climates of the world. Several old crosses are so robust and vigorous that they have outlived their creators and, like Methuselah, seem destined to outlive us all.

🌺 *The Deep Sea Lily*

The most prolific and abundant crinum in Southern gardens is a distinctive species with tapered, blue-green foliage. Each leaf reaches as much as two feet in length and three or four inches in width at the base. These wrap around each other to form a thick column topped with gracefully arching fountains of foliage. In the center of the rosettes, there are usually a few thin, wispy, blue leaves just emerging; this unique appearance makes this crinum easy to distinguish wherever it grows.

Some country folk know these old garden flowers as deep sea lilies. In their native South Africa, they are called veld lilies or Orange River lilies. They may be found growing along banks of rivers in the southern Transvaal, Natal, and the Orange Free State. These robust amaryllids are also common escapes in the South, where they may be seen in April flowering in the shallow water of roadside ditches.

Old garden literature named this species for its glaucous leaves (*Crinum longifolium*) or its homeland (*C. capense*), and these defunct epithets will still be met in many nursery catalogs. Botanists, meanwhile, have settled on the unromantic epithet *C. bulbispermum*. Translated as "bulb seed," this refers to the peculiar, fleshy capsules of this plant. They swell and ripen into large pods, which split and tear open as they mature.

All crinums bear peculiarly large, fleshy seeds, which makes most varieties easy to raise. If left on the surface of the soil in a humid, shady position, the thick, green embryos germinate and form perfect miniature bulbs. These usually send down long roots, which pull the young plants deeply into the soil. Three or four years' growth on rich earth will mature the fledgling bulbs enough to begin flowering. Because of its prolific seed bearing, *C. bulbispermum* has sired numerous hybrids: This species is the forerunner of many of the old garden flowers of the South.

The succulent leaves of *C. bulbispermum* stand more frost than most other crinums, and this is the best variety to plant where freezes regularly penetrate the ground. The bulbs thrive anywhere in the South and are reported hardy in protected situations as far north as Long Island, New York. Blossoms are most prolific in April and May but come almost any season if stimulated by rains. In sheltered gardens *C. bulbispermum* flowers welcomely through December and January.

Flowers vary widely from plant to plant; they may be all white or pale pink with darker pink or wine markings on the keels. A dozen or more trumpet-shaped blooms cluster together, with five or six open at any one time. These lustrous flowers emit a peculiar, spicy odor, a wintry fragrance something like musk and anise mixed together. This is pleasant to some noses, but not all gardeners appreciate it.

The ordinary pinkish forms of *C. bulbispermum* may seem a bit homely, but they return with the trusted loyalty of a cocker spaniel. Even the poorest offer good, gray foliage to mix in a border. Improved selections include some of the finest flowers that may be grown in the South. The old, pure white 'Alba' reflexes luminous, waxy blooms over a period of four or five months. It soon increases into impressive clumps. The wine-flamed 'Sacramento' is a show plant with deeply pigmented blossoms. This variety, descended from a reddish strain of *C. bulbispermum* collected near Kimberly, South Africa, inherits a reluctance to offset from its colorful parent. It may be readily propagated by seed, though, to develop a spectacular group in the garden.

❧ *The Sabie Crinum*

Another crinum seldom, if ever, forming offsets is *C. macowanii.* This species has a wide range through southern and eastern Africa, especially common along the Sabie River in the northern Transvaal. Its big rosettes of foliage are as rank as those of *C. bulbispermum,* but they are dull green in tone, with none of the blueness of the Orange River lily.

The May blooms of *C. macowanii* are tulip-shaped and open widely at the throats to display thick, black anthers set against pale interiors. Light rose stripes line the backs of the petals, so that the buds resemble groups of pink-striped balloons. A sweet fragrance radiates from the rounded blossoms as they open in early evening. Each night several big flowers open and pose in an out-facing circle. The next morning they nod and fold their heads toward the ground. Since the petals recurve at the tips, these pendant, clustered blooms look like bunches of ruffled bells all through the following day.

This species is uncommon in the South but may be found occasionally in old gardens, usually growing as a solitary bulb. It grows easily from seed and, when cared for, assumes enormous proportions. Certain tetraploid *C. macowanii* hold the record for excessive size among hardier crinums. The fountains of leaves exceed five feet in height and spread, while the necks of the bulbs come to look like the trunks of young trees. Despite a near-tropical homeland, this species seems fairly frost tolerant. It performs well on heavy clay soils as well as deep sands.

❧ *Creole Lilies*

The rough-margined, undulating leaves of *C. scabrum* make this old garden treasure easy to recognize even when out of bloom. Although similar to *C. macowanii* when young, this species produces foliage of a brighter green. The wavy rosettes of leaves frequently lie prostrate against the ground and writhe about like lively vegetable snakes.

In the first weeks of June, the globular bulbs send up fat bloom stalks. Each stem carries five or more milky blossoms, which expand into shapely bells marked inside and out with deep stripes of crimson. Scented with a fantastic, spicy aroma, they attract all the hawk moths in the neighborhood and bring to mind visions of lush jungle landscapes illuminated by the gibbous, tropical moon.

Although *Crinum scabrum* is clearly an African flower, the precise origin of the species has long been in doubt. The bulbs described by Dean Herbert and other early botanists were collected from low ground around Rio de Janeiro. Presumably, they had been carried to Brazil along with slaves imported from west Africa. It seems likely that the presence of these beautiful flowers in the South marks our legacy from the African slave trade, as well.

C. scabrum thrives on rich, loamy ground where the bulbs do not lie cold or damp during winter dormancy. This deciduous, semitender species suffers in hard freezes but will tolerate temperatures as low as ten degrees F if planted on acid, sandy soil. Such loose earths hold warmth better than clay and help to discourage bacteria and consequent winter rots.

When well situated, *C. scabrum* multiplies into large clumps that flower generously through early summer. Each bulb produces several spikes of showy flowers, with an occasional late bloom following autumn rains. This spectacular variety is the ancestor of many modern hybrids, and its brilliant wine-red coloring has passed to several beautiful descendants.

🌸 Tender Species

In the warmest parts of the South, gardens often boast prolific clumps of *C. zeylanicum*, a showy native of tropical India and east Africa. This is a variable, frost-tender bulb. The darkest forms are nearly as brilliant as *C. scabrum*, but more ordinary types are only lightly striped with pink. These markings are darkest toward the ends of the petals, which are drawn out in distinctively pointed tips. The leaves of *C. zeylanicum* may undulate like *C. scabrum* or spread in flattened rosettes. They develop a strong central ribbing like leaves of corn, and this character passes to some hybrids. All forms of *C. zeylanicum* have a fine, spicy-sweet fragrance.

Another prominent group of tropical crinums in the South are the forms and hybrids of *C. jagus*, an evergreen species with spoon-shaped leaves and creamy, tuliplike flowers. The name *jagus*, a corruption of *gigas*, or gigantic, refers to the lush, dark green foliage of these bulbs. The fragrant blooms appear in small umbels in early summer. The best ones, such as the cultivar long grown in the South as 'Rattrayi', smell deliciously of vanilla. Another variant, the 'Christopher' lily, multiplies prolifically but is less free with its blooms. 'Maya Moon' is a tender dwarf with large, tulip-shaped blossoms introduced from Guatemalan gardens.

These are choice bulbs for positions in partial shade, valuable for their fine foliage even when they are out of bloom. They resent hard freezes, however, and need rich, acid soil to prosper. They are most valuable in mild, protected gardens near the Gulf and in Florida. They also make fine subjects for large tubs on a warm, shady patio.

🌸 Moore's Crinum

The forests of the eastern Cape Province provide the home to a half-hardy relation of *C. jagus* that has become a favorite wherever it can be grown. It first flowered in Europe from seeds planted in Dr. Moore's Glasnevin, Eire, garden; the seeds had been sent by a British soldier serving in South Africa around 1863. Unlike its tropical allies, *C. moorei* cycles its growth to climax in late winter, with flowers following in early summer. The plants often die down entirely in July and August to await fall rains.

The lush, cornlike rosettes of foliage sit on the tall necks that project from the big bulbs. Glossy, whorled leaves provide fine complements to the tall scapes of bell-shaped blooms. With mild weather the fragrant flowers last several days and assume rich tones of rose, pink, or white, without any of the striping seen in other colored crinums.

In most of the South, winters are a bit too cold and summers much too hot to do justice to these princely bulbs, but a few *C. moorei* succeed in shady gardens along the Gulf. The warm temperatures prevailing in early summer bleach the flowers to a pale semblance of their appearance in California and other cool climates, where this species is better adapted.

For Southern gardens the best variety of *C. moorei* is a snowy white form, var. *Schmidtii*. This variant comes from areas in the species' eastern range where summer rainfall is prevalent. Its growth is more in tune with the South, and *Schmidtii* flowers more reliably. The goblet-shaped blooms, opening one at a time in late May, radiate an ethereal fragrance.

❦ *The St. John's Lily*

In seaside gardens along the Gulf and Atlantic, the old frame houses often have lush plantings of positively enormous crinums. These obviously tropical bulbs develop huge necks topped with broad, green, spear-shaped leaves. The stout stems hold the foliage in a stiffened rosette, which spreads like a big, succulent agave. Several times each year, but especially in fall and winter, these noble bulbs send up scapes topped with clusters of spidery, white blooms.

The gigantic leeklike plants are forms of *C. asiaticum,* a species whose natural range extends across the Indo-Pacific. Various allies of this crinum occur from Japan south to Australia and east to Madagascar, and it's a popular garden plant over much of the Asian tropics. Since the big, green seeds float, they have the capacity to spread from island to island over the waves. Mariners brought this noble bulb to the Gulf and Caribbean basins during the sixteenth century, where they became known as St. John's lilies.

Like many crinums, the succulent stems and leaves of *C. asiaticum* contain an acrid, bitter juice. This has earned these flowers a wide reputation as poisonous plants, and they are called poison bulbs in their native Indonesia. In spite of this ominous title, southeast Asian children often pluck the tubular blooms to drink their sweet nectar, like American kids do from honeysuckle blossoms.

C. asiaticum is one of the few crinums that have entered successfully into the nursery trade. Since it propagates easily from seed and makes a fine foliage plant, it has become popular for poolside landscaping in Florida and other frost-free regions. The bulbs of this species grow more shallowly than other crinum. For this reason they are not reliably hardy where temperatures below twenty degrees F visit on a regular basis.

In addition to the common large green *asiaticum,* collectors of exotic bulbs also cultivate a dwarf ally with spreading foliage (*C. japonicum*) an aquatic relation with nearly erect leaves (*C. pedunculatum*), a stunning, pinkish flowered, red- or bronze-leaf form (*C. procerum* 'Splendens'), and a leafy variant with foliage turning from lime green to golden yellow as it matures (*C. xanthophyllum*). All of these have similar, narrow-petaled blossoms, and all require shelter from hard freezes.

❧ *Swamp Lilies*

The native crinum of the South, *C. americanum,* is a surprising rarity in gardens, although several of its hybrids are common. This stoloniferous wildflower inhabits estuaries in the darkest Southern swamplands and demands similar conditions in the garden. If given adequate flooding in a pond or artificial bog, the leafy bulbs offer fragrant umbels of four to eight spidery flowers in late summer or autumn. Pure white, with reddish stamens, they have a delicious fragrance.

An old garden plant recognized by many collectors as *C. americanum* 'Robustum' is in reality the South American *C. erubescens.* These two species are so close in appearance, it's a wonder botanists ever separated them. Both share blunt-tipped leaves, uniquely marked with paired longitudinal creases. The one important distinction between them is that *C. erubescens* grows happily under average garden conditions, while the native Southern swamp lily must stand in water if it is to blossom. The name *erubescens* means "blushing," refering to the purplish tint of the buds and flower stems in the Brazilian form.

In gardens *C. erubescens* continues in flower from July till frost, and it is well worth having for its sweet-scented blossoms. It quickly runs about the garden to make large patches and will even come up in lawns if conditions are to its liking. It is wise to plant the bulbs in a tub sunk in the ground if the questing roots might present a problem.

There is also a tiny miniature form of *C. erubescens,* imported originally from gardens in the West Indies. This mini-crinum travels underground just like its larger brother. Bulbs as small as a scallion will flower. They yield one, two, or three small blossoms on six-inch stems. Patches of this crinum resemble clumps of spidery white rain lilies. The mini-crinum is hardy in the middle and lower South and may be used as a small-scale groundcover like liriope or ophiopogon.

❧ *Milk and Wine*

The most familiar garden crinums in the South are striped trumpets known as milk and wine lilies. These trusted flowers descend from *C. bulbispermum,* which conveys its tall scape and rugged constitution, and *C. scabrum,* which imparts more or less reddish striping. The hybrids radiate a musky-spicy fragrance recognizably derived from both parents. Although varying from ordinary to extravagant, blossoms nearly always appear on vigorous, floriferous plants. Foliage is impressively rank, tapered, and grassy green.

Dean Herbert originated the first milk and wine lily in 1819. His achievement is commemorated in the "grex" name, *C.* × *herbertii,* which now applies to any hybrid of *scabrum* and *bulbispermum.* Many crosses involving these fruitful parents have followed, and *C.* × *herbertii* now exists in a multitude of forms. It is impossible to know exactly which clone came first, but it seems entirely probable that Herbert's original still grows in gardens. He described the milk

Crinum 'Empress of India'

Crinum x *digweedii*

Crinum 'Twelve Apostles'

Crinum amabile

Crinum x *herbertii* 'Carroll Abbott'

Crinum 'Goweni'

and wine lily in 1836: "A plant of great beauty, bearing 11 flowers on a scape three feet high . . . blush with deep red stripes. It requires a warmer situation where the wall is a little heated to make it flower finely, which it does several times each year."

In 1888 J.G. Baker published a handbook of the amaryllis family, listing many new *Crinum* species. Nurserymen seized on several of Baker's varietal names, applying them to the many different milk and wine forms at hand. As a result, botanical-sounding titles such as *sanderianum, kunthianum,* and *virginicum* became attached to various milk and wine clones. Bulbs still pass under these mistaken names in market bulletins and nursery lists. Since the hybrids rarely produce seed, they make themselves obvious in collections that include honest, fertile species, such as *C. bulbispermum* or *C. scabrum.*

Many *C.* × *herbertii* variants bear light pink-striped blooms, but a few clones are marked nearly as dark burgundy as *C. scabrum*. In most varieties the stripes are strongest near the center of the blossoms, fading gradually toward the petal tips. 'Carroll Abbott' is one of the best, with large umbels of wine-marked blossoms. It's an old heirloom flower of Southern gardens, originally imported from England during the nineteenth century. The vibrant blooms appear in late spring and early summer.

'Goweni' is a milk and wine hybrid with drooping foliage like *C.* × *herbertii,* but its reversed color pattern shows that it descends from *C. zeylanicum,* rather than from *C. scabrum*. The recurved petals, with pointed tips like the elongated fingernails of a Mandarin court official, bear pale exterior stripes, which fade toward the center of the flowers, opposite the true *C.* × *herbertii*. Blooms open several at a time, so that the spikes almost always fall over to the ground unless they are staked. The lightly striped blossoms look nearly white when seen in strong sun.

Especially deep-rooted bulbs make 'Goweni' tough and hardy. Clumps persist, flower, and slowly increase under the most rigorous conditions. Gardeners know these pale trumpeting amaryllids as August lilies, for they often appear after late summer showers. This unique and distinctive hybrid dates from around 1820, bred in England by J.R. Gowen. It has been pictured in several Victorian treatments of garden flowers. The first bulbs probably came to the South in the middle 1800s.

❧ *Nassau Lilies*

There is another, more exotic section of the milk and wine lilies quite different from the hardy trumpets. Their flat, star-shaped blooms begin to appear in the second half of the summer. As they open in early evening, they send forth an intense, delightfully sweet perfume.

The most prolific of these star lilies is a half-hardy hybrid whose presence in the South dates back over one hundred years. At Round Lake, a historic Irish settlement along the Texas coast, settlers planted long rows of these crinums. The bulbs they set around their homes came from the nearby convent of San Patricio, where sisters cultivated the fragrant flowers as early as 1876.

Reasoner Brothers' Royal Palms Nursery of Oneco, Florida, advertised this variety in their catalog of 1900 as:

> *C. fimbriatulum, The Nassau, or Milk and Wine Lily.*
> *A strong grower; not particular as to soil. Flowers in umbels; very large and showy, striped white and carmine; 3 to 4 inches in diameter. Exceedingly choice and desirable as a pot plant or for bedding out during the summer in the North. The fragrant flowers are so different from any of the more common flowers grown North that they produce a sensation when seen.*

Twelve years later the famous Florida plantsman Henry Nehrling lamented the misnaming of this and other crinums. He then compounded horticultural error by making his own guess at the proper name of this flower:

> *There is great confusion in the nomenclature of these plants, scarcely half a dozen being correctly named in the various catalogues . . . .*
> *C. erubescens (usually advertised as C. fimbriatulum). One of the most common species in Florida gardens. Increases rapidly by offsets. Leaves long, thin and narrow, 2 to 3 feet long: flower stem 2 to 3 feet tall, purplish green, carrying usually four to six very beautiful fragrant flowers, pure white with a faint pink keel, outside purplish red. Does not bear seeds, and is useless for cross-breeding. Found everywhere in gardens.*

In truth this old, sterile hybrid is neither *C. fimbriatulum* nor *C. erubescens,* although something close to the latter is one of its parents, the other parent being *C. scabrum.* As evidence for this, the slick, lime green leaves of this Nassau lily bear longitudinal creases characteristic of *C. americanum* and its allies. The Nassau lily may be reasonably identified as a child of *C. americanum* and *C. scabrum,* a cross officially named *C. × digweedii* in 1820. Nevertheless, in collections this old favorite will appear under pseudonyms such as *erubescens, fimbriatulum, submersum,* or 'Royal White' for years to come.

The spindle-shaped bulbs of the Nassau lily multiply by short stolons to form compact, upright clumps. With good care the bulbs offer their fine blooms over a long season from July till frost. Near the coast these classic Southern perennials may be seen marking old property lines from which hurricanes have removed "permanent" structures. There could hardly be a more romantic encounter than stumbling upon a blooming clump among the dunes, with the intoxicating fragrance of the succulent flowers wafting on the sea air.

Recent breeders have introduced hybrids similar to the Nassau lily. All are showy and worth growing, although none can compete in vigor or fragrance with the original. 'Sundance' is a pink-striped, frilly hybrid from *C. scabrum* and the long-tubed, Mexican *C. loddigesianum.* It likes plenty of water but is otherwise easy. 'Stars 'n Stripes', 'William Herbert', and 'Carioca' are three showstopping hybrids from Thad Howard with wine-streaked, starry blossoms.

🐚 *More Star Lilies*

C. zeylanicum has also sired striped hybrids with *C. americanum*, and these may be seen in many gardens in the lower South. 'Maureen Spinks' and 'Veracruz' are two named varieties that may be had from collectors. These crosses, officially known as *C.* × *baconi*, usually prove less cold-hardy than the Nassau lily, but they are fragrant, beautiful, and useful for gardens along the Gulf Coast. They follow the typical *C. zeylanicum* color scheme, with darkest striping on the exterior of the petals, becoming paler toward the center and interior of the blossoms. The petals bear long, clawlike tips, and the flowers always have a deliciously spicy scent. The rounded, globular bulbs should be set deeply to protect them from hard frost and discourage overly rapid multiplication, to which these varieties are prone.

🐚 *The Empress*

In 1906 Reasoner Brothers imported a colorful, fragrant crinum christened 'Empress of India'. This honestly Victorian flower (Queen Victoria *was* the Empress of India) bears huge, wine-striped, powerfully scented blossoms, which rise on tall, dusty purple stems above nearly prostrate, channeled, green foliage. The nine-inch flowers are at their best only on moon-filled nights, for they fold promptly and wither at first light.

The straplike leaves and night-flowering habit make 'Empress' one of the most distinctive milk and wine lilies in Southern gardens. These characteristics imply descent from *C. zeylanicum* and one of the tender, nocturnal Indian species, such as *C. pratense* or *C. amoenum*. Herbert listed several such hybrids in 1836, with names like 'Paxtoni', 'Louisae', and 'Cooperi'. He also reported exchanging bulbs with a horticulturally inclined missionary friend, Dr. William Carey of Serampore, India. It seems quite possible that one of these varieties persisted in India and was imported by Reasoner Brothers at the turn of the century.

🐚 *Queen Emma's Lily*

The last native monarch of Hawaii, Queen Emma, included several favorite bulb flowers in her garden at Lawaikai. She is remembered for her love of these plants, especially a huge, treelike crinum the residents of Kauai call Queen Emma lily. This same crinum, common in the gardens of Florida and the lower South, has long been known as *C. augustum*. In Barbados this famous tropical flower is called the Great Mogul.

Herbert recorded that sailors brought the first bulbs of this exotic crinum to Calcutta from the small island of Mauritius. A similar plant from Sumatra was introduced around the same time and named *C. amabile*. Both of these appeared to be spontaneous hybrids from *C. zeylanicum* and the gigantic *C. asiaticum*.

Trunklike bulbs hold the leaves of *C. augustum* in an erect whorl. Several times each year they send up tremendous, empurpled stalks, which expand into huge umbels of spidery, wine-striped blooms. The fat stems usually lie on the ground, but this does not deter the succulent, twelve-inch blossoms from opening and scenting the air with narcotic sweetness.

Although tropical, *C. augustum* survives modest frost if planted in a sandy bed near a south wall. The shallow bulbs should be mulched or periodically reset at depth to protect against disastrous freezes. Otherwise, they require only a large space in which to sprawl. When well grown, the leaves of this crinum may exceed six feet in height and spread. Offsets form slowly but steadily and, since they grow shallowly, may be carefully removed without disturbing the mother bulb.

❧ *Twelve Apostles*

The oldest building on Mustang Island, Texas, is the historic Tarpon Inn, a long frame structure built in 1886. Its twenty-six small, efficient rooms once housed sportsmen intent on capturing trophy fish from the nearby bays. The pugnacious, silvery tarpons are long gone from these estuaries, and the weathered compound is all that remains of the former town of Tarpon, presently included within the city of Port Aransas.

Along the cypress post foundation of the inn grow several large *C. augustum* and, interspersed with them, fragrant crinums familiar to gardeners under the name 'Twelve Apostles'. The scent of these narrow-petaled, pink-tinged blossoms is sweet and carries a hint of anise or musk. This fragrance and the tapered foliage of the plants identify these old flowers as products of *C. bulbispermum.* The other parent is *C. asiaticum*, as may be seen by the robust size of the bulbs and by their slow rate of increase through vertical fission.

'Twelve Apostles' is a remarkably apt name for this plant, for that is the usual number of blooms found in the umbel. The somewhat homely flowers come periodically through the entire year, so this crinum eventually wins favor by its persistence. The pallid, spidery blossoms do not always show to good effect in gardens, but they last well and will pervade the house with a pleasant fragrance if cut and set in a tall vase.

More glamorous cousins of 'Twelve Apostles', such as the spectacular 'Sangria', descend from the red-leafed *C. procerum* 'Splendens'. This hybrid displays deep wine-red foliage and pink, spidery blossoms, which reflex gracefully like Guernsey lilies. With *C. bulbispermum* ancestry, such plants prove cold-hardy, but they are slow to increase unless the bulbs are sliced to induce multiplication. They remain rare in collections. Gardeners can raise their own hardy, red-leafed seedlings by placing *bulbispermum* pollen on the blooms of the red-leafed *C. procerum* 'Spendens'.

❧ *Miss Elsie*

Much more generous with offsets are several old hybrids of *C. bulbispermum* and *C. americanum*. They have narrow, whitish, spreading petals and clusters of violet-toned filaments. This gives these fragrant crinums a character similar to 'Twelve Apostles', but on shorter, leafier plants. Carolina plantsman William Lanier Hunt describes these flowers as bearing a "decided odor of anise."

Crinum 'Ollene'

Crinum 'Peachblow'

Crinum 'Sangria'

Crinum 'Claude Davis'

Crinum 'Mrs. James Hendry'

Crinum 'Ellen Bosanquet'

Elizabeth Lawrence says the blooms have the "delicious scent of waterlilies." They are certainly pleasant to smell, in any case.

'Miss Elsie', the best known of these near-white hybrids, is common to gardens of Georgia and the Carolinas. 'Catherine', originally from the Natchez garden of Catherine Winston, and 'Seven Sisters', selected by Grace Hinshaw of Mobile, are well distributed in the South. 'Ollene' is a beautiful, ash white descendent of 'Seven Sisters' introduced by Thad Howard. All of these are very hardy, succeeding everywhere below the Mason-Dixon line if given enriched soil and unfailing moisture.

❦ White Zinfandels

One of the most intoxicatingly lovely crinums is an old blushy hybrid from the famous horticulturist T.L. Mead of Oviedo, Florida. Around 1900 Mead imported a collection of nearly one hundred crinums from India and set about making crosses. The bulbs were planted near a small bog, which overflowed during the rainy season, inundating the beds of seedlings. When the waters receded, one of the surviving crinums was rescued and moved to higher ground. Although the exact parentage was lost, this hybrid proved outstanding, with tall stems of huge, pinky-white, scented blossoms. Mead named his cross 'Peachblow'. Although somewhat tender and inclined to flop over if not staked, it is one of the most beautiful crinums, with an exotic appeal similar to the 'Empress of India'.

Mead's contemporary Henry Nehrling introduced another handsome blush hybrid around 1915. This exquisite flower, 'Mrs. James Hendry', ranks as one of the most beautiful and rewarding of Southern perennials. The superb, pink-tinged blossoms appear in tidy umbels, which open so that the flowers face forward together. The buds are set on sturdy scapes amid lush, compact, green foliage, with none of the untidiness seen in other hybrids. The flowers are spicily scented but never overpowering. They grace garden borders with their tender colorings from May till frost. 'Mrs. James Hendry' multiplies at a steady pace and seems hardy anywhere frost does not penetrate the ground.

'Alamo Village' is another blush-colored hybrid from various older Southern gardens. Its spiky umbels of narrow-petaled, near-white flowers radiate an intense, spicy fragrance. The bulbs are vigorous, everblooming, and surprisingly hardy. Deep wine-colored buds and long, clawlike petals suggest parentage from *C. zeylanicum*.

'H.J. Elwes' is a famous blushy pink selection raised by the English horticulturist Henry John Elwes. In the lower South, this fragrant offspring of *C. moorei* and *C. americanum* makes a fine border plant, with short rosettes of thick, spreading leaves. In colder areas it does well in pots—and is one of the few sufficiently compact crinums for this use. In 1908 it received a Royal Horticultural Society Award of Merit.

'Summer Nocturne', a Thad Howard cross of *C. moorei* and *C. erubescens*, is similar to Elwes's plant but has paler, whitish blooms and blunt, grass green foliage. The sweet-scented flowers begin appearing in early July following summer rains and continue till frost. Larger blush hybrids from *C. moorei* include 'Maiden's Blush' and 'White Mogul'. The especially lush foliage of these varieties makes them outstanding choices for edging a bed in semishade.

'White Mogul' is unususal in that it descends from *C. yemense*, a rare variety from the deserts of the Arabian Peninsula. The foliage of this species resembles *C. zeylanicum*, but blooms are entirely white, with long petals and olive-toned floral tubes. After flowering in early summer, this remarkable plant ripens several lumpy seeds the size of tennis balls. In its desert homeland, this allows this crinum to reproduce in periods of extended drought, for the seeds germinate and form sizable bulbs without need for rain. Although better adapted to areas with dry, mild winters, such as California, *C. yemense* will succeed in the South if planted in deep, sandy soil.

🌸 *Powellii*

When *C. moorei* is bred to other crinums, whether striped or plain, the offspring usually develop self-colored flowers, rather than a milk and wine pattern. This can be seen clearly in the numerous pink or white *C.* × *powellii* forms descended from *C. moorei* and *C. bulbispermum*. Like the *C.* × *herbertii* hybrids, these are hardy workhorses among crinums. Their tapered, lush, green clumps of foliage may be seen in many older gardens.

C. × *powellii* 'Album' is a plant of superlative quality, with tall scapes bearing large umbels of shapely, snowy blooms. Introduced as long ago as 1888, it is now common in gardens, performing equally well in sun or shade. The rich pink 'Cecil Howdyshel', was developed in the 1930s by a California nurseryman. This outstanding hybrid has earned a niche in Southern gardens through its tremendous vigor. Large bulbs of 'Cecil Howdyshel' reliably send up eight or more stalks in a season, remaining in almost perpetual bloom. 'Claude Davis' is a wine purple *powellii* type with contrasting, brownish floral tubes. This prolific Louisiana selection descends from a colorful, but rare and slow-to-offset, *yemense* hybrid, 'Cape Dawn'.

The famous plant breeder Luther Burbank worked his genius on crinums, as well as on many other flowers, and a few lucky gardeners still grow some of his creations. 'White Queen' is a frilly, snow-white hybrid of *C.* × *powellii* 'Alba' and *C. macowanii*, arguably the most lovely crinum ever bred. The blossoms retain the bell-like petals of *C. macowanii* but have the fine form and fragrance of *C. moorei*. These large bulbs are tough and long-lived, with good fountains of glossy, green foliage. Offsets appear slowly, so this fine white remains a collector's item.

🌸 *Shell Pink*

The most ubiquitous of all the *C. moorei* offspring is 'J.C. Harvey', a turn-of-the-century cross from *C. zeylanicum*. This half-hardy hybrid inherits clear pink, goblet-shaped blooms and lush foliage. This foliage is heavily ribbed, like leaves of corn, and makes these crinums easy to identify, even when they are out of bloom. With only a little encouragement, 'J.C. Harvey' multiplies like the devil, so it has become especially common in Southern gardens. Partial shade and deep planting in rich soil are needed to encourage free blooming, but this old shell pink crinum is otherwise fantastically easy to grow.

❧ Reds

'J.C. Harvey' is one probable parent of a famous wine-red clone called 'Ellen Bosanquet', first listed in the Reasoner Brothers' catalog of 1930 as 'Mrs. Bosanquet'. This lovely plant was bred by an English plantsman, Louis Percival Bosanquet, who resided in Fruitland Park, Florida. Mr. Bosanquet named his creation for his wife.

The lush foliage of 'Ellen Bosanquet' resembles 'J.C. Harvey', and the two plants can be readily confused when out of bloom. The rich burgundy flowers are distinct, however, and appear punctually in the first weeks of June. This points to C. scabrum as the other probable parent of this colorful hybrid. Slightly ruffled leaves, spicy fragrance, and shortish scapes support this theory, as well.

This invaluable crinum multiplies nearly as well as 'J.C. Harvey' and is even more tolerant to cold and drought. Shade from the hottest sun will allow the big, wine-colored blooms to open to perfection. You could hardly wish for a showier, more affable garden flower. This crinum is one of the South's greatest horticultural treasures. Although flowering is heaviest in June, established clumps continue to bloom into autumn.

In an attempt to exceed 'Ellen Bosanquet' in depth of coloring, several breeders have continued to hybridize with C. scabrum and other colored crinums. 'Elizabeth Traub' is a tall, wine-tinted variety nearly as dark as 'Ellen', but with foliage more like C. × powellii. It is probably descended from 'Cecil Howdyshel' and scabrum. 'Summer Glow' is a Grace Hinshaw cross of 'Ellen' and 'Cecil Howdyshel', with large, red-pink blooms that fade to old rose in warm weather. Both 'Elizabeth Traub' and 'Summer Glow' make fine hardy plants for the rear of summer borders, useful where 'Ellen' would prove too short.

❧ Bicolors

Katherine Clint crossed 'Ellen Bosanquet' with C. × powellii 'Alba' to produce 'Walter Flory', an unusual bicolor with exquisite pink blossoms accented by burgundy stripes and green petal tips. This early-flowering variety has excellent lush, green foliage and, like its parents, succeeds in both sun and shade. C. × worsleyi, a cross of moorei and scabrum, has similar pink, wine-striped blooms that appear later in summer. The tremendous fountains of foliage and waxy blooms of this variety are at their best in half-day sun or partial shade. Also worthy of special favor is the novel 'Carnival', a curious C. × herbertii hybrid from Thad Howard with spectacularly variegated red blooms.

❧ Walking Sticks

H.B. Bradley, a barrister residing in Sydney, Australia, developed several colorful crinums that received Awards of Merit from the New South Wales chapter of the RHS in 1927. 'Bradley' has deep wine, open-faced blossoms that appear on tall, slender scapes, inspiring the Australian colloquial name, "walking stick lilies."

These waxy flowers bear spreading, rounded petals, and the bulbs produce fountains of bright green, narrow foliage. This suggests descent from *C. scabrum* and the rare Australian native *C. flaccidum*, a species famous for its rounded blooms that vary from sulfur yellow to white and pink. *C. flaccidum* is, unfortunately, ill at ease in the South. Its hybrids thrive, however, and breeders may one day use it to bring yellow pigment into their crosses.

In addition to 'Bradley', two other Australian hybrids are offered by American dealers. 'George Harwood' is one with slender leaves like *C. flaccidum* and wine-red, white-centered blooms. These goblet-shaped flowers open one at a time like *C. moorei*. 'Bradley Giant' has larger, redder flowers and lush, spreading foliage. All of Bradley's hybrids are vigorous garden performers, multiplying with long-necked, globular bulbs.

❧ *'Emma Jones'*

If forced to choose among the colored crinums, the most satisfying of all might be 'Emma Jones'. This blousy pink hybrid originated in the Corpus Christi garden of Fred Jones from an improbable cross of 'Peachblow' and 'Cecil Howdyshel'. Although saturated with the deep pink, velvety color of its *powellii* parent, the ruffled blooms also carry the exotic fragrance of Mead's old Florida hybrid. The tall stems and large umbels inherit the 'Peachblow' fault of flopping over, but who could imagine a more cheerful necessity than to be forced to tie up the huge, pink buds as the scapes rise in succession through the summer?

❧ *Amarcrinums*

When temperatures climb near 100 degrees F in mid-July, even the heartiest flowers lose their enthusiasm. By midmorning the majority of crinums fold up and limply hang their heads. Any fragrance left from the night before steams away on the noon air, and the best colors of the succulent blossoms swoon away.

At such times it is congenial to have blooms such as the × *Amarcrinum*, which defiantly surmount the trials of summer. These tough, lilylike blossoms belong to an intergeneric hybrid of *Crinum moorei* and a related bulb from South Africa, the Cape belladonna (*Amaryllis belladonna*). Heat and strong sun are the very conditions they savor, and their delightful fragrance could cool the fiery breath of a dragon.

There are several different × *Amarcrinum* clones, but the most famous is a pale pink variety developed by the California plantsman Fred Howard. It's one of the finest flowers any Southerner can hope to bloom, regardless of weather. A flowering stalk of this × *Amarcrinum* lasts for a month in the hottest season. Sixteen or seventeen buds appear on each two-foot scape. They open to waxy, pink, blunt-petaled blossoms accented with white throats and radiating a refreshing bouquet that smells like a gentle mixture of vanilla and lemon chiffon.

The oversized bulbs of × *Amarcrinum* 'Fred Howard' seem a little clumsy attached to their modest tufts of straplike, leaves. Inheriting the character of the belladonna parent, these leaves set themselves in more or less opposite ranks, rather than in rosettes. It takes a hard freeze to knock this compact, glossy foliage down, and in mild winters these plants remain nearly evergreen. Lean, sandy soil seems to encourage more generous growth and flowering.

In California, where *Amaryllis belladonna* and various *Crinum* × *powellii* clones often grow together, several additional × *Amarcrinum* have been introduced by alert gardeners. 'Delkin's Find' is a fast-offsetting, pale pink with well-formed flowers. 'Born Free' is a near-white. 'Dorothy Hannibal' is a midget, late-flowering selection with raspberry blossoms. These hybrids lack the size and intense fragrance of 'Fred Howard' but are useful additions to this valuable section.

The Cape belladonna (*Amaryllis belladonna*) is itself sometimes planted in the South, but it may rot from excess moisture unless planted by a dry foundation or on a raised bed of sand. If winter temperatures fall below twenty degrees F, leaves may be damaged, preventing bloom the following summer.

Southerners sometimes succeed with vigorous forms of the Cape belladonna, such as *Amaryllis* × *parkeri*, 'Hathor', 'Rubra bicolor', or 'Purpurea Major', but flowering is hardly a consistent event. It is often necessary to lift the bulbs in early summer to enforce a dry dormant period. If replanted in September, blooms appear quickly. The lovely blossoms are like elegant versions of × *Amarcrinum*, with ruffled clusters of pink or white, scented blooms. They appear on bare stems unaccompanied by foliage, so, like *Lycoris*, they are often called "naked ladies." Other related hybrids, such as × *Amarine* (*Amaryllis* × *Nerine*), are equally lovely but also ill-suited to the South. It would be desirable to breed these, and related genera such as *Brunsvigia*, *Nerine*, *Ammocharis*, and *Scadoxus*, with crinums. This might eventually develop a range of colored hybrids suited to humid climates.

❧ *Ballerinas of the Garden*

The spider lily clan (*Hymenocallis* spp.), comprised of uniquely graceful evening flowers, offers some of the garden's most exquisite summer fragrances. Like crinums, these easy-growing flowers are characteristically Southern. Although neglected and overlooked by many horticulturists, native *Hymenocallis* species include the most elegant and beautiful of wild bulbs. The subtropical American forms contribute some of the most pleasing and dependable perennials to summer borders. Common names for the various species include "spider lily," "basket flower," "crown beauty," "Peruvian daffodil," and "chalice lily." In Latin America they are often called *flor de San Juan*, or "St. John's lily," a name widely applied to any fragrant, nocturnal bloom.

Hymenocallis derives from the Greek *hymen kallos*, literally "beautiful membrane," a reference to the gossamer cups of webbing centered inside the spidery white petals. These bizarre blooms have an exotic, mysterious quality, which makes them especially choice. Although several amaryllids share the common name, "spider lily," *Hymenocallis* deserves first claim on this title. It would be hard to imagine a blossom built more like a daddy longlegs.

Each flower has a tapered, usually greenish tube, which expands to six slender segments. These are ordinarily white, but one or two yellow or greenish flowered species are known. The petals surround spidery, dark green stamens, which in turn unite to form the diaphanous, white or yellowish cup, or corona. On the tips of the stamens, maneuverable anthers dusted in orange or yellow pollen dangle and swivel with each passing breeze or buzz from a hawk moth's wings. From the center of the cup rises the greenish style, tipped by a drop of clear, sticky liquid.

Once pollinated, these amaryllids rapidly ripen their seed. Fleshy and green, like those of crinum, these seeds usually have the capacity to float. As the seeds swell, they burst from the pods at the ends of the long stems. During the heat of the day, the stalks lie flaccid on the ground, releasing a few seeds at a time. At night the flower stems become turgid and rise upward. As they repeatedly move up and down over several days they describe a small circle, releasing seeds at intervals to assure an even distribution around the mother bulb.

If placed in a humid, shady position free from marauding slugs, the seeds quickly germinate to form miniature bulbs. Evergreen types begin growth immediately, sending out leaves and roots and pulling down into the soil. Deciduous species usually remain dormant, waiting till the following spring before leafing out in earnest. With three or four years growth, the young bulbs come into flower.

Like other subtropicals, *Hymenocallis* species relish rich soils. Most thrive under boggy conditions, and several Southeastern species require aquatic culture for best growth. Heavy clays are to their liking, but sandy ground is usually fine, so long as it is well watered.

Spider lilies range from big, bulky tropical evergreens to tiny, daffodil-like miniatures. Nearly all make fine foliage plants. The blossoms of the various species have much the same appearance but differ in fragrance and in season of bloom, so it rewards gardeners to include a wide array. With careful selection, Southerners may enjoy these flowers from early March till frost. It's thrilling to watch the nightly ritual of the blossoms as they actively swell, cling for a moment, half-open by the petal tips, and then burst wide apart to admit the first hawk moths of the evening.

❧ *Ismenes*

The most common *Hymenocallis* in horticulture are the deciduous Peruvian daffodils. Botanists once placed these distinctive South American flowers in a separate genus called *Ismene*, after a daughter of Oedipus and Jocasta in Greek literature. These Andean species differ from other *Hymenocallis* in their large, trumpetlike coronas and short stamens. The anthers bend inward over the centers of the flowers, instead of sprawling outward. The overlapping leaves of the bulbs also form a unique neck or stem.

In the warm climate of the South, these mountain-dwelling bulbs require deep planting and heavy mulching to ensure a suitably cool root run. The bulbs should be reset every other year in fresh, well-manured ground to discourage splitting to less than flowering size.

Small species, such as *H. pedunculata* (*Ismene macleana*), are now and then offered in the bulb trade, but the best known and most readily available of the ismenes is the large-flowered *H. narcissiflora* (*Ismene calathina*). The common horticultural strain is sterile and routinely produces blooms with five petals instead of the customary six. The funnel-like coronas, attractively fringed, are shaded with green along the ribs of the stamens. The blooms radiate a thickly sweet, nocturnal fragrance.

Because they are naturally deciduous, these subtropical natives of Peru and Bolivia may be grown in cold climates by digging and storing, as with gladioli. In this fashion, bulbs may be scheduled to bloom on command. They reliably flower within a week if planted during warm weather.

The famous clone 'Festalis' was bred by the English bulb fancier Arthington Worsley from a cross of *H. narcissiflora* and the strange, greenish flowered *H. longipetala*. This curious species was once segregated into its own genus, *Elisena*, which is an ancient word meaning "romance." Although *H. longipetala* is more intriguing than beautiful, it imparts a graceful, orchidlike curling to the petals of 'Festalis'. Unfortunately, this hybrid tends to increase at the expense of bloom. 'Advance' is a better-behaved seedling of 'Festalis' backcrossed to *H. narcissiflora*.

'Sulfur Queen' is a popular, light yellow selection descended from a cross of *H. narcissiflora* and the "lily of the Incas," *H. amancaes*. This three-flowered species and its one-flowered cousin, *H. heliantha*, are the only golden yellows in this otherwise ghostly white, nocturnal genus. These brightly colored species, denizens of high deserts around Lima and Cajamarca, Peru, prove ill-suited to the humid lowlands of the Southern United States. The hybrid 'Sulfur Queen' is more forgiving and rates as the most reliable of the ismene group in the South, forming impressively large bulbs. 'Sulfur Queen' has a pleasant primrose scent to complement its attractive flowers.

During the 1960s the Cincinnati, Ohio, breeder Len Woelfle created a series of flowers from the same parents as 'Sulfur Queen', the finest of which was a yellow-and-white bicolor named 'Pax'. He also developed several graceful, greenish gold flowers from crosses between *H. amancaes* and *H. longipetala*. These long-necked plants are known as the 'Dancing Dolls'. These Woelfle varieties have never become common in the bulb trade, but they are grown by a few fanciers of the genus. They seem to thrive in the South and are entirely hardy.

In the mildest parts of the Gulf Coast and Florida, the magnificent hybrid 'Daphne' is also worth planting. This treasure, raised by the Dutch bulb firm Van Tubergen before 1900, is descended from a difficult cross of *H. narcissiflora* and the Caribbean *H. speciosa*. It combines the large cup of its ismene parent with the elegant form and evergreen foliage of *H. speciosa*. The lush, spear-shaped leaves renew themselves in autumn; they should be protected from strong sun and hard frost. The ravishing clusters of sweet-scented blossoms appear in early summer.

Double-flowered tropical *Hymenocallis*

Hymenocallis sp. "Tropical Giant"

Crinum 'Carnival'

Hymenocallis 'Daphne'

Crinum x *worsleyi*

🌺 *Tropical Spider Lilies*

Most of the cultivated *Hymenocallis* in the South are old, heirloom flowers, originally brought from the tropical shores of the Antilles and the Spanish Main. The early explorer Oviedo initiated the long garden history of these bulbs when he encountered his first *"lirios blancos,"* or "white lilies," growing on beaches near Porto Bello, Panama, in 1535. Spider lilies were also reported by later English and French explorers, and they were soon spread widely by sailors. As with crinums, the identities of many of these flowers have been obscured in the tangled web of early horticulture. Although naturally evergreen in frost-free climates, the more vigorous tropical spider lilies endure the annual loss of their foliage in winter.

The most widespread *Hymenocallis* in gardens is also the variety for which there is the least certain information. This frustrating plant, distinctive enough to be readily recognized anywhere, matches none of the descriptions of known species. It might be one of Herbert's old Puerto Rican or Jamaican varieties, *H. expansa* or *H. caymanensis*, but unless a botanist arranges an expedition to visit the Caribbean, he or she can do little to resolve this question. Early descriptions of spider lilies are imprecise, and dried *Hymenocallis* specimens in herbaria are so shriveled and distorted that they bear little resemblance to the living plants.

All that can be done is to note everything that may be observed in garden cultivation, in hopes that others may someday fill in the gaps to our knowledge. We can attempt to arrange our cultivated *Hymenocallis* into more or less sensible species, but Nature incessantly reminds us,

I own not any name,
Neither order nor degree.

Botanists and nurseries generally list this familiar garden flower as *H. littoralis*, *H. caribaea*, *H. rotata*, or *H. tenuiflora*, titles rightly applying to four unrelated plants. Since no honest botanical name is forthcoming for this venerable spider lily of Southern gardens, the most acceptable and least confusing tag to apply is an old horticultural nickname, "tropical giant."

Tropical giant is a favorite landscape ornamental, perhaps the finest of all foliage perennials in the South. The lush fountains of glossy, sword-shaped leaves arch gracefully, and the generously proportioned bulbs soon multiply to form imposing clumps. This abundant foliage sets off the sweet, spicily fragrant, white blooms, which appear in early July. These blossoms sit atop flattened, sharp-edged scapes, which are typical of Caribbean *Hymenocallis*. Their moderately long tubes and large, spreading coronas are distinct, well proportioned, and lovely. The slender petals, set in two ranks of three, one recurving and one spreading, are unique to the species. Tropical giant might be an old garden hybrid, but when well grown it ripens glossy, green seeds, like other wild *Hymenocallis*, which sprout and grow up to look much like their parents.

Queen Emma cherished this plant in her Hawaiian garden, and it is widely distributed around the world in warm climates. The bulbs, apparently hardy anywhere the ground does not freeze deeply, may be planted on any damp soil. In addition to the ordinary luxuriant tropical giant, a few gardeners maintain stock of a rare double variety. The extra set of petals makes the flowers less graceful, but they are well worth including in gardens for the sake of novelty.

❦ Island Beauties

On the white, coral sands of the Florida Keys, large, succulent-leafed *Hymenocallis* are often the first plants to colonize the salty, wave-tossed beaches. When they flower in July and August, the thick bulbs send up elegantly long-tubed blossoms. These support erect, gobletlike cups and trail spidery, dangling petals that swirl around the tubes. In September, the stalks ripen large, gray-green seeds, which may often be seen floating among the waves and drifting up on the beaches.

This bulb occurs widely over the Caribbean, flowering from midsummer till autumn. It escapes and persists around old settlements near the Gulf. For the moment, botanists have attached the name *H. latifolia,* or "wide-leafed" spider lily. This is an apt description of some forms of this species, but in natural colonies the foliage is diverse, varying from blunt to pointed, flattened to rolled, and glossy green to ashy gray. Although typically a denizen of dry, sunny beaches, this species is as apt to be met in shady mangrove swamps or along freshwater ponds.

A wonderful old garden form of *H. latifolia* is commonly planted in sandy beach gardens along the Gulf. This cultivar has stiffly erect, green leaves. Because its floral tubes are exceptionally long (seven or eight inches), it is sometimes segregated under the name *H. pedalis.* The enchanting fragrance of the blooms, suggesting vanilla or buttered pecans, scents the evening air for nearly a month in the middle of summer. This old garden form remains seedless unless planted near other clones of *H. latifolia.*

Another cultivar, usually listed incorrectly as *H. caribaea* 'Variegata', develops a beautiful ivory variegation. Unfortunately, it lacks sufficient strength to survive the open sun and inclines to rot if left cold and damp over winter. It is most useful in honestly tropical gardens, or as a pot or greenhouse subject given rich, acid soil.

❦ The Big Fatty

Several gardens around Jacala, in the east Mexican state of Hidalgo, include a large, early-flowering spider lily with especially fine blooms and foliage. This spectacular variety, *H. imperialis,* was apparently collected by gardeners from the local region, for it may occasionally be seen growing on nearby hillsides. The huge bulbs and enormous, spear-shaped leaves resemble tropical giant, but the foliage has a slight grayish tinge. The late April or May blossoms of *H. imperialis* have wide petals for a *Hymenocallis,* which makes them particularly showy.

When given rich soil and partial shade, this species is among the largest that may be grown. Aficionados of *Hymenocallis* know it by the nickname "big

Hymenocallis maximiliani

Hymenocallis latifolia

Hymenocallis eucharidifolia

Hymenocallis glauca

Hymenocallis acutifolia

Hymenocallis imperialis

fatty." Like other Mexican plants, it seems rather hardy. Well suited to garden use through the South, it reproduces easily from large, gray-green seeds, as well as offsets.

Even tougher is an old spider lily common to turn-of-the-century gardens in South Texas and northern Mexico. Nicknamed the "New Lion" for the state of Nuevo Leon, Mexico, this variety blooms in May, like *H. imperialis*, but the snowy flowers show themselves against foliage that is particularly blunt and dark green. Bulbs are enormous, with a squared, globular form and thick, blackish coats. The flowers never set seed, so this may be an old hybrid. It is of special value for its drought-resistance, an uncommon attribute in this genus of water-loving flowers.

🌿 *The Clumper*

One of the mystery plants of subtropical gardens is an old *Hymenocallis* with lushly narrow, arching leaves. This glossy foliage makes a striking fountain effect in the garden, like an exotic giant *Liriope*, but the globular bulbs remain perpetually desolate, without a hint of bloom. This old variety is one of the most hurried offsetters, and it seems likely that lack of flowers is the price exacted for hasty multiplication. The many offsets assure wide distribution, and "the clumper" is ubiquitous in gardens of the subtropics. Although flowerless, it merits use as a foliage plant.

In the benevolent climate of the swamps of Iberia Parish, Louisiana, the tropical *H. littoralis* has become widely naturalized. This glossy-leafed variety is similar in foliage to "the clumper" and is probably the species Oviedo met in Panama. The slender petals adhere to the cup of the bloom and make *H. littoralis* easy to distinguish from other tropical spider lilies. The snowy blossoms appear in August, accented by bright orange pollen.

H. littoralis is fairly tender to cold. It comes into its own in the South only when set in a watery tub or shallow pond. When grown aquatically, it shows gratitude by forming dense, tangled mats of underwater roots, which completely envelope the pots. The bulbs may be left submerged through winter, so long as ice forms only on the surface of the water. Some nurseries offer this fast-multiplying spider lily for use in landscaping, but the trade generally confuses it with a native Southern species, *H. caroliniana*.

A hardy Mexican and Guatemalan cousin of this plant flowers in October and November—usually the last spider lily to bloom in Southern gardens. It has been aptly named *H. acutifolia* for its long, pointed leaves. The grand, frilled cups and drooping or spreading petals look sensational against the slender, dark green foliage. They are especially welcome during their late season.

Like *H. littoralis*, this species may be grown aquatically, but it also performs well when planted on damp clay soils. In its native habitat *H. acutifolia* grows along jungle streams in deep shade, and it enjoys shade in cultivation, as well.

The river spider lily, *H. acutifolia* v. *riparia*, is a smaller, earlier-flowering edition from western Mexico. Remarkably hardy and prolific, it self-sows under ordinary garden conditions. Nice frilled blooms appear in early summer.

🐚 *Mexicans*

The seasonally dry hills of western and southern Mexico are especially rich in deciduous *Hymenocallis* species, including some of the gems of the family. Native habitats extend from just south of the Arizona border down to the volcanic mountains of the Isthmus of Tehuantepec, where more than twenty species of spider lilies grow in varied conditions among forests and scrublands. The bulbs remain dormant during a long winter season. They leaf out briefly to flower and set seed with summer rains. Like all *Hymenocallis*, these species are more or less poisonous and bitter. Tarahumara Indians consume bulbs of their local *lirio del rio*, or "river lily," by boiling them twice to rinse away and destroy toxins, and slicing and frying them like potatoes.

Most of these fascinating plants are hardy in the South, if given sun or part shade and ordinary garden soil. Perhaps because of their diminutive stature, they remain rare in cultivation. Although slow to offset, many Mexican *Hymenocallis* set abundant seed, and several may be propagated quickly by slicing or coring the bulbs.

H. maximiliani is a narrow-leafed species from the state of Guerrero, superficially much like *H. acutifolia* v. *riparia*, but with long, shiny, green foliage and petals that dangle freely from the cups. The graceful, white blooms appear prolifically from May into July or later, ripening generous clusters of seed. This robust variety thrives in the South like a native. The botanical name recalls a tragic figure of Mexican history, the Emperor Maximilian.

Although hardly common, the most cultivated of the Mexican species is the *estrella de San Nicolas*, or "St. Nicholas' star" (*H. harrisiana*). This modest dwarf was originally described in 1840 from plants imported by a Mr. T. Harris, Esq., of the Grove, Kingsbury. They probably came from the Valley of Mexico, where this plant once grew abundantly on swampy plains. Much of the natural range of these bulbs has been covered in the sprawl of Mexico City, but these flowers still occur in a few adjacent valleys and southward to near Acapulco.

The tongue-shaped leaves of *H. harrisiana* cluster together to form a short false stem, which is typical of several of the Mexican spider lilies. Foliage is a dull, dusty green in the common garden strain, but forms from lower elevations have glossy green leaves. A pair of longitudinal folds, or creases, marks the foliage of all types and distinguishes this species from others. The spidery blossoms carry pendulous, dangling petals crowned by ridiculously tiny, white cups. They appear in May in slender groups of six or less and later ripen abundant seed.

Showier for garden use is the gray-foliaged *H. glauca* (*H. choretis*). The large-cupped, snowy blooms of this southern Mexican flower appear in pairs in early summer, while the emerging stems are still quite short. Gray, spear-shaped leaves elongate afterward, eventually reaching two feet in length and offering an interesting accent for a shady or partially sunny corner. The attractive flowers have orange pollen and smell strangely of ammonia or chlorine.

H. cleo (*H. chiapasiana*), from the beautiful uplands of the state of Chiapas, is similar, but smaller in all parts.

The fabulous *Hymenocallis eucharidifolia* is a rare, shade-loving species with rosettes of unusually broad, green, hostalike foliage. Although unknown to cultivation since its description in 1884, this remarkable bulb has been recently imported into the lower Rio Grande Valley of Texas. The slender flowers, held upright in groups of two or three, look very small set against the large leaves. The vigorous bulbs thrive in rich, leafy soil and seem as hardy as other Mexican species. They offset at a steady pace, so they may one day become more common in gardens.

H. leavenworthii and *H. azteciana* are exotic varieties from high, cool woodlands near Patzcuaro and Guadalajara. They have unusual, spreading, long-stemmed, or petiolate, leaves; this beautiful foliage has an elegant, satiny dusting of gray overlaying dark green. Small clusters of erect blooms, rising between the flaccid foliage, open together like miniature, midsummer bouquets. These varieties enjoy shade and cool, loamy soil.

H. guerreroensis is a delightful miniature with slender, paired leaves like a tiny daffodil. One to three good-sized blooms appear in early summer. *H. araniflora* and *H. sonorensis* produce larger clusters of long-tubed, sweet-scented blooms, with somewhat wider, pale green or grayish foliage, respectively. These species proliferate locally on coastal prairies and upland volcanic soils in western Mexico. They make intriguing subjects for early summer borders and reproduce easily from seed.

❧ Native Spider Lilies

When Mark Catesby wrote his *Natural History of Carolina, Florida, and the Bahama Islands* in 1731, he described an exotic flower found blooming in a bog "on the Savannah River within the precinct of Georgia." Catesby noted that the plants resembled the sea daffodil (*Pancratium maritimum*) of southern European coasts but had deep, shining green foliage, rather than gray leaves.

This American spider lily eventually became known as *Hymenocallis caroliniana*. In the two-and-a-half centuries since Catesby's work, an amazing eighteen additional species of *Hymenocallis* have been described as natives of the South. Most are more or less aquatic, and several are small plants of modest garden merit. There are at least a half-dozen, however, with good-sized, showy blooms. Some of these plants adapt to general garden culture as well as to ponds and bogs. They have some of the most elegant blooms that may be grown, so these wildflowers deserve to be planted with pride in Southern gardens.

❧ Lily-Scented Hymenocallis

From Mobile Bay westward to Texas, the most abundant spider lily on the coastal prairies is *H. liriosme*. This early-blooming species is distinctive for its yellow-centered, frilled cups. The glossy, dark green leaves, emerging in spring along with the blooms, vary in length from a modest eight inches to nearly three feet in the most vigorous forms.

This species often stands in shallow water and invariably grows in thick, heavy clays. Although most common near the Gulf, this beautiful flower ranges as far inland as southern Arkansas. The black-coated bulbs seem entirely hardy and will succeed anywhere in the South if given ample moisture through spring and early summer. The lovely blooms appear during March and April. The clusters of buds sit atop razor-edged stems, which range from less than a foot to two feet tall. They have the fragrance of Easter lilies and make a fine complement to Louisiana irises. If summers are wet, *H. liriosme* may rebloom sporadically in summer and autumn.

❧ Galveston Lilies

There is long-standing confusion between this *H. liriosme* and another widespread spider lily, *H. galvestonensis*. Both were collected originally by Thomas Drummond in the vicinity of Galveston Bay. Dean Herbert successfully grew one of Drummond's bulbs long enough to observe its gray-green, deciduous leaves. Herbert reported, "Having been forced early out, it has gone to rest before the end of July." Although he saw no fresh blossoms, one of Drummond's sheets bore a pressed flower stalk, so Herbert was able to describe the plant, giving it the name *Choretis galvestonensis*.

J.G. Baker later transferred this species to *Hymenocallis*, but in doing so he included another Drummond specimen with both leaves and flowers together. Unwittingly, he had combined the dark green-leafed, spring-flowering *H. liriosme* with this very different gray-leafed, summer-flowering spider lily.

The true *H. galvestonensis* (*H. eulae*) is a native Southern bulb that behaves much like the oriental *Lycoris squamigera*, putting up foliage in spring, dying away, and then blooming in response to summer rains. The species is unique among *Hymenocallis* for flowering on rounded, naked stems, which makes it especially exotic and beautiful in gardens. Although locally common in parts of the South, *H. galvestonensis* is generally considered to be rare. It may sometimes be seen in July flowering in thick clumps around old homes or cemeteries in open woods of loblolly pine. The jaunty, angled petals and lavish, spreading cups make a memorable summer show.

Culture for this species is different from other Southern spider lilies, for *H. galvestonensis* naturally grows on reddish, friable, upland soils. It needs plenty of water during the spring growing season, but it may be left to dry out after May. It has no tolerance for heavy, waterlogged clay or for alkalinity.

Mention of such summer-blooming spider lilies as *H. occidentalis* and *H. moldenkiana* may actually refer to environmental forms of *H. galvestonensis*. With ample rainfall, these bulbs sometimes retain foliage while flowering, presenting a very different appearance and leading to misidentification.

❧ River Lilies

The showiest of the strictly aquatic spider lilies is *H. coronaria*, a species named for its especially large, frilly cups. This variety grows in clear, flowing streams with its bulbs nestled firmly between rocks, bound against the current by masses

Hymenocallis araniflora (in seed)

Hymenocallis araniflora

Hymenocallis leavenworthii

Hymenocallis traubii

Hymenocallis liriosme

Pancratium maritimum

of strong, twining roots. It is locally common on watercourses from Alabama to North Carolina. Its early summer flowering creates an annual floral event.

In the brackish water of the Everglades and south Florida, the alligator lily (*H. palmeri*) is the most common aquatic spider lily. This very fragrant variety has odd, green-tinged blossoms, which appear singly along with its sparse, narrow foliage. The bulbs are stoloniferous, so they multiply into patches among the native reeds. The coronas of the alligator lily usually have several prominent teeth, but this character varies widely in *Hymenocallis*.

In eastern Florida's lake country, two dwarf spider lilies, *H. floridana* and *H. traubii*, proliferate in calm fresh water. Both are lovely, with large, fringed cups appearing in early summer. Of the two, *H. traubii* is the miniature, usually flowering with just two oversized blossoms to each six-inch scape. Both species have narrow, dark green leaves and multiply steadily by stolons, like the alligator lily.

The late hybridist Luther Bundrant of Poteet, Texas, used the tiny *H. traubii* to create a beautiful flower named 'Exelsior'. The other parent of this cross was the Peruvian daffodil, *H. narcissiflora*. 'Excelsior' inherits the dwarf stature of the hardy *H. traubii*, but the huge, frilled, fragrant blossoms it produces are up to eight inches across, with four-inch cups. Like all of the aquatic Southeastern species, 'Excelsior's thrive under boggy conditions and make excellent subjects to set at the edge of garden ponds. They are perfectly hardy as long as the bulbs themselves are preserved from frost.

❧ Sea Daffodils

The barren, sandy beaches of the Greek islands are the home of one of the hardier members of the Old World genus *Pancratium*, the *krinos tis thallasas*, or "lily of the sea" (*P. maritimum*). These interesting plants, cousins of the American *Hymenocallis*, have flowers like small Peruvian daffodils. Their seeds are flat and black, and their thick, evergreen foliage is fleshy and straplike. Often tangling in a spirally twisted mass, the unique leaves are dusted in a silvery gray bloom, which helps conserve moisture.

In the South, sea daffodils are easy to grow on sandy soil in full sun, but they flower only if kept fairly dry over summer. They need very little moisture to get along and make excellent subjects for beach plantings. The sweet-scented blooms appear in July. Seed ripens in autumn and may be planted immediately to sprout and grow through winter. This very odd bulb is fairly easy to locate in nursery lists. Dioscorides reported using it medicinally to control asthma and coughs.

P. illyricum and *P. canariense* are related, winter-growing, deciduous bulbs suitable for near frost-free conditions. *Vagaria parviflora* and *Calostemma purpurea*, allied plants from the Mediterranean and Australia, grow and flower in winter and enjoy poor, sandy soils. Their small, clustered blooms resemble *Narcissus tazetta*.

❧ Amazon Lilies

In tropical Florida the Amazon lily (*Eucharis grandiflora*) is a popular perennial for shady beds. Its hostalike leaves form thick clumps. Modest-sized, waxy, ismenelike blooms appear in fall and winter and emit a powerful, sweet fragrance. Plants weaken if they lose their evergreen foliage, so Amazon lilies must be relegated to pot culture where frost visits regularly. The common form in cultivation appears to be an old, sterile hybrid. There are several smaller species native to the forests of South America.

8

Summer Glories

If true lilies (*Lilium* spp.) had ordinary bulbs like daffodils and could withstand the same rough handling, they might rank as the most popular of summer bulbs. As it is, the majority of these aristocratic perennials call for more careful treatment. Lilies come primarily from temperate woodlands, and their primitive, loose-scaled rootstocks suffer if allowed to dry excessively, either in the garden or in storage. Some of the most beautiful, such as the golden rayed lily of Japan (*Lilium auratum*), are famous for their exacting requirements: well-aerated, humus-rich, unequivocally acid soil and generous positions in cool, filtered sun.

Not all the members of this genus are so particular, and several are suited to ordinary garden situations, even on heavy clays or on limy soils. If Southerners dedicate their efforts toward these vigorous lily varieties, their plantings can be gloriously enhanced with nominal effort. The fussier Oriental hybrids can usually be accommodated in the same beds that house azaleas. This combination works well for the lilies, which enjoy rooting among the bushes, while their tall, elegant blooms help relieve the tiresome summer greenery of the shrubs.

Most lilies require several seasons to mature before giving their best performances. With good care the bulbs become truly enormous, and they will send up proportionally large stalks of bloom. If for some reason they must be moved, it is best to treat established lilies as if they were mature shrubs: A generous portion of earth should be taken up along with the delicate roots. As long as this is done, the clumps may be moved at any season, even while in full bloom.

Lilies look their best when massed, so that the towering stems do not appear overly gaunt. The initial expense of bulbs might dissuade gardeners from planting enough for good effect. Fortunately, these bulbs are among the most readily propagated flowers.

Many lilies grow quickly from seed, and all varieties may be started from bulb scales. In addition, several types form tiny bulbils in the axils of the leaves, which may be carefully removed to start new plantings. By peeling away the outer sections of the bulbs as if preparing an artichoke, several scales may be procured. Scales, seeds, or bulbils should be set in pots of rich, leafy soil and grown on for the summer. They may be set in permanent quarters in autumn. After three seasons of good care, the young bulbs will be large enough to begin blooming. Such homegrown plants establish readily and often outproduce purchased bulbs.

When propagating these flowers, it is important to secure virus-free parent stock, for mosaic disease is a serious problem of some lilies. Viruses express their presence in visible streaking of foliage, followed by loss of vigor. There is no remedy, and infected plants must be destroyed to prevent the spread of disease.

Choice lilies may be preserved by growing new, virus-free bulbs from seed. Keeping a fresh batch of seedlings coming along at all times provides an excellent long-term strategy to defeat disease. Many commercial lily growers follow this ploy, producing named strains from seed, rather than clonal hybrids.

Due to their tall, weighty stems, most lilies benefit from planting with three or four inches of soil above the tops of the bulbs. The emerging stalks often develop bulblets and roots in this zone that help to anchor the plants against wind and rain. After a season in the ground, the bulbs adjust themselves to their preferred depth. The Madonna lily (*Lilium candidum*) is an exception: it should be set with its bulb just below the soil surface.

In spite of, or perhaps because of, their temperamental reputations, lilies occupy a special place in the hearts of all lovers of floral beauty. With their leafy stems and loosely built blossoms, they unabashedly reveal the primordial structures of their family. Stamens, pistils, petals, and leaves all combine in a fascinating array of colorful designs, as if they had been painted and assembled from separate pieces by troops of imaginative children.

❧ *Madonna Lilies*

The white, funnel-shaped blooms painted on the walls of the Minoan palace of Knossos belong to the Madonna lily (*L. candidum*), and this sentimentally romantic flower has been pictured innumerable times since. These fragrant, immaculate blossoms have long been emblematic of purity. Medieval depictions of Mary usually show her clutching a bouquet.

The Madonna lily is unique among the genus *Lilium* in its habit of leafing out in fall, and the species is also unusual in its preference for limy soils. The frostproof foliage, forming tidy rosettes like small green hostas, is an asset to the winter gardens all by itself. In April the leafy stems elongate, eventually reaching two feet or more in height. These are topped by several waxy blossoms, which scent the air sweetly in all directions.

In the middle and upper South, wherever soils include a measure of lime, the Madonna lily features in old, country gardens. It often keeps company with pink and purple shrub roses. In April or May the chaste torches of glistening white bloom may be seen lighting the grayed monuments of colonial cemeteries.

Unlike most other lilies, these natives of the eastern Mediterranean flourish on the same dryish, sunny slopes as bearded irises. They sometimes prove mysteriously difficult to establish in new gardens, even in districts where ancient colonies flourish. Viruses may be the culprit, so it is useful to look for the 'Cascade' strain, which is raised from seed. This oldest of garden flowers prospers on benevolent disregard—and on the liberal dousings of soapsuds, tea slops, and rotted horse manure that ordinary gardeners offer their most cherished possessions.

There is a very old hybrid of the Madonna lily, the lovely, apricot Nankeen lily (*L. × testaceum*). Six to twelve blooms appear on top of its tall stems and nod like the Turk's cap (*L. chalcedonicum*), its other parent. The soft chartreuse 'Limerick' and pale yellow 'Uprising' are more recent cultivars of similar parentage. These are seldom planted in the South but should succeed in the same gardens in which *L. candidum* prospers.

🐚 *Trumpets*

Nearly all the trumpet-shaped lilies of the Far East flourish in the South, and many of their hybrids do, also. The most famous of this group is the old Bermuda, or Easter lily, *L. longiflorum* v. *eximium*, formerly raised commercially on the island of Bermuda and forced by florists for its pure, fragrant blooms. Although slightly tender, this showy flower performs well in Florida and the lower South. Any soil, including heavy clay or barren chalk, seems suitable. The bright grassy green leaves and snowy blossoms fill Gulf Coast gardens in April.

L. longiflorum naturally inhabits subtropical brushlands in Japan and Taiwan. Bulbs often grow in shallow pockets of soil formed in volcanic or coral rocks. They sometimes appear just above high tide line, where the spray from the waves splashes on the foliage and impregnates the soil with salt and lime. In the South these flowers make excellent choices for seaside plantings.

Modern cultivars of *L. longiflorum*, such as the dark green-leafed 'Croft' variety, have supplanted the Bermuda lily (var. *eximium*) in greenhouse culture and are now the Easter lilies most popular for forcing. Although hardier and blossoming later, they are not so vigorous as the Bermuda lily. A recent hybrid with pink trumpeting flowers, 'Casa Rosa', would be worth trying.

The most prolific Asian trumpet is *L. formosanum*. No lily could be easier to grow than this, and it is sufficiently hardy to survive everywhere in the South. The graceful, narrow-leafed stems may be counted on to provide a wealth of summer and autumn blooms much like the Easter lily in appearance. Afterward, the plants swiftly ripen capsules of papery seeds, which sow themselves delightfully into any partially shaded corner. This lily is famous for its rapid growth, and seedlings generally come to flower in their second year. *L. formosanum* is sometimes listed as a variety of the similar, but more tropical, *L. philippinense*.

Gloriosa rothschildiana

Gloriosa 'Wilhelmina Green'

Lilium henryi

Lilium lancifolium

An oriental hybrid lily

Lilium longiflorum var. *eximium*

Other members of the trumpet group include *L. brownii, L. sargentiae, L. leucanthum, L. sulfureum,* and *L. regale*—the types that have been most developed through hybridizing. All were collected from the Chinese mainland by the famous explorer E.H. Wilson, who discovered and imported to America nearly one thousand Chinese plants in the early years of the twentieth century.

The regal lily (*L. regale*) is the member of this group most planted in its natural, unhybridized form. This beautiful flower deserves its royal title, for it is at once easy to grow and thoroughly lovely. The vigorous, sturdy stems reach three or four feet in height. In May they bear several pearly, funnel-shaped blossoms. These are flushed with lilac purple on the backs of the petals and are warmed by a yellow zone at the throat. In the heat of the sun these colors may fade, so it is customary in the South to provide partial shade for these and all other lilies flowering after mid-May. 'Album' is a snowy cultivar that lacks the external striping.

In the mid-twentieth century, the famous Oregon breeder Jan De Graaff began hybridizing trumpet lilies, bringing into existence a spectacular race of garden flowers. The trumpets themselves were intercrossed to produce the Olympic hybrids, or centifolium lilies. These are larger, more vigorous versions of their wild predecessors but they inherit susceptibility to virus.

Better and healthier are the Aurelian lilies. These bowl-shaped flowers descend from crosses with the vigorous Oriental Turk's cap lily, *L. henryi.* This small, brown-freckled, orange-yellow blossom imparts virus resistance to its offspring; most of the Aurelians inherit strong constitutions. The first breeder to develop this section, M.E. Debras, named the group for his hometown, Orleans, France.

L. henryi is itself a fine garden lily and tolerates a wide range of soils and positions. When established, the tall stems bear several nodding, apricot-yellow blooms, curiously marked and relieved with papillae, or small bumps. The petals completely recurve in the typical Turk's cap manner, with the orange-tipped anthers projecting merrily downward.

These blossoms appear in early summer and combine well with the snowy summer phlox, 'Mt. Fuji'. The selection called 'White Henryi' is a sport with larger, ivory blooms. It sometimes reverts to the ordinary form, which is only a small disappointment, since both versions of this plant are lovely. This flower was introduced by Dr. Augustine Henry, an Irish physician and forester who explored central China and Formosa in the late nineteenth century.

The Aurelian hybrids are often sold as strains named to designate their various color forms. 'Pink Perfection', 'Green Magic', and 'Golden Splendor' describe themselves. 'African Queen' is a rich golden yellow. 'Black Dragon' is streaked darkly on the petal exteriors but, in the warmth of Southern summers, often fades to white. Best of all is 'Thunderbolt', a huge, strong grower with fragrant, wide-open, apricot-orange blossoms.

🌿 *Tiger Lilies*

The familiar spotted orange tiger lily (*L. lancifolium*) is a sterile hybrid that has been grown for centuries in Japan. It is probably a cross of *L. leichtlinii,* an

Oriental Turk's cap, and *L.* × *maculatum,* an old Japanese garden flower with blooms that face up. Tiger lilies carry extra chromosomes (a triploid set), and resultant vigor and resistance to virus. Gardeners still call this beloved flower by its old name, *L. tigrinum,* and they cheerfully share and multiply their stocks by means of the prolific, dark green bulbils.

This most reliable of all the spotted lilies in the South accepts the widest range of conditions. If offered any modestly prepared soil, tiger lilies will flower freely through summer. They ask for little added attention beyond shade from the hottest sun. Up to twenty nodding blossoms appear on strong stems above the handsome, dark green leaves.

In addition to the common bright orange red tiger ('Splendens'), there are a rare double form and an unusual variegated selection. A race of varicolored tiger lilies may also be had from bulb dealers. "Yellow Tiger" ('Yellow Star') is bright, buttery yellow with black dots. "White Tiger" has maroon speckles and stamens; "Pink Tiger" ('Tigrinum Rose'), "Red Tiger" ('Red Fox'), "Cream Tiger" ('Torino'), "Orange Tiger" ('Tigrinum Fortunei'), and "Gold Tiger" ('Sunny Twinkle') are additional, colorful variations of this old garden flower.

Some of the well-known Asiatic hybrids are descended in part from the tiger lily. A few of the most vigorous, such as 'Enchantment', succeed in the middle and upper South. For the most part, however, these up-facing "candle-stick lilies" perform better in cold climates.

The Oriental hybrids of the pink and red showy Japanese lily (*L. speciosum rubrum*) and the yellow and white gold-rayed lily (*L. auratum*) are better in cool climates, also. Nevertheless, vigorous selections sometimes succeed in the South without undue difficulty. They are so beautiful that every attempt should be made. Well-drained, acid soil, and partial shade are requisite. Some gardeners also employ the technique of tilting bulbs when setting them out. This prevents the loose scales from collecting water and remaining overly moist or soggy.

The same kind of careful treatment suits the rare native lilies of the South, for they are also denizens of rich, peaty woodlands. The leopard lily (*L. catesbyi*), Carolina lily (*L. michauxii*), royal lily (*L. superbum*), pot of gold lily (*L. iridollae*), and roan lily (*L. grayi*) are widely distributed through the damp forests of the Southeast. All of these have spotted, fragrant, Turk's-cap-style blooms in early summer, from small, often stoloniferous bulbs. Wild colonies should not be disturbed, but bulbs may be raised from seed, or obtained from wildflower specialists who propagate their own stock.

Climbing Lilies

Some of the most exciting lilies adapted to the South have adopted the novel habit of vines and will climb on a trellis or post. These spectacular flowers offer an exotic way to dress up a wire mesh fence. Their botanical name, *Gloriosa,* means "glorious," and so they are.

The glory lilies include several species native to subtropical Africa and India. All have weak, trailing stems with elliptical, tendril-bearing leaves. They sprout from odd, L- or V-shaped tubers, which travel slowly under the ground. These may be dug and divided, making sure that each severed piece includes an eye, or growing point. The tubers replace themselves each season, so they should only be disturbed after the plants have completely ripened their foliage.

In the wild these rhizomatous flowers grow in scrubland, where they remain dormant through a long, dry winter season. In gardens they thrive on rich soil and summer moisture. They may be left in the ground over winter if sheltered from cold, damp conditions.

The showiest of the climbing lilies, *Gloriosa rothschildiana*, reaches three to six feet in height and enjoys full sun or partial shade. The flowers are like bizarre Turk's cap lilies, with yellow, undulating petals flamed red on their upper two-thirds. The fleshy, green stamens and pistil curve and splay outward from the center of the nodding blooms. This popular species originates from Uganda.

G. simplex (*G. plantii*) is a dainty species from the eastern Cape, Natal, and tropical east Africa. Its orange and yellow blooms are undulate only near the tips of the petals. The flowers open with a pale greenish yellow tone, for which reason this species is sometimes called *virescens*. The vining stems reach about three feet in length.

G. superba, with a wide range from the Transvaal through tropical east Africa to India, varies in color. Some forms have the same red and yellow pattern as *G. rothschildiana*, but the best-known cultivar, 'Lutea', is valued for its lemony yellow blooms. All forms of *G. superba* have especially narrow, crisped petals.

Wyndham Hayward used a rare yellow gloriosa discovered in an old Trinidad garden by the flower painter Wilhelmina Greene to create a series of tall, late-blooming hybrids. The other parent of this cross was the central African species *Gloriosa carsoni*, a medium-sized variety with prominent claret markings on the petals. The strain, 'Wilhelmina Green', includes clear sulfur yellows and selections with slight wine featherings. Although rare in the bulb trade, they are still grown by some Southerners. Similarly beautiful plants were once bred by Sidney Percy-Lancaster and his son, Alick, and may persist in the gardens of India.

All the glory lilies ripen large pods of reddish, marblelike seeds. These may be saved in autumn for planting in pots in March. They are slow to germinate, and it is wise to allow at least four months for them to sprout. The young plants rapidly form tubers and will be ready to bed out in their third season.

Climbing bell lily, or *geelklokkie* (*Littonia modesta*), is a rare relation of *Gloriosa*, with similar wants and habits. The flowers are bell-shaped, with six tapering petals of a beautiful golden yellow. The flowers ripen to form decorative seed pods. 'Keitii' is a robust selection of this South African perennial. Another *Gloriosa* ally, the Christmas bell or Chinese lantern lily (*Sandersonia aurantiaca*) produces small, clear orange blooms that puff out like little bells.

❧ *Parrot Lilies*

Tropical America, too, has unusual vining lilies, but these lush perennials ramble about, rather than honestly climb. Their thickened rootstocks wander vigorously under good conditions. Best known are the florist's Peruvian lilies (*Alstroemeria* cvs.), natives of the cool, high Andes Mountains.

The Peruvian lily does not succeed as a garden plant in the warm South, but its lowland cousin from Brazil, the parrot lily (*Alstroemeria psittacina*), prospers mightily. This curious flower has six petals compressed laterally so that the blooms resemble orchids. The coloring of the flowers is a Christmasy red with green tips and chocolate freckling on the interior. This mix of tones seems fairly lackluster in the garden but serves to attract hummingbirds, who are the principal pollinators of these flowers.

Parrot lilies grow vigorously in moist soil and partial shade, and they are quite capable of taking over an embankment or other rough position. They are perfectly hardy in the South and flower reliably through summer. The whorled, green foliage is attractive even when the plants are not in bloom, remaining in good condition through the growing season. This flower is sometimes listed as *A. pulchella. A. braziliensis* is another similar species.

Also hardy and adaptable in the South, but rarely grown, is the "white Jerusalem artichoke" (*Bomarea edulis*). This is a cousin of *Alstroemeria* from Mexico, the West Indies, and tropical South America. A leafy plant rises from a thickened tuber. The outer petals of the flowers are pink; the inner, yellowish green with purple spots. This uplander needs rich, moist soil and partial shade but is tough and long-lived once established.

🌸 *Blue Gingers and Dayflowers*

Many perennials of the dayflower family (*Commelinaceae*) have thickened roots, but these rhizomes are usually poorly developed. Only in the the so-called blue ginger (*Dichorisandra thyrsiflora*) of Brazil are the tuberous roots really substantial.

Although not a true ginger, this South American is as glamorous as any summer flower, with smooth, shiny, green leaves arranged spirally along a stiff, two- to three-foot, jointed stem. At the top, five-inch heads of rich blue-violet, white-centered blooms appear in late summer. This tender perennial grows easily in rich soil, sprouting stems from its creeping rootstock like *Alstroemeria*. It is hardy along the Gulf, but it resents freezes and needs most of the summer to build up strength for bloom.

Although they're overly free with self-sown seed, gardeners sometimes admit the related, native dayflowers, or widow's tears (*Commelina erecta*), of Southern fields. The celestial blue, two-petaled blossoms are certainly worth having in early summer borders, although they remain open only during the cool morning hours. The nutlike tubers have strong roots, which tend to pull down into crevices and other hard-to-weed places. Some varieties also root from the trailing, jointed stems, forming a sort of succulent groundcover.

🌸 *Potato and Madeira Vines*

Potato vines (*Dioscorea bulbifera*) and Madeira vines (*Anredera cordifolia*) are old-fashioned, tuberous climbers popular in the South for their lush, green summer foliage. In the era before air conditioning, these fast-growing vines provided the very functional service of screening and shading porches. They are still popular for this purpose among country people.

The potato vine, or air potato (*Dioscorea bulbifera*), is remarkable for its production of aerial tubers. Looking like small, brown Irish potatoes, they develop over summer along the vining stems. They remain hidden behind the glossy, heart-shaped leaves until fall, when the foliage yellows and dies away. The "potatoes" may then be gathered and saved for planting the following season or left to fall in place. They will sprout on their own if not frozen during winter.

Potato vines belong to the tropical yam family, which includes several lily-like, tuberous climbers. The tiny flowers of all varieties are insignificant. Roots of the edible Chinese yam, or cinnamon vine (*Dioscorea batatas*) may sometimes be found in Asian or Latin markets. If set in rich soil after danger from frost, they make attractive, leafy vines for summer gardens. The drought-loving elephant's foots of Africa and Mexico (*D. elephantipes, D. glauca, D. sylvatica,* and *D. macrostachya*), are also easily grown in summer, but their exotically corky, protruding tubers must be sheltered from damp and frost over winter.

The Madeira, or mignonette, vine (*Anredera cordifolia*) has succulent, glossy foliage similar to the air potato, but it lacks the prominent, parallel veining of *Dioscorea*. This South American also imitates the air potato in forming occasional aerial tubers, although these are not so large or prolific. The sprays of flowers are pale, greenish white and too small to be noticeable, but they emit a penetrating, nocturnal fragrance that endears this plant to all. Rude vigor and heat- and drought-tolerance are other valuable attributes of *Anredera*.

❧ *Asparagus*

Asparagus is a large genus of lily-type perennials, many of which bear attractive, feathery foliage and showy berries. The true leaves of these plants are tiny and scalelike, and their function is largely replaced by modified branchlets called cladophylls. Fleshy roots support the matted crowns; these perennials may be cut apart with a sharp knife for increase. All varieties grow readily from seed.

Along the Gulf several tender, evergreen asparagus ferns are popular for landscaping. Basket asparagus (*Asparagus densiflorus* 'Sprengeri') is best known. Its sprays of prickly, emerald green cladophylls, resembling pine foliage, cascade gracefully to form mounds three feet across. These rugged natives of Natal endure drought and poor soil and thrive in seaside gardens. Their rootstocks are rather hardy, but slow to recover when frozen. If the prickly stems and tender foliage are sheltered from frost, small, creamy blooms appear in spring and form bright red berries in autumn. Foxtail fern (*A. densiflorus* 'Myers') is a stiffer, more compact cousin.

The climbing asparagus (*A. setaceus*) is another rugged African variety popular in Florida and Gulf Coast gardens. Its flattened sprays of luxuriant, dark green foliage form horizontal pyramids at intervals along the wiry, twining stems. These leafy sprays look good trained on trellises in deep or partial shade, or they may be cut for floral arrangements. Like *A. densiflorus*, climbing asparagus resprouts if frozen, but it is most valuable in gardens where freezes seldom visit. The tiny, sweet-scented flowers ripen to black berries.

Sickle thorn (*A. falcatus*) is another half-hardy climber suited to the lower South. Although beautiful and robust, it should be planted with caution. The dark green, yewlike foliage disguises vicious thorns, which make this robust plant unfriendly to garden around.

One of the most beautiful of the many South African asparaguses is *A. virgatus*, a feathery, sprawling variety with dark green sprays of foliage. The tough, wiry cladophylls stand up to hot sun and remain evergreen to frosts as low as eighteen degrees F. They carry small, greenish white blooms in spring and pea-sized, orange-red fruits in autumn. Any soil seems satisfactory.

The hardy, deciduous species of asparagus are seldom planted in flower gardens, although they often escape and persist around old plantings in the South. Common table asparagus (*A. officinalis*) makes a beautiful plant, with waving, ferny foliage that turns a fine yellow tone in autumn. The shiny, red berries are showy, also. There is no reason why plants grown for their tender spring shoots cannot be sited where their summer greenery can contribute to the garden as well. For those not interested in harvesting for the table, a Romanian variety of *A. officinalis* called *psuedoscaber* may be planted strictly for ornament. An especially graceful selection is called 'Spitzenschleier' in Germany.

A. filicinus is a charming dwarf asparagus from India and China with low, compact mounds of fresh green foliage. Although deciduous and hardy, in the South this variety remains dormant for only a short time. It is very suitable for bordering beds in sun or partial shade. The stems are thornless and the fruit is black. The southern European *A. tenuifolius*, with red, marble-sized fruit, is another hardy type that would be worthy of trial.

❧ *Equestrian Star Flowers*

The American belladonna (*Hippeastrum puniceum*) was long ago robbed of its birthright by Dean Herbert, who maintained that the South African belladonna, instead, should bear the beautiful name *Amaryllis*. The strange substitute title, *Hippeastrum*, means "horse star," apparently inspired by the two-parted spathe valves surrounding the thick buds. These open "like ears" to "give the whole flower a fancied resemblance to a horse's head."

Gardeners are rightly skeptical of such foolishness and still universally refer to these beloved flowers as amaryllis. Within the ranks of this vast tropical American genus may be found the most splendid of flowering bulbs. In the native Quechua tongue of the Andes, where most wild amaryllises grow, they are known as the *aputika*, or "flowers of God."

❧ *St. Joseph's Lily*

In 1888 the future nurseryman Henry Nehrling, just beginning his teaching career, traveled to Houston to assume a position with the Lutheran schools. This was Nehrling's first trip to the South, and, as he stepped off the train from chilly Chicago, he was thrilled by the lush gardens greeting him.

Hippeastrum x *Johnsonii*

Hippeastrum 'Ackermanii'

Sprekelia formosissima 'Orient Red'

Hippeastrum 'Sumac Pinini'

Hippeastrum puniceum

Hippeastrum vittattum

Nehrling enjoyed his first experience of Southern magnolias and sweet-scented gardenias. He marveled at the lush, tea-scented China roses and long borders of aspidistra that filled every neighborhood. What especially caught his fancy was a clump of flaming red amaryllises. These beautiful flowers later became the focus of his career; Nehrling eventually moved to Florida and authored a treatise, *Die Amaryllis,* on these favorite blooms.

The flowers Henry Nehrling beheld in those early gardens still grace Southern plantings today, although they have long since disappeared from nursery catalogs. They belong to a familiar, deep crimson, trumpet-shaped amaryllis with white keels and bronze-tinted foliage. Sources differ on the date of introduction (Herbert says 1810; Baker records 1799), but they agree that this is the earliest of all amaryllis hybrids. Raised in a Lancashire garden by an English watchmaker named Johnson, it is known in horticulture as *Hippeastrum* × *johnsonii*. Gardeners call these beautiful flowers St. Joseph lilies.

Several *Hippeastrum* species were discovered during the eighteenth-century explorations of the wild territories of South America. These were introduced to Europe, and Mr. Johnson used two to create his lovely hybrid. The Queen's amaryllis (*H. reginae*) from Peru contributed its gorgeous, satiny red petals to the cross, while the Brazilian *H. vittatum* gave its hardy constitution, many-flowered umbel, and white, central stripes. This species also seems to be responsible for the trumpet shape of the blooms and for the tolerance for heavy clay soil evidenced by the black-coated bulbs.

After nearly two hundred years, *H.* × *johnsonii* remains the most prolific and hardy garden amaryllis. Its bold, crimson trumpets rise in clusters of four to six atop two-foot stems. In most of the South, these blossoms appear in early April. They offer exotic companions, to irises, columbines and other hardy perennials of the season.

H. × *johnsonii* is one of the most cold-hardy *Hippeastrum* cultivars, succeeding wherever the ground does not freeze deeply. Partial shade suits the bronze foliage best, but the handsome fountains of leaves will accept direct sun if watered generously through the summer. A good bulb will frequently throw up four spikes of flowers.

❧ *Garden Amaryllises*

Amaryllises respond readily to the gardener's hand, and the many beautiful species intercross with ease. Large bulbs can be swiftly raised from the papery, black seeds, so long as they are very fresh. Half-sterile hybrids, such as *H.* × *johnsonii,* may be shy to bear seed, but most amaryllises ripen fat pods like gigantic rain lilies.

Fanciers of *Hippeastrum* customarily float seeds in cups of water for a few days to induce germination. Sprouted plantlets may then be potted individually, rather than in flats. This avoids disturbing the young bulbs as they grow.

Seedling amaryllises flourish in containers filled with rich, well-drained compost and topped by thin layers of sphagnum moss. The pots of tiny bulbs should be set in a warm, brightly lit area, such as an interior windowsill or outside in bright shade. The seedlings may be covered with plastic bags to retain humidity until they have formed their second sets of leaves. With generous feeding and shelter from frost, seedlings may reach flowering size in two years or less.

In the garden a raised position in good, rich loam, heavily manured and sheltered from strong sun, gives the best results. In the lower South most amaryllises may be left in the ground over winter, if provided good drainage and protective mulches of straw or bagasse. Where the soil remains cold and damp for long periods or where frost penetrates to any depth, only hardier types, such as *H. × johnsonii,* may be trusted.

Most garden amaryllises are hybrids descended from various South American species. Some of the pioneer work with these plants was performed by Henry Nehrling at his nursery near Gotha, Florida. Nehrling's plants were developed further by T.L. Mead of Oviedo eventually becoming the "Mead strain" of amaryllis. These tough, hardy plants became popular during the early twentieth century. Their small- to medium-sized, mostly pink-striped blooms may still be seen in gardens of the South.

After World War II nurseries began distributing the fabulous, large-flowered amaryllis of Holland, which descend from *H. leopoldii,* a huge, scarlet-flowered species. This was collected around 1870 by Richard W. Pearce, who journeyed to South America on behalf of the House of Veitch, a famous English horticultural firm.

The immense, showy Dutch hybrids have become the common amaryllises of gardens. In addition to fine reds, pinks, salmons, and whites, the modern hybrid strains include colorful doubles and unique picotees. When properly grown, most varieties send up at least two four-flowered scapes.

Although this group has been bred mainly for pot culture, vigorous clones such as the favorite pink, 'Appleblossom', make good border flowers in the lower South. Similar crosses developed in South Africa also show excellent vigor and work well in gardens. Homegrown hybrids between the Dutch and African strains and *H. × johnsonii* or the hardy Mead strain are usually excellent landscape performers.

❧ *Species and Species Crosses*

Of the fabulous wild amaryllis species, the belladonna lily (*H. puniceum*) is the most cultivated in gardens along the Gulf Coast. Its lilting, scarlet blossoms, usually appearring in pairs, have an exotic, orchidlike personality. In the wild this species ranges from the West Indies to Bolivia and varies in color from red to pink and near-yellow. There is a very old double selection called 'Semiplenum' or 'Albertii'. The common, orange garden strain appears to be a sterile triploid. Although bulbs of *H. puniceum* endure considerable cold, they often flower poorly after harsh winters. A multiflowered, orange strain of this species is marketed by the Dutch under the clonal name 'Charm'.

The yellow-flowered belladonna of Bolivia, *H. evansiae,* was used by a California breeder, C.D. Cothran, to give the sulfury 'Yellow Pioneer'. This is a unique color break in amaryllis and is now available from Holland. Another primrose-toned selection with trumpet-shaped blooms is sold under the trade name 'Germa'. This variety, descended from the desert-dwelling Argentinean *H. parodii,* should tolerate more drought and cold than most amaryllises.

H. striatum is a nasturtium-red variety from the Cerro del Mar of southeastern Brazil. The old selection 'Fulgida', is marked with radiating bands of scarlet, creamy keels, and a pale star in the center of the blooms. This strain has been a popular houseplant in America for generations. The easy-growing bulbs summer happily in the ground, but they usually rot over winter if left cool and damp. The miniature Dutch amaryllises sold as 'Gracilis' or 'Scarlet Baby' descend from *H. striatum* and have similar wants. *H. blossfeldiae* and *H. petiolatum* are other related types.

Although spectacularly prolific as a parent of hybrids, the original *H. leopoldii* disappeared from cultivation during the nineteenth century. Afterward, nothing like the species was seen in the wild until the 1960s, when Dr. Martin Cardenas collected bulbs in the department of La Paz, Bolivia.

With his re-collected "*H. neoleopoldii*" and the related leopard amaryllis (*H. pardina*), he developed a gorgeous hybrid, which he christened 'Sumac Pinini'. In the native Aymara language of Bolivia, this means "most beautiful flower."

Dutch nurserymen have propagated this lovely amaryllis and made it widely available under a less romantic name, 'Spotty'. The spreading blossoms are dotted and dashed all over with terra-cotta freckling. The small bulbs grow easily and offset swiftly.

Even more exotic are species such as the spider amaryllis (*H. cybister*), with naked stems topped by narrow-petaled, tan to maroon, insectlike blossoms. It is native to dry areas of southern Bolivia. The aquatic *H. angustifolium,* from southeastern Brazil, looks like a bright red, narrow-petaled orchid. Although difficult to obtain, it is easy to grow in a garden pond and seems entirely hardy in the lower South.

With its long-tubed, white flowers, the fragrant *H. brasiliensis* resembles an Easter lily more than an amaryllis. It may be hybridized to create novel, trumpeting amaryllises in a range of colors. The old, tropical evergreen cultivar 'Mrs. Garfield' bears small, pink-flecked blooms and wide, oval leaves with distinctive white stripes. This tender variety is descended from a cross of the Brazilian *H. reticulatum striatifolium* and an old red hybrid, 'Defiance'. The green amaryllis (*H. calyptratum*) is a bizarre evergreen with orchidlike, chartreuse blossoms. Although this species is a tree dweller and entirely frost-tender, it may be intercrossed with garden amaryllises to produce intriguing hybrids.

The greatest challenge to growing all of these botanical amaryllises lies in their susceptibility to mosaic viruses, for *Hippeastrum*, like *Lilium*, often succumbs to this disease. Strong-growing hybrids such as *H. × johnsonii* may continue to multiply and flower even when leaves are visibly streaked with mosaic, but their performance will be a pale shadow of uninfected bulbs. Diseased bulbs should be discarded and replaced with healthy seed-grown stock at the earliest opportunity.

❦ *The Lily of the Palace*

One section of *Hippeastrum* seems resistant or tolerant to virus infection, offering hope for developing healthier hybrids. These are the forms and relatives of the winter-growing lily of the palace (*H. aulicum*), comprising the subgenus *Omphalissa*. An old hybrid between *H. aulicum* and *H.* × *johnsonii* called 'Ackermanii', a forerunner of the Mead strain, probably accounts for the vigor of these old varieties.

H. aulicum itself is an easy-growing, odd flower with a muted, red and green color scheme. The thick, sturdy foliage comes up in autumn, with the blooms following before Christmas. With its winter growth cycle, this species must be protected from hard frosts.

A spectacular mahogany and chartreuse cousin of *H. aulicum*, the butterfly amaryllis (*H. papilio*) has recently become popular as a pot plant, and as a garden flower in near-frostfree regions. This amazingly striated blossom was discovered in the state of Santa Catarina, Brazil, by the Argentine collector Dr. Carlos A. Gomez Rupple. Another beautiful *aulicum* relation, *H. bukasovii*, should become popular when better known. It is an arresting Peruvian amaryllis, with petals changing abruptly from dark red to greenish yellow at the tips.

More in tune to the South's summer schedule of growth is the spring-flowering *H. iguazuanum*, a rare variety from the famous Iguazu Falls on the Rio de La Plata. The parrot amaryllis (*H. psittacinum*), which grows in the region between Rio de Janeiro and São Paulo, is similar. These species have waxy foliage like *aulicum*, but they are deciduous in winter and may be counted hardy. The flowers look like gigantic versions of *Alstroemeria psittacina*, which inhabits the same region.

Best of all is a hybrid of *H. aulicum* with a rare miniature, pink-flowered belladonna, *H. traubii f. doranianum*. The resulting cross is a tough, vigorous plant with glossy, flattened, red-edged leaves and gorgeous, twin-flowered scapes of rosy red blooms. These appear in midsummer, long after most amaryllises have finished for the season. This variety, which makes an excellent subject for the foreground of a subtropical border, is hardy all along the Gulf.

❦ *Aztec Lilies*

One of the most beautiful flowers of the Americas, the Aztec lily (*Sprekelia formosissima*), can often be found in the wild growing along with crowds of rain lilies, lording over the hillsides like motherly orchids set among the rocks. The deep-rooted bulbs seek out shallow pockets of soil, seemingly enjoying the same rugged terrain and semiarid conditions as many *Zephyranthes*.

The Aztec lily ranges widely across Mexico, as well as through the mountains of Central and South America. Orchidlike, crimson blooms rise from the sides of the black-coated bulbs in response to rain, appearring in both spring and fall. When seen in the sun, the flowers appear to be dusted with gold. The specific name, *formosissima*, describes these plants aptly as "most handsome."

Long, green, upright leaves sprout from the necks of the bulbs all summer, and offsets appear at a steady pace. If differing clones are intercrossed, seed readily ripens and grows off quickly, in the same way as amaryllises.

'Orient Red' is a richly colored selection that bears white stripes on the keels of the petals in fall, but not in spring. 'Peru' is a dark, velvety red throughout. Both of these varieties are good garden strains in the South. They perform better than the common commercial cultivar, 'Superba', which has been developed for pot culture and often must be dug and stored to induce bloom. Like most Mexican plants, *Sprekelia* is rather hardy.

A bigeneric hybrid called × *Hippeastralia* 'Mystique' derives from the Aztec lily and Dutch amaryllis. Its broad, red flowers show both the orchidlike beauty of *Sprekelia* and the improved size of the amaryllis. Surprisingly, 'Mystique' sets abundant seed when pollinated by either *Sprekelia* or *Hippeastrum*. Although this flower has not been in gardens long, it seems vigorous and hardy, and it should survive open borders in the lower South.

❧ *Veld Lilies*

The summer-rainfall regions of South Africa around the *Drakensberg*, or "dragon mountains," house a number of bulbs adaptable to the South. All are exotic and well worth including in summer gardens. Most respond to more careful care than crinums and demand rich soil and abundant moisture. They prefer cool root runs in the warm season and need sheltered, well-drained positions in winter. Partial shade is usually helpful.

The red Ifafa lily (*Cyrtanthus obrienii*), a showy amaryllis relation from Natal, has grassy leaves like rain lilies and curved, tubular blossoms colored an electric orange-red. The blooms and foliage appear together in early summer. After the leaves ripen in autumn, it's best to keep the bulbs as dry as possible, so sandy soil is preferred.

The torch lily or *bloedblom* (*Scadoxus multiflorus*) has similar wants. Its magnificent globes of spidery, red florets appear in late spring, followed by attractive rosettes of dark green, oval leaves. These distribute themselves in a whorl on top of a short false stem formed by the leaf bases. In full shade the beautiful foliage remains dark, glossy green all summer. In autumn the stems may bear ripe, bright orange-red, globular fruits.

These showy tropical bulbs, formerly included in the genus *Haemanthus*, are still listed by most nurseries under the name *Haemanthus katherinae*. Gardeners usually keep the bulbs in pots, bedding them under trees for summer, but in the lower South they are hardy on deep sand. In the wild, *Scadoxus* ranges from the eastern Cape north to Zimbabwe, eastern Transvaal, and Natal.

The pineapple lily, or *wildepynappel* (*Eucomis* spp.), is a curious, subtropical member of the lily family. Long-lasting, clustered summer blooms resemble the fruit of a pineapple. The globular bulbs are easy growing on well-watered ground, either clay or sand, and remarkably hardy if mulched for the winter.

The variegated pineapple lily (*E. bicolor*), introduced from Natal in 1878, is the most common variety. Its ample flower stems reach eighteen inches and bear many tightly packed, greenish, nodding blossoms. These are edged in purple and topped with a tuft of green leaves. The wavy-edged basal rosettes are attractive and structural in appearance. This is a choice specimen plant for a sunny, damp position.

The wine eucomis (*E. punctata*) has the most beautiful flowers of the group, varying from white to pink or wine-purple. Foliage also varies in tone; the variety *striata* has given rise to several showy, bronze-leaf forms. The leaves of the wine eucomis are more flaccid than in *E. bicolor* but still make a good summer showing. This species was formerly known as *E. comosa*. There are several other species of *Eucomis*, such as the six-foot *E. pole-evansii*, that are also worth planting.

Another useful lily from the same region of South Africa is the monarch-of-the-veld (*Ornithogalum saundersii*). This relative of the star of Bethlehem has grayish rosettes of blunt leaves that appear much like *Eucomis*. Soaring, three-foot stems carry globular clusters of milky flowers in midsummer. This variety grows easily on any soil but winters best on dry, sandy ground.

The famous chinkerinchee (*O. thyrsoides*) grows readily on sand or stiff clay, but the blooms come in winter when they are liable to be damaged by frost. In the South this long-lasting cut flower survives in the warmest parts of the Gulf Coast and Florida. The related yellow and orange "chinks" (*O. maculatum* and *O. dubium*) have been crossed with *O. thyrsoides* to widen the palette of colors in these fragrant plants; they promise to become popular with florists. The common name, chinkerinchee, is said to derive from the sound made by the dry flower stalks rubbing together in the wind.

In the semiarid regions of South Africa, a number of *Scilla*-like lilies have evolved bulbs to store water. In nature these usually rest above the surface of the soil. At least one such plant, *Drimiopsis maculata*, thrives in the South if the bulbs are set deep enough or mulched to protect them from frost.

The bulbs of *Drimiopsis* are fleshy, primitive affairs, with large, visible scales like true lilies. In summer they carry nondescript spikes of small, white blooms and attractive rosettes of hostalike foliage. The leaves, speckled prominently with maroon dots, luxuriate in full or partial shade. With rich soil the bulbs multiply at a terrific pace. The clumps stay low, six inches or less, and make an intriguing edging for summer borders.

🌺 Lily of the Nile

The splendid *Agapanthus*, the lily of the Nile, is the best known and most cherished of South African blossoms. Invaluable stems of blue or white blooms bring a cool, bright loveliness to summer gardens unmatched by other flowers. The lush tufts of slick, green leaves provide an attractive feature in themselves, besides making a perfect foil for the globular clusters of bloom. Set in a tub on a terrace, a flowering *Agapanthus* always looks smart, requiring no companion or ornament to enhance its flawless beauty. The botanist Charles Louis L'Heritier de Brutelle, with appreciation for the special qualities of these plants, named the genus from the Greek words *agape* and *anthos*, meaning "flower of love."

The individual blossoms of *Agapanthus* resemble lily blooms but sit in large umbels like *Allium*. Some varieties have more or less drooping, tubular florets, some of which spread widely like bells or funnels. The blue coloring is usually darkest on the keels. Flower stems may reach up from two to six feet. In most varieties they arch gracefully toward the strongest light, so this should be taken into account when positioning clumps in the border. Fleshy roots spread widely over the surface of the soil and support a short, more or less tuberous rootstock holding several leeklike stems.

Few flowers are so badly confused in horticulture as *Agapanthus*. Navigating the treacherous botany of this genus is, however, a necessity for Southerners. Only a handful of varieties truly prosper in this climate, and these have many impostors.

The more common nursery strains in America are derived mostly from the tender *Agapanthus orientalis*, an evergreen variety from the eastern Cape. This species and its common cultivars, such as the dwarf 'Peter Pan', succeed in mild parts of the South, but they tend to rot away during the winter if subjected to hard frost or planted on heavy soil.

Large-statured *orientalis* varieties, such as the old, white 'Albus', cream-striped 'Variegatus', or double blue 'Flore Pleno', are slow growing but more enduring than common seedlings. These robust forms are sometimes listed as varieties under the names *A. umbellatus maximus*, *A. giganteus*, or *A. praecox*. The California nurseryman J.N. Giridlian developed several hybrids in this section, including 'Albatross', a gigantic white with over 150 blooms to a cluster, and the brilliantly colored, five-foot-tall 'Blue Skyrocket'.

Gardeners often treat *A. orientalis* as an annual, keeping the roots in pots or bedding fresh plants out for summer in part shade. Mulching sometimes helps to bring clumps through winter, but it may do more damage than good if the ground remains soggy.

More cold-hardy, deciduous *Agapanthus*, such as the Headbourne hybrids, are descended from *A. campanulatus*, a Natal species requiring rich, peaty ground and unfailing moisture. Although winter-hardy, these are only likely to succeed in the coolest, most temperate parts of the South.

The old, successful *Agapanthus* of Southern gardens is usually listed as a form of *A. africanus*, an evergreen species from the mountains of the Cape peninsula. Since this name is often mistakenly applied to *orientalis* varieties, and since both species are sometimes listed as *A. umbellatus*, it is a challenge for ordinary gardeners to ascertain whether they have the true *A. africanus* or not. One way to tell is to count the flowers. There are generally less than thirty in an umbel of *A. africanus*, while *A. orientalis* has between forty and one hundred.

The best known *africanus* form is 'Mooreanus', an old selection made by Sir Frederick Moore of Glasnevin in 1879. This dwarf variety is also known as 'Minor', and some authorities list this semideciduous form under *A. campanulatus*. In midsummer the narrow, deep green leaves send up several straight, eighteen-inch spikes topped with radiant clusters of exquisite, blue flowers. 'Mooreanus' grows readily on rich, well-watered soil and makes a beautiful summer companion for orange montbretias.

During the 1960s Mary G. Henry raised several *africanus* seedlings in her garden at Gladwyne, Pennsylvania. A particularly lovely white was named 'Henryae' in her honor. Proven hardy to zero degrees F, it has had wide distribution among gardeners and nurseries. In the present era it may be more easily obtained than the blue 'Mooreanus'.

Divisions of 'Mooreanus' or 'Henryae' should be made immediately after flowering. Plants may take a year to settle in before blooming at full capacity, but they are otherwise simple to grow in part shade. Seedlings are also easily raised and may be expected to flower in their third year. Good soil preparation and ample watering will be repaid in a refreshing abundance of cool, midsummer blossoms.

🌺 *Tuberoses*

In 1519 the army of Cortez descended to the beautiful, lake-filled Valley of Mexico. The Spaniards walked in wonder over well-built causeways ushering travelers to the fearsome, skull-topped walls of the Aztec capital, Tenochtitlan. As they entered the gates of the city, the soldiers marveled at lush gardens and wondrous markets filled with fruits and flowers. One of the blossoms they encountered was a surpassingly fragrant, waxy, white bloom that grew from a clustering, spindle-shaped bulb.

The Aztecs cultivated many flowers, and they appreciated the poetic contrast of beautiful, ephemeral blossoms with the gruesome, moribund traditions of their religion. Captives were taken in mock battles called "wars of flowers," then prepared by priests for sacrifice with obsidian knives. Glistening white *omixochitl*, or "flowers of bone," associated with these rituals, were held sacred to Xochiquetzal, the patron deity of art, beauty, and love.

The Aztecs' universe crumbled at the hands of the *conquistadores*, but the flowers of their gardens continued to grow and blossom and soon passed to many other lands. Ninety years after the conquest of Mexico, Clusius wrote the first full account of the *omixochitl*, now known to gardeners as the tuberose (*Polianthes tuberosa*).

As early as 1530 a missionary returning from the Indies, Father Theophilus Minuti, introduced tuberoses to his garden at Toulon, France. The variety he grew was the type now known as 'Mexican Single', which has narrow, grassy foliage and long, tubular florets. The individual blossoms, radiating stiffly from the tall, slender stems, expand six short petals at their tips, forming a small, white star. Parkinson knew this flower as the "greater Indian Knobbed Jacinth" and said that it had a "very sweet scent, or rather strong and heades."

In addition to the 'Mexican Single', early gardeners also grew a variegated sport with creamy margins on the leaves. The first double originated as a seedling raised by M. Le Cour of Leyden, Holland, who considered the plant to be the finest flower in the world and hoarded his stock for many years. In 1870 the Flushing, New York, nurseryman John Henderson discovered a dwarfer, larger-flowered double tuberose with especially broad, dark foliage. This he named 'Pearl'. It soon became the most popular of all Victorian blossoms, widely marketed under the trade name "Excelsior."

The lovely, waxlike flowers of 'Pearl' are fully double and resemble spikes of miniature gardenias. Their rich, exotic fragrance makes them highly prized cut flowers, as well as garden ornaments. Both the single and double tuberoses have been embraced by flower-loving countries such as India, where they are cultivated for use in religious ceremonies. Although centuries old, 'Mexican Single', 'Variegated', and 'Pearl' are all still widely grown.

Each flowering tuberose produces many offsets in a season, and any reaching or exceeding thumb size may be expected to flower the following summer. One common pest, the soil nematode, or eelworm, sometimes attacks old clumps of tuberoses in the garden, preventing the bulbs from properly sizing up and ripening for the following year. As long as the bulbs are annually dug up and reset in fresh, well-manured ground, this pest can be kept at bay, and blossoms may be expected in abundance.

In summer heat the 'Mexican Single' is the most reliable variety; this is the most "perennial" type suited to the South. Doubles respond to more careful handling. Large bulbs of 'Pearl' should be held for delayed planting in June, so that the blossoms will not open until cool, autumn weather prevails. Small bulbs may be set out earlier, having time to mature before September flowering. Nothing could be more wondrous than the fragrances of these evening flowers wafting on fresh autumn breezes.

Around the famous town of Grasse, in Provence, the French perfume industry annually harvests 2.2 million pounds of tuberoses. Within hours of picking, the blossoms travel to nearby "houses," or factories, where they are laid between layers of refined Italian lard. The petals are allowed to remain for forty-eight hours, so that the blooms may continue to manufacture and exhale their perfume for the fat to absorb. This is then slightly melted and reformed and frozen into the waxy concentrate known as "pomade." From pomade the perfumeries produce alcoholic washings of fragrance, which are in turn distilled to obtain the pure flower oils called "absolute of pomade." Only the most perfect blossoms are used for this process. Tuberose is usually harvested at night, since it is especially fragrant after sunset.

Although widespread in gardens, the cultivated tuberose (*P. tuberosa*) has never been collected in habitat; it may have been driven to extinction in pre-Columbian times. It has several beautiful wild relations that are little grown but adaptable to Southern conditions. Some of these, such as *P. nelsoni*, *P. palustris*, and *P. pringlei*, are fragrant, white, night-bloomers like small versions of 'Mexican Single'. Others, such as the scarlet Mexican twinflower (*P. geminiflora*), have colorful, paired blossoms attractive to hummingbirds. A sunset-colored hybrid is called *P.* × *blissii*.

P. howardii, a unique tuberose variety from the state of Colima, Mexico, is especially easy growing and garden-worthy. It produces two- to three-foot wands of solitary, red and green blossoms with near-black interiors. A vigorous series of pastel orange, red, and purplish hybrids with the 'Mexican Single' is called *P.* × *bundrandtii*. This group makes suitable garden flowers for the South and multiplies rapidly with good care. The shallow-growing bulbs may be protected from hard frost by resetting at depth each autumn or covering with thick mulches of straw.

🐚 *Rattlesnake Master*

Gardeners are usually surprised to learn that a close cousin of the tuberose is native to the South. The rattlesnake master, or American aloe (*Manfreda virginica*), is a very neglected wildflower. It is known to botanists mostly as a stepchild of the century plant genus, *Agave,* and to gardeners hardly at all. Although tough, interesting, and attractive, manfredas have yet to be widely appreciated.

These relatives of *Polianthes* prosper in the South and are especially enduring in drought. Nematodes occasionally cause difficulty, inhibiting proper blooming and growth, but they may be simply and easily discouraged by planting the massive, tuberous roots on raised beds of lime rubble or decomposed granite.

The odd nicknames of these plants derive from their use among native peoples of Mexico and the Southeastern United States. The Catawba Indians of North and South Carolina mashed the starchy rootstocks of the local *M. virginica* and drank its juice as an antidote to snakebite, hence the title "rattlesnake master."

Huaco and *amole* are aboriginal Mexican names. Tradition holds that a snake-eating bird called the *huaco* uses manfreda to cure itself when it has been bitten. *Amole* refers to a cleansing lather made by crushing the swollen roots. Commercial preparations of amole soap harvested from native manfredas were once sold in Texas for use as shampoo.

Tall, honey-scented, green and cinnamon bottlebrushes rise from the succulent, leafy rosettes of *M. virginica* in early summer. These odd flowers lack obvious petals, but thickened, waxy stamens project to form the feathery blossoms.

The substantial, pointed leaves offer an attraction, perhaps greater than the blooms, forming neat rosettes like dwarf aloes or agaves. This waxy, deciduous foliage is usually slick and gray, but it may be marked with interesting, maroon blotches or dots. Clumps multiply and serve admirably as edgings for beds in partial shade. In the wild, *M. virginica* ranges from the Atlantic seaboard to central Texas. It grows happily on poor, dry soil and frequents mixed-oak woodlands, prairies, and railroad embankments.

Even more beautiful are the evergreen, succulent-leafed manfredas of Texas and Mexico. Their fleshy rosettes are uniquely handsome, and their spicily scented blossoms develop thick, waxy petals like tuberoses. In the tall-growing varieties, these are furthur enhanced by long, projecting stamens. These manfredas endure frost as low as twenty degrees F with little damage to their fleshy foliage. They recover quickly if frozen back to the bulb. A winter mulch of straw will see them through more severe cold.

The spice lily (*M. maculosa*), the most widespread species in southern Texas, may be seen blooming in summer or fall following periods of rain. Fragrant blossoms open creamy petals, which fade gradually to somber purplish olive, so that the two-foot spikes grade from dark to light as the buds open from the

Flowers of *Manfreda sileri*

Polianthes tuberosa

Manfreda longiflora

Flowers of *Manfreda undulata*

Manfreda maculosa

bottom. The very fleshy foliage usually has rows of soft teeth on the margins and abundant brownish red spots.

In nature *M. maculosa* grows in the shade of shrubs and dwarf trees, but it will accept sun if given plenty of water. The same conditions suit Runyon's manfreda (*M. longiflora*), a rare miniature variety from the lower Rio Grande Valley. It has night-scented blooms like *M. maculosa*, but with long tubes and starry petals that fade to pink, rather than brown. The foliage is very slender and striated with tan pencilings.

The large-growing manfreda of the the lower Rio Grande, *M. sileri*, bears oddly flaccid, bluish leaves, marked with large purple blotches. The five-foot spikes of flowers are especially beautiful, carring dozens of upward-facing, chartreuse blossoms, which open gradually over a period of three weeks.

Night-flying hawk moths are frequent visitors to these summer or autumn blooms. Hummingbirds seem to love them also, often perching on the stalks in early morning. The stiff, slightly woody flower stems never need staking and are a welcome addition to windy gardens, where these elegantly tall flowers provide some of the most graceful that can be grown.

Several manfredas from Texas and Mexico send up equally tall stems topped with modest groups of brownish green blooms. One variety has been grown in Texas gardens for many years as *Manfreda variegata*. This clone makes valuable clumps of evergreen leaves that are more succulent and narrow than *M. sileri*. This old garden plant refuses to set seed and displays all the vigor one might expect from a garden hybrid. It may be an old cross of *sileri* and *maculosa*.

Farther south in Mexico in the lush Sierra Madre, plants with very different, unspotted foliage grow on the rugged slopes. An especially beautiful form with undulating, silvery green leaves is common in the oak woods near Monterrey. In 1903 J.N. Rose applied the name *Manfreda undulata* to a plant that had flowered in a greenhouse in Berlin during 1869. It seems hard to imagine a more appropriate epithet for the Monterrey manfredas, and they may be the rightful owners of this old title.

In the state of San Luis Potosi, spots return to leaves. The manfreda varieties that grow in this area show great vigor and the capacity to multiply by stolons. An old horticultural strain of this type was distributed by J.N. Giridlian of Oakhurst Gardens under the name 'Maculata Gigantea.' This form has had wide circulation and seems very cold-hardy. Like *M. virginica*, 'Maculata Gigantea' is naturally deciduous. Its grayish blue leaves are heavily spotted with brown and make a showy patch of succulent herbage, useful for covering dry banks.

Strange as it may seem, the weirdly beautiful manfredas confirm their relation to the tuberose by hybridizing if offered the opportunity. The black, flattened seeds grow easily and flower in their second or third year, so this is a good project for home gardeners. Hybrids recorded so far involve *M. virginica* and the 'Mexican Single' tuberose. Although these are not particularly showy, they are vigorous. A cross using the maculate, yellow-green *M. sileri* might be spectacular. Here is an area where Southern gardeners can get busy.

🌸 *Naiads*

There are some tuberous flowers whose personalities are so sprightly and lithe, one is loath to consign them to the garden border. Even when planted en masse, the slender stems and leaves of the Mexican star (*Milla biflora*) practically disappear from view until their flat, white blossoms expand. Ordinarily, such gracefully carried flowers would be best displayed in pots, but they seem to grow more successfully if plunged in cool ground for summer.

The growth of millas, allies of brodiaeas, is geared to the alternating wet and dry cycles of their homes in Mexico and the Southwest. Most varieties need a profound winter rest and a sudden jolt of summer rain to get them growing and flowering on schedule. Although these flowers are hardy in the South, the flattened corms should be dug in autumn and stored over winter to enforce dormancy. Otherwise, even large, healthy roots may fail to leaf out, sleeping quietly underground for years, until they finally waste away.

A gigantic, night-flowering species from southern Mexico, *Milla magnifica* is one of the few types successful without winter storage. Gray, hollow, onionlike leaves reach three feet in height. Equally tall umbels carry a dozen or more long-tubed blossoms, which are white, with green stripes on the reverse of the petals like *Ornithogalum*. Their fragrance is rich and cloying. Both leaves and flower stems flop over untidily if not supported, but this is a minor fault in an otherwise glorious summer flower. If well treated, the corms reach the size of gladiolus roots. They offset freely and usually multiply by self-sown seed.

A beautiful companion for *Milla* that enjoys the same treatment is the coral drop (*Bessera elegans*). Dealers in rare bulbs occasionally offer these natives of western Mexico, and gardeners should jump at any opportunity to possess them. There is nothing like a *Bessera* in the floral kingdom.

Threadlike foliage and wiry stems suspend small umbels of incredibly graceful, drooping flowers. They are marked like little birds with bright scarlet or rich purple. Creamy white stripes run through each tiny petal. Slender, dangling, purple stamens and a miniature corona protrude from the center of the blossoms to complete the fantastic accouterments.

Coral drops, reaching twelve inches in height, appear for several weeks in summer. They need the same dry rest as most *Milla* varieties and may be kept in pots or dug and stored. Although rather hardy, they are too beautiful and too difficult to obtain to risk leaving in the ground over winter. The tiny, black seeds grow readily and will bloom in their second or third season.

Another small Latin American treasure, the glory of the sun (*Leucocoryne ixioides*) offers exquisite, satiny blue blossoms. They have the fragrance of freesias and appear in April or May if corms are planted in January or February. The roots tend to pull the plants deeply into the soil over the growing season. It is useful to contain them in a mesh or wire bag to make retrieval of the corms easier in early summer. These beguiling Chilean flowers must be kept dry after their leaves die down in summer, but they are otherwise hardy and unparticular. As with many *Brodiaea*, increase comes by seeds, rather than offsets.

❧ Star Grass

Although not a flower of great glamour, the yellow star grass (*Hypoxis hirsuta*) is a stalwart performer in Southern gardens, quietly blossoming through spring and summer, with an occasional appearance in fall or winter, as well. The little star-shaped blooms have six petals, which are green and slightly hairy on the back but clear yellow on the face. They appear without protest on the heaviest clays and poorest sandy soils. Shade and competition from oak roots hardly slow them down.

The entire plant scarcely passes a foot in height, and the leaves of the yellow star grass resemble hairy, green clumps of grass. The cheery, yellow blooms, coming in small groups, stand out in spite of their small size. They make a nice contrast with the succulent foliage of purple heart (*Setcreasea pallida*). Although formerly classified in the Amaryllis family, these cormous flowers now belong to their own family, the *Hypoxidaceae*, and ripen small pods of seeds that look like black grains of sand. They grow throughout the eastern United States and are entirely hardy.

The showiest members of the star grass family come from Latin America and Africa. The Argentinean *H. decumbens* seems nearly as tough as the native yellow star grass, but it forms lush clumps with much larger, richer, golden blossoms. In early summer these appear in masses large enough to smother the foliage. *H. decumbens* makes a superb foreground specimen, beautiful associated with mounds of sky blue *Plumbago capensis*.

The red star, or *rooisterretjie* (*Rhodohypoxis baurii*), is a related, rose-colored flower from South Africa that has become popular as a subject for pots. Charming, solitary, rosy pink blooms appear all summer on stems only four inches high. Although rather hardy, the tubers are liable to rot over the winter if not kept dry, so they should be lifted or placed in raised beds of gritty soil.

❧ Orchids

The South has several beautiful wild orchids that grow from tubers. Unless you garden in a boggy meadow filled with insect-eating pitcher plants, however, or a deep, shady glade beneath gigantic stands of beech, these flowers are unlikely prospects for cultivation. Even with the best care, most orchids transplant poorly. Wild stands should be noted and cherished in place, but they are best left to bloom unmolested. These shy blooms are happier without undue human attention.

The one tuberous orchid that takes kindly to the gardener's hand is the Chinese ground orchid (*Bletilla striata*) and this should be in every garden. All it asks is a bit of shade in the hottest part of the summer and an annual dressing of autumn leaves. This helps to shelter the precocious spikes of bloom, which come too early in spring to be safe from late frosts. In return the gardener will enjoy several dainty, true orchid blossoms and a long summer of attractive, pleated leaves. Looking like rich green, dwarf aspidistra foliage, they spread luxuriantly in any shady position.

The common form of the ground orchid is rosy purple, but there is also a good white, which has the added attraction of a creamy picotee margin on its foliage. The blooms have the typical orchid shape, with furrowed lower lips and five spreading petals. They appear in March or April, held in clusters of five or six just above the leaves.

In China these robust flowers grow on the margins of thickets, occurring from sea level up to 10,000 feet in the mountains of western Yunnan. The fleshy, U-shaped tubers divide annually, so the clumps increase at a steady pace. *Bletilla* orchids are entirely charming and rewarding flowers. They are almost foolishly easy to grow yet convey an air of distinction to shady borders, where they make a handsome textural combination with ferns, boulders, or other natural features.

❦ *Magic Flowers*

It is hard to imagine anything more appealing than a brimming potful of *Achimenes* in full bloom. Gardeners show their universal approval of these flowers in the many nicknames they bestow: "magic flowers," "widow's tears," "cupid's bow," "monkey-faced pansies," "Japanese nut orchids," and "kimono plants." These hardy relatives of gloxinias and African violets are of easy culture. In the South they have long been popular for pots and porch boxes. Although tropical in origin, the underground bulbs remain safe from frost, so *Achimenes* may be used as perennials in shady beds filled with rich soil.

Achimenes are leafy, hairy herbs that grow about a foot tall. Species come mostly from Mexico and Guatemala, with a few varieties introduced from the West Indies. The long-tubed flowers, varying from an inch to three inches in diameter, resemble pansies or petunias. In color they are always vibrant, with a velvety, substantial depth and intensity. They may be seen in a pleasant, naturalized condition about older gardens, once being more popular than today. During the nineteenth century over four hundred different cultivars were offered by bulb dealers.

The oblong tubers are composed of many scales, which overlap in a unique design like the pollen-bearing cones of a pine tree. With warmth, shade, and rich, moist soil, they begin growth in early summer. After several weeks, flowers begin to appear and continue until the plants are dried off in early fall.

It is important to provide a constant supply of moisture through the blooming season, for drought signals the plants to rest and begin forming tubers. These develop not only in the soil, but also at nodes along the stems. The fragile bulbs may be gathered in autumn and saved for replanting in rich compost the following summer. They store best in pots or bags of soil, sphagnum moss, or vermiculite. This prevents undue dessication.

The common "magic flower" seen everywhere in older gardens is a large, hyacinth blue, trailing selection of the Mexican *Achimenes longiflora*. This easy, vigorous, old cultivar is 'Galatea', also called 'Blue Beauty' or 'Mexicana.' Another old purple-blue, *A. grandiflora* 'Atropurpurea' is distinctive for the bronzy green tone of its heavy foliage.

The original rosy scarlet introduction is *A. coccinea* 'Major'. This Jamaican species has smaller petals and a longer tube than most *Achimenes*. *A. candida* is a large-flowered, white species from Guatemala. All of these and several other types have been widely hybridized, so these blossoms are now more often seen as colorful strains than as named species or varieties.

A notable recent development is a beautiful, double-flowered race of *Achimenes*. These prized, patented varieties, known as the Rose Series, come in lavender, pink, and white, as well as white with a lilac picotee. The lovely blooms look like varicolored, miniature gardenias and compete in beauty with any summer bedding flowers. In the South they may be used freely for summer color in the same way as *Impatiens*.

🌺 *Begonias*

Many exotic begonias thrive on porches and in summer window boxes in the South, but these are not the tuberous varieties of the genus. Hybrid tuberous begonias descend from species native to the cool mountains of Bolivia, which were collected originally for the House of Veitch by Richard Pearce, the same gentleman who introduced *Hippeastrum leopoldii*. As might be expected, these Andean forms and their progeny sulk in the sultry climate of the lowland South. In frost-free regions of Florida and the Gulf Coast, they may be attempted for winter bedding in rich, moist soil, but they are otherwise valueless in this climate.

There is a tuberous begonia from Asia that may be planted as a hardy perennial. So unique and vigorous that it deserves to be in all Southern gardens, this is the famous *Begonia grandis* (*B. evansiana*). The modest sprays of tiny, pink blooms are not as showy as those of the hybrids, but the luxuriant, embossed foliage, red tinted beneath, makes a fine addition to any shady nook. There is a rare white-flowered form ('Alba') and a selection with reportedly larger blooms ('Simsii').

B. grandis enjoys a cool position with rich, leafy soil and abundant moisture. Where it is happy, it quickly spreads to form large patches. In late summer small tubers form along the stems; they may be gathered and potted immediately for increase. The plant yellows and dies down entirely in autumn. Since this hardy begonia emerges fairly late in the spring, it is a good choice to follow early-blooming woodlanders, such as *Trillium*.

In the lower South, gardeners may also experiment with some of the rhizomatous begonias. These mostly Mexican plants endure heat and heavy soil better than other begonias. Their creeping rootstocks, resting on the surface, should be protected from hard frost with a mulch of straw over winter. All varieties propagate readily from leaf cuttings, so gardeners can quickly produce spare plants to set out for trial. Among the most beautiful of all foliage plants, they have a uniquely succulent, watery character.

The star begonia (*B. heracleifolia*) is a tremendous, vigorous type with deeply lobed, pale green leaves and light pinkish blooms in early summer. 'Selph's Mahogany' is a strong-growing hybrid from this, with dark, heavily veined, bronzy foliage. Although these are tender evergreens, they resprout readily even when the leaves are frozen. *B. crassicaulis* is naturally deciduous, so it should not mind occasional frost during its dormant period. The pink sprays of bloom appear in early spring before the deeply cut, shining green leaves.

❧ *Dahlias*

The hybrid Dahlias of summer gardens are descended from plants originally domesticated by the natives of Mexico. Like tuberous begonias, they are flowers for cool, pleasantly mild regions and do not generally thrive in the torrid, steamy weather of the South. Since these daisy-type blooms are closely related to annual *Cosmos* and *Coreopsis*, both of which thrive in heat, it is tempting to forego this genus altogether. Purists will point out that *Dahlia*, like other tuberous genera, has a unique succulent quality. This gives the blooms a translucent depth and color not found in other daisylike blooms.

Although the hybrid strains of *Dahlia* are poorly suited to the South, some of the wild Mexican species may be tried. *Dahlia merckii* is a modest-sized variety with lilac ray florets, pointed at the tips. *D. coccinea* is single, scarlet with a bright yellow central disk. These two species were the forerunners of the modern single and collarette dahlias, and these strains might perform acceptably in the South. *D. imperialis* is a tall-growing, white variety with reddish disks, suitable for shady gardens in the lower South. A cool root run in rich, well-drained soil and a position with shade from the hottest sun offer the best prospect for success. Most varieties grow easily from seed. The clustered tubers may be separated with a knife in early spring, making sure each division has a growing eye.

❧ *Yellow Show & Coral Flowers*

There are other summer-flowering Mexican tubers better suited to the warmth of the South, but these are little known as garden plants. They are most commonly grown by succulent enthusiasts, who pot the enlarged roots in an exposed position to display their narled, bonsailike swelling. As long as the tubers are planted safely underground in well-drained soil, these plants may be treated as perennials. They revel in heat.

Yellow show (*Amoreuxia wrightii*) is a small plant that belongs to a curious, tropical American family, the *Cochlospermaceae*. It makes a round tuber the size of a walnut. After summer rains, short stems with gray-green, palmate leaves come up and bear bright yellow, nasturtiumlike blossoms. These open freshly in the morning and fade in early afternoon. Interesting, transparent, egg-shaped capsules follow, containing numerous hard, brown seeds. If planted in ordinary garden soil, these grow rapidly, forming flowering-size plants in their first season. Old tubers sometimes succumb to nematodes, but this plant is easy to keep coming from fresh seed.

Tougher and equally exotic is the coral flower, or *jicamilla* (*Jatropha cathartica*). This relative of the common bull nettle forgoes the painful thorns of its cousin. Instead of fragrant, white blooms, it sends up a succession of small, coral red blooms. These ripen into three-sided capsules bearing nutlike seeds.

If gathered before the capsules burst, the seed can be set straight in the border where the plants are desired. Growing well in dry, sandy soil in full sun, they have attractive, gray, palmlike leaves. The tubers are long-lived and eventually become six or eight inches in diameter. The coral flower is hardy wherever the soil does not freeze.

🌸 *Wood Sorrels*

With over eight hundred species, *Oxalis* is a huge genus that has scarcely been explored by gardeners. Although several common horticultural species prefer cool, maritime climates, a goodly number come from warm regions, especially Mexico and South America. These revel in the Southern climate and make fine garden material.

Nearly all *Oxalis* have ornamental, divided foliage, either like clover or much dissected to resemble tiny windmills. Leaves are often further ornamented with markings of bronze or purple. The attractive clusters of five-petaled blossoms furl themselves tightly while in bud, and both leaves and flowers exhibit strong sleep movements, twisting and closing at night. Flowers ripen to oblong pods, which burst as they dry to scatter the seeds.

The common name shared by *Oxalis* species is "wood sorrel," a designation apparently borrowed from true sorrel, which is a very different-looking plant in the dock genus, *Rumex*. What sorrel shares with *Oxalis* is the pleasantly acid, mustardlike flavor in its leaves. True sorrel is often harvested for use as a potherb. The more strongly flavored *Oxalis* may be used in small doses as a condiment, but the concentration of oxalic acid in the leaves is usually too high to permit more liberal consumption. *Oxalis* comes from the Greek *oxys*, meaning "sour."

🌸 *South Americans*

One *Oxalis* in particular is outstanding for its widespread use in borders and as low edgings. Most gardeners simply know this ubiquitous, mounding flower as pink wood sorrel, but this risks confusion with several other varieties.

Its botanical name, *Oxalis crassipes*, translates as "thick foot," referring to the swollen, tuberous roots of this species. Although many *Oxalis* develop simple bulbs composed of scales, *O. crassipes* goes beyond this with its starchy rootstock and potatolike swellings. These storage structures help make this species especially drought-tolerant. The clumps can be easily divided at any season, and it is a simple matter for gardeners to propagate all they might desire.

Gazing out at plantings of the small, rounded clumps of *Oxalis crassipes* on a frosty February morning, a hasty observer might fail to notice the folded, nodding buds. With the warmth of the noonday sun, these turn upward to display cheerful, magenta pink funnels. This resolute bloomer graces gardens in earliest spring, continuing well into summer where it receives shade from the western sun, opening its flowers progressively earlier in the day and closing them in afternoon heat.

A tough, thrifty native of the Argentine pampas, *O. crassipes* often returns to bloom in late fall, persisting through the winter on sheltered sites. This is an invaluable plant for Southern gardens, a prime choice for edging beds or path-

Oxalis regnellii 'Triangularis'

Oxalis crassipes

Bessera elegans

Hypoxis decumbens

Milla magnifica

Oxalis pes-caprae

ways. Its lightly felted, cloverlike leaves make handsome mounds even when not in bloom.

The common form of *O. crassipes* has especially vibrant, wine-striated blooms. These sometimes clash with other flowers or red brick, but there is a lovely white form, 'Alba', which can be used in any scheme. It has fresh, green foliage and replaces the wine pencilings of the common form with light gray striations.

O. braziliensis is a beautiful ally of *O. crassipes* with a dwarfer, more spreading habit. Instead of thickened roots, this variety spreads from small, scale-covered bulbs. The leaves have the same mounding quality as *O. crassipes*, overlapping like shingles to form a solid groundcover. This handsome foliage has a lustrous, waxy greenness that bespeaks the tropics, and it is indeed tender to hard frost. The rounded leaflets provide an ideal background for the glowing cerise blossoms, which appear from March through May.

O. braziliensis is one of the most beautiful species if given its preferred moist, acid soil. It makes a charming filler for crevices between stone pavers, although no one would want to step on its leaves or flowers. Like *O. crassipes*, this species grows in winter, becoming dormant with the heat of June. The small bulbs should be planted in the fall.

O. regnellii is another South American that takes to the climate of the South. It has become fairly popular as a bedding item for its attractive, three-parted foliage. If watered and shaded from hot sun, the leaves hold up through summer as well as winter. The white flowers of common *O. regnellii* look rather ordinary, but they show off against the triangular green leaflets, which are purple underneath. 'Triangularis' is a splashy introduction with brilliant reddish purple leaves throughout and pale pink blossoms.

These varieties grow easily on rich, moist soil, spreading steadily to form dense patches in full or partial shade. The fresh green or purple, flattened foliage contrasts happily with southern shield fern (*Thelypteris kunthii*) or orange shrimp plant (*Justicia fulvicoma*) and makes a good filler for foregrounds of shady bedding schemes.

O. corymbosa (*O. martiana*) is the common houseplant oxalis, a native of tropical America. It is like a taller, looser *O. crassipes* with pale pink blossoms and small nutlike bulbs. In the South this species survives in shaded, protected nooks. The most interesting form to grow is 'Variegata', an old selection with yellowish reticulated veins.

The candy-striped oxalis (*O. versicolor*) is one of the South American species with heavily divided leaves. These are usually so furled and tossled that the clumps look like moss. In late winter the flowers begin expanding on warm days. The backs of the petals are deep pink and the faces white, so in opening and closing an unusual peppermint effect predominates.

This winter-growing species seems entirely hardy in the middle and lower South, but it has no tolerance for summer rains during its period of dormancy. It is best grown in a pot plunged into the ground over winter. This may be lifted and dried off in early summer for replanting in the coming fall. If used in this way, these pink and white beauties are as valuable as pansies for cool-season color.

🌸 *Bermuda Buttercups*

In the lower South the pale yellow blooms of the Bermuda buttercup (*O. pes-caprae*) are a regular feature of late winter. They often punctuate old lawns and are almost as common as *O. crassipes*, although they are less prominently used in borders. This South African variety makes lax clumps that lean nonchalantly in the direction of the February sun. The leaves have the same clover like appearance as *O. crassipes* but are peppered all over with brown freckles.

The clustered yellow blooms are at their best at ten in the morning and look especially pretty when massed under the gaunt bareness of a rugged, old elm. Unless it is a misty, overcast day, they fold up and rest after midday. An old name for this flower, *O. cernua*, means "nodding," referring to this afternoon siesta. The present Latin title, *pes-caprae*, "goat foot," refers to the heart-shaped leaflets.

Although this species is a vigorous spreader, hard frost is its enemy, and in cold years it is a struggle to see the tender foliage through the winter. There is a beautiful double form ('Flore Pleno'), which tends to rich, golden yellow. It is a choice, early flower and makes a deserving subject for a sheltered position at the foot of a south-facing wall.

🌸 *Southerners*

The wild purple wood sorrel (*O. violacea*), a delightful woodland flower, makes a dainty spring garden subject, useful to combine with the yellow stargrass. The cloverlike leaves are pale green, and the blooms are rosy purple (not violet). The small, scaly bulbs spread by rhizomes but are seldom invasive.

More glamorous is the Southern yellow wood sorrel (*O. priceae*). Its foliage and build are like *O. violacea*, but the blooms are rich, golden yellow. The root is a slender, creeping rhizome. Flowers appear in April and May on poor, sandy ground.

This fine flower should not be confused with the ubiquitous *O. corniculata*, which makes a taproot instead of a tuber and often has purple-tinted leaves. This native is too well known to most gardeners to need more definite introduction. Well-nigh ineradicable, trailing stems make it a frightful weed, and it is capable of seeding itself through an entire bed in short order. Any decent garden will inevitably have to endure its onslaught, for *O. corniculata* seems to come as a free plant in every nursery pot.

🌸 *Texicans*

The Southwestern and Mexican *Oxalis* carry the blooming season into summer and fall. Many of these are especially choice flowers suited to a special niche on the rockery. All grow from true bulbs and tolerate considerable drought. They enjoy rich, clay soils with a measure of lime but will succeed on sand, also.

O. lasiandra sends up charming, many-parted leaves on tall stems like little palm trees. This species is widespread over the semiarid uplands of Mexico. Some forms reach nearly a foot in height, but other strains remain much shorter. The blooms appear on six- to eight-inch stems carried among the leaves in early summer. They are a very bright cerise pink, almost electric in tone. The slender carriage of these plants suggests display against lichen-covered boulders, so that their strong form will not be hidden by leafier neighbors.

The iron cross oxalis (*O. tetraphylla*) produces foliage like a four-leaved shamrock, but with dark purple stains marking the base of each leaflet. This coloring defines the iron cross pattern, making the mounds of leaves stand out boldly in the garden. In May and June satiny, rose blossoms join the foliage. *O. deppei* and *O. nelsonii* are similar but with deeper red and purplish blooms, respectively. All are natives of western and southern Mexico.

O. latifolia is a fast-spreading, tropical American variety with leaves composed of three wedge-shaped leaflets. In the common form, these are green, but there is a striking burgundy-leafed selection that looks much like the purple-leafed *O. regnellii*. It is smaller and more drought-tolerant, with lilac-pink blossoms in late summer and fall.

A Texas relation, *O. drummondii*, also spreads vigorously, and it may be unwelcome in some gardens for this attribute. Nevertheless, it sends up redeemingly large, lilac-rose blooms in September and October. The foliage comes up at the same time and remains through the winter. It is so low growing that it is only a nuisance in the most manicured gardens, and the blooms are pleasant if allowed to naturalize in a rough lawn.

A form of *O. drummondii* from the mountains of western Texas and northern Mexico was once given the name *O. vespertilionis*, which means "batlike." The narrow, V-shaped leaves sometimes look like the wings of bats, and this form is worth cultivating for its unusual foliage, as well as its autumn blooms. In some clones the leaves are also marked with bars of purple.

9

Cannas, Arums, and Gingers

In the warm climate of the South, a few families of tuberous plants go beyond the ordinary parameters of perennial flowers. Although they die down at some point in the season, they make their presence felt in such a way as to almost commend use as shrubs. Cannas, gingers, and members of the arum tribe afford basic garden architecture as well as exuberant displays of bloom.

🌸 *Cannas*

The original garden cannas were not planted for their flowers at all, but for their exotic, tropical foliage. Tall, leafy varieties were especially favored in Victorian bedding schemes. Cannas proudly combined with castor beans, begonias, and other bold growers to effect the tropical style of summer bedding.

The original species of the genus *Canna* come from moist, upland forests, mostly in Asia and Latin America. Two aquatic, yellow-flowered varieties, *Canna flaccida* and *C. glauca,* are natives of Southern swamps. All have thick, branching rhizomes, with upright stems, sheathed by large, alternate leaves. The stems sprout at intervals from the roots like shoots of bamboo and give the plants a very lush appearance. Cannas are hardy anywhere in the South if mulched in winter to ward off penetrating frost.

These robust flowers are tremendously free growing; since gardeners know this, cannas are often relegated to less than ideal conditions. Although the plants will endure drought and poor soil, they prefer steady, abundant water and rich ground. The luxuriant performance of properly cherished cannas amply repays gardeners who offer good care.

The blossoms of cannas are curiously built

affairs in which enlarged, sterile stamens (staminodia) take the place of petals and sepals. The true petals are tiny and form a narrow tube from which the showy, orchidlike staminodia protrude. There are usually four of these petal-like structures together, with one bent and reflexed to form a sort of lip.

The first hybridizer of cannas, M. Annee, had been the French consul-general at Valparaiso, Chile. He returned to Europe in 1846 with a collection of species, which he used as breeding stock. Some of Annee's early crosses and the wild species used to create them may still be seen in older Southern gardens.

🌸 Indian Shots

The best known of the cannas from Annee's breeding stable is the tropical American Indian shot (*Canna indica*), so called for its hard, round seeds resembling buckshot. Typical forms of the species have very glossy, green leaves and grow between two and six feet tall. Narrow, up-facing blooms appear at the tops of the stems. They usually have yellowish to orange lips and are frequently spotted with red.

Annee also used the tall, bronze-leafed *C. warscewiczii* in his breeding; this tropical American species may be the source of the colored foliage seen in many garden cannas. The blossoms of *C. warscewiczii* are bright scarlet, but they appear very small in relation to the tremendous foliage.

An especially fine, purple-leafed canna, perhaps the old cultivar 'Robusta', is in many gardens in the South. It is among the tallest, achieving nine to twelve feet on rich soil. The substantial, veined leaves hold their color in sun or shade, asking only for shelter from strong wind. This variety makes an ideal specimen plant, with graceful, outward-arching stems, superb as a dark-colored center-piece for a bed of bright summer flowers.

A different canna sold as *warscewiczii* today has broad, fluted leaves tinged red on the midribs and stems, a color pattern that matches the description of another tropical American species, *C. edulis*. A similar plant is cultivated in English gardens under the name *C. indica* 'Purpurea'. These types make exotic foliage accents and bear slender clusters of rich red or orange blooms.

There are several old, green-leafed cannas nearly as tall as these bronzy types. One of Annee's famous hybrids, 'Imperator', was such a plant, and was derived from a cross of two other South American forms, *musaefolia* and *gigantea*. All three of these were popular nineteenth-century companions for the purple-leafed cannas.

🌸 The Iris-Flowered Canna

The largest blooms among the tall cannas belong to the pendant, rosy crimson *C. iridiflora*. This distinctive Peruvian is one of the few wild types still in cultivation. Its Latin name means "iris-flowered" and refers to the showy, large-petaled blooms. The broad, smooth leaves have a handsome blue-green tone and are especially sturdy. They appear along five-foot stems, topped by the long-tubed, cardinal rose blossoms. These dangle on slender stalks that curve like swan's necks. Throughout summer a succession of warmly colored blossoms suspend

Canna 'Erebus'

Canna 'Cleopatra'

Zantedeschia 'Galaxy'

Hedychium coronarium

Arisaema flavum

Zantedeschia ethiopica 'Green Goddess'

themselves like bright butterflies over the foliage. Swarms of hummingbirds follow the brilliant blooms.

Around 1860 Annee used *C. iridiflora* to produce the hybrid 'Iridiflora Rubra', better known in horticulture under name 'Ehemanni'. It has the same brilliant rose crimson flowers as *C. iridiflora*, but the vigorous plants hold their blooms in upright clusters. 'Ehemanni' became popular in the late 1800s for its rich, heavy foliage and abundant bloom.

Both 'Ehemannii' and *C. iridiflora* may still be had from nursery sources, although their names are apt to be confused. The very husky roots of both varieties prefer cool, moist conditions, and they should not be allowed to dry out completely when dug and separated for increase. Although leaf-rolling insects plague many modern canna hybrids, they usually ignore these old, tall varieties, which bear much tougher, more leathery foliage.

❧ Crozy Cannas

Several French gardeners worked to develop cannas for their floral beauty, but M. Crozy of Lyon is usually credited with breeding the large-flowered race that now dominates gardens. Showy Asian species such as the tiger canna (*C. childsii*), with yellow, crimson-spotted blooms, and the dwarf *C. limbata* (*C. aureo-vittata*), with slightly variegated foliage and red and yellow blossoms, probably contributed to Crozy's hybrids. A five-foot, orange- and yellow-flowered selection, 'Florence Vaughn', is thought by some to be his famous, old variety 'Madame Crozy'.

❧ The Harlequin Canna

Another old Crozy-type canna may be seen everywhere in Southern gardens, and it is always an attraction. The four- to six-foot stands of leaves are topped abundantly in early summer by massive, orchidlike blooms. Normally, these flowers have yellow petals covered with red dots and accompany clear green foliage. With amazing regularity, however, various shoots develop spontaneous variegations in which the leaves become wholly or partly purple. At the same time, the blooms change to vermillion. Individual stems may sometimes be found with bronze and red on one side, green and yellow on the other, as if they had been cut vertically and sewn together from two separate plants.

No one seems sure of the proper title or ancestry of this harlequin, but it is widely sold under the name "Cleopatra" and has also been called "Spanish Emblem." In its green-leafed phase, this fascinating canna answers the description of an old Crozy hybrid called 'Admiral Courbet'. The red-leafed form could be another nineteenth-century variety, 'Edouard Andre'. Under any title, this is one of the most rewarding cannas, always outstandingly brilliant and exotic, no matter which aspect it chooses to display.

❧ Asiatics

The pin-striped variegation seen in 'Striped Beauty' suggests that this Asian cultivar may be close to the wild *C. limbata*. In America this beautiful dwarf is also sometimes called 'Nirvana' or 'Bangkok Yellow'. The lance-shaped foliage is attractive by itself and usually remains under two feet tall. The yellow, white-striped blooms are lively and refreshing—bright, yet with none of the gaudiness seen in more common canna hybrids.

Brilliant orange flowers top the five-foot, leafy stems of 'Pretoria', another hybrid with obvious golden pin-stripes. The contrast of leaves and flowers is especially rich. Although 'Pretoria' exhibits no more love for water than other cannas, it has become popular for poolside plantings. An even more opulent selection, 'Durban', appears to be a bronze sport of 'Pretoria'. Yellow stripes remain visible against its purplish foliage, making a truly festive appearance.

In addition to these variegates, a few other imports from India and South-east Asia are worthy of note. 'Cupid' is a delicate, porcelain pink dwarf with lightly speckled, orange-throated blooms. 'Pride of India' ('Taj Mahal') reaches four to five feet and bears rich, rose-pink blooms. Both of these are outstanding.

❦ Orchid-Flowered Cannas

The native *C. glauca*, an interesting, pale yellow flower in itself, has been used by breeders to develop what are called orchid-flowered cannas. These inherit the upright, lance-shaped leaves of *C. glauca* and the long-tubed aspect of its flowers.

The first cannas of this type were introduced in the 1880s by Dammann & Co. of Naples, Italy. Few remain in commerce, but recent breeding by Robert J. Armstrong at Longwood Gardens, Pennsylvania, has introduced a new race of orchid-flowered varieties, all with the attractive, blue-gray foliage of *C. glauca*. An especially choice clone is 'Erebus', with delicate, salmon pink blossoms.

❦ Modern Varieties

Most recent hybrid cannas have been developed for use as summer bedding plants. Shapeless masses of brilliantly colored blooms have been the breeders' principal aim. Although most varieties remain more or less "dwarf" in Northern gardens, in the generous climate of the South it is not unusual for bedding cannas to exceed four or five feet.

Standard, green-leafed selections, such as the rosy pink 'City of Portland', golden yellow 'Richard Wallace', and scarlet 'President', all achieve good size, as do the bronze-leafed, orange-flowered 'Wyoming' and vermillion 'King Humbert'. These are harshly brilliant flowers but have great vigor. They have long asserted supremacy over the mass bedding displays of public parks, combining strikingly with bold foliage plants such as yucca or pampas grass.

The popular Pfitzer and Grand Opera series are slightly shorter and come in a range of pastel shades more easily placed in home gardens. The warm apricot 'Stadt Fellbach' is particularly fine. 'Lucifer' is a brilliant red with striking yellow borders.

In addition to these named varieties, nurseries also offer strains that may be raised from seed. 'Seven Dwarfs' includes a mix of reds, roses, oranges, yellows, and salmons, all of which remain eighteen inches tall or less. 'Tropical

Rose' is a recently introduced variety growing so rapidly from seed that it may be used as a bedding annual. Glowing, opalescent blossoms appear on lush green, two-and-a-half foot plants.

When planting the seeds of these and other cannas, it is best to file or break the hard coats first. Seeds may then be soaked in water and allowed to swell before planting in individual pots. With warm conditions, growth is amazingly rapid.

🌸 Fragrance

As active and successful as breeders have been with cannas, one characteristic they have neglected is fragrance. Enhancing it is not an impossible wish, for the Venezuelan *C. liliflora* produces long-tubed, creamy blossoms with the sweet scent associated with nocturnal flowers. It has seldom, if ever, been cultivated in America, but it should certainly be tried in the South. If crossed with our present colorful races of hybrids, what wonders it might produce.

🌸 Aroids

The arum family (*Araceae*) offers gardeners a sort of herbaceous analog of the palms. Although soft and succulent in leaf and stem, many varieties develop a lush fountain of growth and large fronds of foliage. In the mildest parts of the South, a few approach tree proportions.

The typical aroid "flower" is formed by a leafy bract, or spathe, which may be brightly colored. This enfolds a slender spike called a spadix. The spadix is closely packed, forming a compound "bloom" made up from the inconspicuous true flowers. In some species all the blossoms on the spike produce both stamens and styles. In others the spadix divides into male and female sections. Often these strangely built flowers function as insect traps, attracting flies or midges with the scent of fungus or carrion. After pollination they ripen compact clusters of fleshy berries. Generally a showy red, they appear in autumn like scarlet cobs of corn.

The arum family includes classically tropical genera, such as *Philodendron*, and also harbors hardy flowers, such as the jack-in-the-pulpit (*Arisaema triphyllum*). Several tuberous forms, including the genus *Arum*, favor cool Mediterranean climates. Nearly all varieties enjoy rich, boggy conditions during their growing season.

🌸 Tree Philodendrons

Philodendrons are not really tuberous plants, but at least one species, the Brazilian tree philodendron (*Philodendron selloum*), produces such a heavy, swollen stem that it functions, in effect, as a tuber. This enables this erstwhile tropical vine to recover from periodic bouts of frost. In the lower South the tree philodendron is popular as a foliage plant for shady courtyards. The big, glossy green, scalloped leaves have a luxuriant appearance and illustrate the palmlike character of tropical arums.

❧ '*Ape*

More honestly tuberous, yet still treelike in near-tropical climates, is the Asian '*ape* (*Alocasia macrorhiza*). This is one of several aroids with large, spade-shaped leaves and edible, tuberous roots. The small, greenish flowers are of little importance in the landscape. It's the bold greenery that gardeners enjoy. The '*ape* is one of the plants affectionately known as elephant ear. The starchy corms provide an important subsistence food throughout tropical Asia. In legends of Rartonga, a South Pacific island, the hero Ru used '*ape* to hoist the heavens above the earth.

The shiny green blades of this *Alocasia* spring from a thick stem, which may remain below ground or extend a few feet upward as a ringed trunk. Bold, succulent leaves on long stalks point upward, adding several feet of height. Small strains of '*ape* remain only two to three feet high, but large forms reach four to five feet before they begin to form a trunk, eventually ascending to ten feet if not halted by frost.

The common '*ape* is hardy in the middle and lower South. With its arrow-shaped leaves pointed to the heavens, it offers one of the most striking of summer foliage plants. Ordinary garden conditions produce grand success, and either sun or part shade is satisfactory. A favorite use is in or near ponds. Aquatic culture yields prodigious growth from these and most other elephant ears.

Collectors cultivate several additional selections of '*ape*. 'Jungle Gold' is a variety with yellow-flecked leaves and stems. 'Variegata' is the best known of the variegated elephant's ears, with a mix of rich green, celery, gray, and cream marbled over each leaf. 'Violacea' produces dark green blades with blackish purple stems and veins. These select forms respond to more careful care than ordinary '*ape*. The variegated types, especially, should be sheltered from sun and hard frost.

❧ *Taro*

The '*ape* and its varieties are often confused with taro (*Colocasia esculenta*), which is equally robust and leafy. The plant known to many American gardeners as elephant ear is a large-growing strain of taro. In the tropics this staple has been cultivated for its edible roots since ancient times. It was once known in the South as tanyah. The potatolike tubers were boiled and eaten, and the tender leaves were cooked to provide nutritious greens. During the era of slavery, these easy-growing plants provided a large part of the diet of African-Americans. Taro is still a popular food in the Carribean.

Although casually similar to '*ape*, taro holds its leaves perpendicular to its stems, so that the blades face outward and point to the ground. Botanists call this arrangement peltate. It's worth a gardener's time to learn this term, for the contrasting leaf designs offer a simple method for distinguishing the various common elephant ears of Southern gardens. The leaves of taro also differ from '*ape* in their color, being a soft, velvety green.

Ordinary taro roots found in grocery stores may be planted for ornament, but the edible strain, dasheen, is usually fairly small. Gardeners want to grow the biggest, grandest elephant ears possible, so large-leafed horticultural forms are preferred. Florida growers send out the heavy, brown, globular tubers in spring, and these are widely available at nurseries and garden centers. The most massive roots give the best results.

A place should be chosen out of strong wind or hot sun, with deep, rich soil and plenty of moisture. A single tuber will grow up to six feet in height, with leaves four feet long and three feet wide. To develop such a specimen, the plant should receive a thorough watering every day it does not receive rain. In the South taro is completely hardy if mulched to preserve the fleshy roots from frost.

Among several ornamental selections, *C. esculenta* 'Illustris' is especially valued for its apple green foliage marked purplish black between the veins. 'Chicago Harlequin' is variously blotched with green and yellow. 'Jet Black Wonder' is entirely black-purple. 'Red Dot' has maroon and pink stems and a tiny reddish splash in the middle of the blade. The water taro (*C. esculenta* v. *aquatilis*) is a purple-stemmed variety that has run wild along the banks of Southern streams. This popular water garden subject runs rapidly by stolons.

❧ Yautia

The Latin American elephant ear, or *yautia* (*Xanthosoma saggittifolium*), is close in appearance to the taro but has triangular leaves dulled by a white powder when young. Close inspection also reveals prominent veins running along the margin of the blades, yet for garden purposes the *yautia* is simply another in the herd of elephant ears. As with 'ape, the tubers may sometimes elongate to form a short trunk.

The blue elephant ear (*X. violacea*), an especially vigorous relative of *yautia*, has purplish stems and leaves covered in a waxy, bluish powder. The golden elephant ear (*Xanthosoma muffata* 'Aurea') produces large, chartreuse yellow leaves.

❧ Exotics

Aficionados of the arum family cultivate several other beautiful elephant ears. *Alocasia* × *amazonica* is a gorgeous, tropical hybrid with arrow-shaped, blackish green leaves. These are scalloped and bear raised veins and margins of silver. 'Hilo Beauty' forms medium-sized clumps of soft green, heart-shaped blades, splashed and mottled with beige. The Javan *A. plumbea* (*A. indica* v. *metallica*) raises large, upright leaves with a blue-gray, metallic sheen.

Although these unusual varieties are not difficult to grow in shady summer gardens, their tubers usually rot if left in the ground over winter. North of Florida these exotics might be used as arresting summer bedding items, but this is rarely tried. The tubers store poorly unless kept in a warm greenhouse.

❧ Caladiums

It is the fancy-leafed caladium that offers the bedding plant par excellence. The flattened, knobby tubers handle with ease and swiftly grow into the most splendid of summer foliage plants. Although not hardy north of the Gulf, these dwarf allies of the elephant ears are particularly fine in the South. Reveling in warmth and humidity, they give a long season of beauty in return for a minimal investment of the gardener's effort.

The green- and red-spotted heart of Jesus (*Caladium bicolor*) was the first caladium introduced to horticulture, appearing as early as 1769. This native of the Para state in Brazil is the principal ancestor of the many heart-leafed hybrids now grouped under the name *C. × hortulanum*. Breeding of modern, fancy-leafed varieties began in the mid-nineteenth century with the introduction of species from the Amazon region. Louis Van Houtte and Alfred Bleu in France, and several breeders of German descent, C.J. Bause, J. Luther, Adolphe Jaenicke, and Adolph Litze were active during the Victorian era. At the turn of the century, Henry Nehrling and Theodore Mead made important contributions. Several of their hybrids remain in cultivation.

Although wild caladium species are rarely planted in present-day gardens, the jewel-like *C. humboltii* is one that is still worth growing. Its six-inch, heart-shaped leaves are boldly splashed with white, contrasted against dark green veins. This Venezuelan miniature was once known as *C. argyrites*, the "silver caladium."

The color patterns of *C. humboltii* are preserved by the famous variety 'Candidum'. This hybrid from 1868 juxtaposes rich green veins against its large, silvery white leaves. It is still the most popular of all caladiums, the cool whiteness of its foliage refreshing numerous summer-bedding schemes. 'Candidum' is especially strong growing and stands direct sun better than many of its colorful brethren.

'Carolyn Wharton', 'Pink Beauty', and 'Red Flash' exhibit patterns more like *C. bicolor*, with vivid splashes of pink, red, and green together. 'Blaze' ('T.L. Mead'), 'John Peed', 'Frieda Hemple', and 'Postman Joiner' produce wine-red leaves edged in green. All of these are vigorous, reaching twelve to eighteen inches in height. They make beautiful beds nestled among the feathered greenery of river ferns (*Thelypteris kunthii*).

With the first cool breezes of autumn, caladium leaves begin to flop or wilt; at this time the tubers may be taken up for winter storage. The tender roots should be kept dry and warm over winter, placed in boxes of sphagnum moss or rice hulls to absorb excess humidity. Although the effort required to conserve them is small, many gardeners choose to purchase fresh tubers each season. Roots may be started into growth in early spring if potted and kept near warm, bright windows.

It is tempting to set caladiums out when the first sunny days of spring arrive, but if the ground has not warmed completely, tubers will rot in short order. A single breath of cool air from an April norther is all that is needed to check the growth of a young plant, and it will not develop properly thereafter. To grow as beautiful as they are capable, caladiums must be given rich soil, unfailing warmth, abundant moisture, and bright, filtered light.

The large-growing eyes visible on the tops of the dormant roots contain buds of flower spikes for the coming summer. Most gardeners plant caladiums for their showy, variegated foliage and remove the greenish flowers as they appear. Knowledgeable planters sometimes use a sharp knife to remove the larger growing points from the tubers. Done several days or weeks before the roots are to be planted, this stimulates side branching, developing a lusher, leafier appearance. Roots sprout from the tops of the tubers, so they should be covered by at least an inch of soil when planted.

❦ Lance-Leafed Caladiums

Among the novelties developed by Theodore Mead is a race of lance- or strap-leafed caladiums. Descended from the narrow-foliaged *C. albanense* crossed among the larger hybrids, they inherit much tougher constitutions than ordinary, heart-leafed varieties. As a group, the strap-leafed caladiums are more tolerant of direct sun and less likely to flag in drought. These hybrids rarely bother to flower, so they do not need to be disbudded.

'Jackie Suthers' is a choice white "strap" with green-edged, ruffled leaves. 'Miss Muffet' is an amazing greenish cream, flecked all over with purplish pink. 'Rosalie' and 'Red Frill' are deep wine. All of these are easy, low-growing plants, with interesting mounds of slender foliage. They are ideal to bed among odd boulders or dwarf ferns, such as the Venus' maidenhair (*Adiantum capillus-veneris*).

❦ Snake Palms

One of the truly bizarre tuberous plants of the subtropics is the devil's tongue, or snake palm (*Amorphophallus rivieri*). The globular corms send up only a single leaf, but this is so marvelously built and branched as to suggest a small palm tree. If the tubers are large, the foliage may reach as much as four feet in height. The rounded, fleshy stem of the blade is mottled all over with olive and purple. At its top it divides again and again to form a broad, leafy umbrella of dark green. In a sheltered spot in the shade, this novel foliage remains in good condition all summer, yellowing and dying down in autumn.

If the tubers are kept dry over winter and are of sufficient size, a flower spike will appear in spring before the next season's leaf emerges. The bloom is constructed on the typical arum plan, with a large, central spadix surrounded by a fleshy bract. In this strange genus the flowers are so enormous that they always provoke comment. Blackish red goblets up to three feet tall rise from the bare earth and emit a foul stench.

Although the snake palm is usually kept as a collector's curio for pots, it is fairly cold-hardy if planted in well-drained, sandy soil. In Southeast Asia and Japan, the cormous roots are grown as an edible. The common spotted-stemmed form is the variety 'Konjac'. There is also an interesting cultivar with all-black stems.

❦ Monarch of the East

Another equally sinister-looking aroid, also hardy in the South, is known variously as red calla, monarch of the East, or voodoo lily. The botanical name of this Indian perennial, *Sauromatum guttatum,* means "spotted lizard."

Although the leaves of *Sauromatum* are not so spectacularly divided as those of the snake palm, they are still substantial and exotically lush. The compound leaves radiate in a distinctive pattern, as if the lobes were attached to the back of a horseshoe. The large, central segment extends up to eighteen inches from the middle of the blade, with six to ten smaller lobes distributed on either side, grading down to the tips. In the common horticultural variety, *venosum*, the leaflets bear prominent veins. The husky, three-foot leafstalks are marked with dark purple spots.

One of the weird attributes of monarch of the East is its capacity to flower as an unplanted tuber, and this is the primary reason nurseries bother to sell this oddity. The evil-smelling blooms produce bracts that are green outside, yellow and reddish purple on the interior. These bracts surround long, blackish purple central spikes. Well-grown tubers reach five inches in diameter and will throw up twelve- to twenty-four-inch flowers.

Although these plants are entirely perennial in the South and enjoy moist, shady conditions, they need a well-defined, dry rest period to induce bloom. If, for curiosity's sake, the malevolent-looking flowers are desired, it is best to take up the tubers in autumn. They may be replanted in spring and will flower before the leaves emerge.

❧ *Garden Dragons*

The temperate relations of *Sauromatum* belong to the large genus *Arisaema*, embracing a tremendous variety of forms, both strange and beautiful. Most species are modest in foliage compared to their tropical allies, but many retain the horseshoe pattern of the leaves. With their smaller stature, this radial foliage looks remarkably like that of another woodlander, the Lenten rose (*Helleborus orientalis*).

The most widespread of the South's native *Arisaema* species is also the easiest to grow. It has the alluring common name of green dragon, and this reptilian title is codified in its botanical name, *Arisaema draconitum*. In the wild, green dragon occurs in damp woods along streams, but the tubers endure ordinary garden conditions in bright shade. They will accept summer drought, so long as they are watered during the spring growing season. The leafy green, many-parted foliage comes up in midspring, with the flowers following in May or June.

The modest blooms are dominated by pale green, tubular spathes, which fold forward at the top, as if to cover the spadix and shield it from rain. The wayward spike will have none of this and escapes upward as a prolonged, tapering "dragon's tongue" five to six inches long. Although these blooms are hardly showy, they are certainly intriguing; they often ripen attractive, scarlet fruit in the fall. A cousin of the green dragon from Mexico, *A. macrospathum*, has slightly larger, greenish blooms, which appear before the foliage.

The better-known jack-in-the-pulpit (*A. triphyllum*) is a more beautiful flower, with an equally hooded spathe, striped vertically with purple and green, and surrounding a thick, purple spike. In the South it occurs naturally only in

Hedychium gardnerianum

Curcuma elata

Curcuma petiolata

Curcuma roscoeana

Kaempferia rotunda

the richest, dampest woods. In garden culture the roots must never suffer drought. The three-parted leaves, handsome accents for a shady bed of ferns, are not so exotic as the green dragon's. With luck, attractive red fruits appear in autumn. The five-leafed jack-in-the-pulpit (*A. quinatum*) is a similar native with greenish white spathes and five-parted foliage.

Most of the beautiful Asiatic *Arisaema* species enjoy the same retentive soils and cool, shady positions as the jack-in-the-pulpit. Few have been tested for their heat-endurance in the South, but beauties such as *A. candidissimum* certainly warrant trial. The hooded, white spathes of this Szechuan species are delicately striped pink inside, with pale green markings outside. They appear in late spring before the three-parted leaves expand. Another Chinese species from the same general region, *A. flavum* does well in the South, producing greenish yellow spathes, marked inside with yellow and purple.

All *Arisaema* gradually form clumps of offsets, which may be divided. The red berries, containing a single, stonelike seed, will grow to flowering size in three seasons.

Such close cousins of *Arisaema* as the Asiatic *Pinellia pedatisecta* multiply more rapidly, running underground on short stolons. The foliage is trilobed and makes a short, exotically leafy groundcover for a shady bank. The interesting, greenish blooms are like small versions of the green dragon and appear sporadically through the summer. If not picked, they often set seed and will volunteer in moist, shady nooks. *P. tripartita* is similar, with broad foliage and waxy, green blooms. *P. ternata* has interesting purplish blossoms but may become a dangerous weed in gardens that are to its liking.

Perhaps the most dragonlike of all the arums is *Dracunculus vulgaris*, which differs from these forest flowers in its preference for sunny, Mediterranean slopes. It certainly looks menacing, with its monstrous, deeply divided foliage and velvety, blackish purple spathes. The whole curious plant may reach three feet in height, with the blooms achieving half this stature.

Like other Mediterranean tubers, *Dracunculus* grows in winter, with flowers following in midspring. The foliage is handsome and seems proof against ordinary frosts. The odor of the dark-plum colored blooms, and of the plant as a whole, is fetid, but the stems may ripen weighty heads of attractive berries. These change gradually through the summer from green to shades of red.

This coarse perennial increases swiftly from offsets formed at the base. In the South the dormant tubers may be protected from excess summer moisture by planting in raised beds of limy soil. Several seasons are usually required for the young tubers to gather strength before flowering, but the attractive leaves may be enjoyed while awaiting the dragon's emergence from his cave.

❧ *True Arums*

Of the true arums only *Arum italicum* is much planted in the South, but it is such an unqualified success, gardeners should be enthusiastic to explore the genus further. The Italian arum is a plant of quiet beauty, but it appears when it is of the greatest value, during fall and winter. The arrow-shaped leaves unfurl in November, rising from the small, rounded tubers. In the popular garden form, 'Marmoratum', their shiny green surface is marbled with gray and cream veins.

The groups of leaves form lush, eight- to ten-inch clumps, which are suited to positions under trees or almost anywhere else they might be desired for winter interest. The flowers follow in midspring, just before the leaves die away for summer. Greenish white, with a creamy spadix, they are not particularly showy but very ready to set fruit. When the berries turn to waxy scarlet in autumn, they are often the brightest stars in the garden.

More unusual arums might also succeed in the South but have rarely been tried. Green-leafed lords and ladies (*Arum maculatum* v. *immaculatum*) is one very similar to *A. italicum* but with plain unspotted foliage. It seems just as easy and permanent.

The Mediterranean black callas (*A. palestinum* and *A. pictum*) have shiny green, arrow-shaped leaves and chocolate-colored flowers like *Dracunculus*. *A. creticum* produces a striking, creamy yellow spathe around a golden spadix— a truly beautiful flower. All of these are frost-hardy and ought to survive in the South if sheltered from excess summer rain.

❧ *Callas*

White calla lilies (*Zantedeschia ethiopica*) are beautiful, easy, winter growers, but they are not so hardy as arums. The common strains will tolerate modest frosts but are sufficiently hardy only for the lower South. The semiaquatic tubers revel in the black muck of ponds, and it is customary to set these plants in or near water when possible. This helps to ward off unusually hard freezes. Either sun or shade is usually satisfactory.

The glossy, arrow-headed foliage remains in growth through the winter, all year if the tubers are planted aquatically, forming lush clumps one-and-a-half feet tall. In the spring the clumps are joined by a succession of three-foot flower stems, each with a showy white spathe surrounding a thick, creamy spadix. These make magnificent cut flowers, lasting a week or two in a vase.

Florists in the lower South have long grown a semidwarf white calla called 'Godfrey', a variety that will sometimes be met in gardens. Sir Cedric Morris's introduction 'Green Goddess' is an especially robust clone, standing more cold than many others. Its spathes are suffused almost entirely with green, white appearing only in the throat. The dwarf or "baby calla" ('Childsiana') makes an attractive pot plant but is generally too weak-growing to be recommended for gardens.

In their native South Africa, white callas grow in both winter- and summer-rainfall areas, although only the Cape forms appear to have been introduced to garden culture. *Z. ethiopica* populations from northern Transvaal and the Natal coast extend their flowering into midsummer, tending to die down during the coldest parts of the year. These types might prove more adaptable to Southern conditions than current garden strains. Except for *Z. ethiopica,* all other *Zantedeschia* species grow and flower in summer. They may be counted entirely hardy in the South.

The white-spotted calla (*Z. albo-maculata*) is like a smaller version of *Z. ethio-*

pica, but it flowers only once, making it somewhat less valuable. Flower stems appear in early summer and usually reach eighteen inches. They carry milky blossoms with purplish blotches inside at the base. The arrow-shaped foliage has curious transparent zones, which give the enjoyable effect of white spots. The plants are not particular as to soil or exposure.

The golden calla (*Z. elliotiana*) and its hybrids are the best varieties for hot, sunny positions, but they also grow well in partial shade. The original yellow form appears in May, sending up deep golden blooms accompanied by spotted leaves like those of *Z. albo-maculata.*

This species has been widely hybridized with the white-spotted calla, the strap-leafed, pink calla (*Z. rehmanii*), and the golden, black-centered *Z. pentlandii.* Varieties available to gardeners today come in an astounding array of warm colors and deserve wider appreciation than they presently enjoy.

'Flame' is a gorgeous orange-apricot, 'Galaxy' a deep pink. 'Red Beauty' is cinnabar, with golden shadowing, and 'Lavender Gem' a dusty shade of rose. 'Cameo' is creamy apricot with black purple throats. All of these have lush, white-spotted leaves for contrast and produce heavily textured blooms, which last for many weeks in midsummer.

❧ *Gingers*

The hardier gingers, natives of warm temperate forests in Asia, show a special affinity for the similar, balmy climate of the South. Just as camellias command the winter scene with their glittering leaves and silky blossoms, gingers take charge over summer plantings, affording both luxuriant foliage and tantalizingly fragrant blooms. While climbing temperatures exhaust the wills of lesser garden flowers, these robust exotics seem to grow and blossom ever more profusely.

Each genus of this large family exhibits its own personality, varying in growth and degree of cold-tolerance. The grand, subtropical gingers, such as *Alpinia,* manifest an almost military bearing, with towering, bamboolike stems up to nine feet tall. These are furnished with alternate ranks of broad, spear-shaped leaves, which smell of cinnamon when crushed or bruised.

In contrast, the shy, deciduous *Kaempferia* hugs the ground with its flattened, stemless foliage, forming compact rosettes. The curious *Costus* chooses a wayward path to the sky, arranging oval leaves in a gentle helix along a stiff, spiraling stem. This stalk reaches upward for several feet and supports a brilliant cone of colored bracts with flowers protruding from among the overlapping scales.

In habitat, gingers often grow as understory plants, thriving in warm, humid enclaves, where they drip away the daily afternoon rains with the long, pointed tips of their foliage. In gardens the creeping rhizomes prosper in any moist soil that has been enriched with organic matter. For most varieties, open shade or part sun is ideal.

❧ *Sweet Snow*

The nearly hardy, large-flowered genus *Hedychium,* offers a dizzying range of beauty and variety. These elegant, cannalike perennials are cherished in the

South as ginger lilies or garland flowers. Their sweetly fragrant blossoms appear in exotic spikes borne at the tips of graceful, leafy stems. The four- to six-foot canes begin to bear flowers in the first weeks of summer and continue with increasing intensity until silenced by frost. A white-flowered species inspired the botanical name of the group, which means "sweet snow."

Most *Hedychium* are hardy wherever the ground does not freeze. In colder zones the roots may be taken up in autumn. Storage is best accomplished in pots of barely moist soil, assuring that the roots never dry completely. Flowering improves if the clumps are lifted and thinned every three or four years. The branched, creeping rhizomes may be divided in early spring before growth begins. The roots should be planted shallowly, with soil just covering the thick tubers. A good autumn mulch may be applied, or the dried foliage of the previous summer may be left to help shield the roots from penetrating frost.

❦ *Butterflies*

The irregularly shaped blooms of *Hedychium* species have enlarged, often beautifully marked upper segments, which give them the appearance of orchids or colorful insects. This exotic character is particularly eye-catching in the favorite of the group, the white butterfly ginger (*Hedychium coronarium*). The two-inch, snowy blossoms, appearing a few at a time, emit the most alluring fragrance of any summer flower—sweet and intense, yet always refreshing. In Hawaii the soft-petaled blooms are strung in leis and used to make perfume. In its native India it is considered the most charming of gingers.

The common strain of *H. coronarium* is white, with a greenish, heart-shaped "eye" in the center of the upper segment, or lip. In the variety *chrysoleucum* this central spot is glowing yellow. The similar yellow ginger lily (*H. flavescens*) produces blossoms that are entirely yellow, with light orange-toned eyes. These flowers are especially fragrant and slightly larger than those of the white butterfly, expanding up to three inches across.

❦ *Bottlebrushes*

Other species of *Hedychium* group their blossoms into large spikes of smaller, spidery blossoms, which often have long, projecting stamens and resemble bottlebrushes. They are very attractive to hummingbirds and butterflies.

The richest colors among these belong to *H. coccineum,* a narrow-leafed species from India and Burma. The six-inch floral spikes are composed of small, slender blooms. In the standard variety *carneum,* the blooms vary from pink to coral, with extending reddish stamens. The best clones of the vibrant variety *angustifolium* approach cinnabar.

The orange delta ginger (*H. greenei*) enjoys moist, shady positions, where its lush, five-foot canes develop into flourishing stands of polished foliage. The backs of its leaves reveal a handsome, dark red coloring, complementing five-inch spikes of fiery orange flowers with dark red lips.

Kahili ginger (*H. gardnerianum*) borrows its name from the plumed standards carried in native processions before Hawaii's kings. This giant of a plant attracts attention with its broad, blue-green foliage, forming canes up to six feet tall. In late summer the lemony, precisely spaced flowers appear in foot-tall spikes, with bright red, two-inch stamens extending outward into the air. These magisterial heads of bloom radiate a heavenly aroma and shame any lesser flowers foolish enough to bloom nearby. 'Fiesta', a beautiful hybrid from Margaret Kane of San Antonio, is similar to this, but with drooping foliage and red-throated, deep yellow blooms.

The white pincushion ginger (*H. thyrsiforme*) offers pale bottlebrushes made up of tiny, all-white flowers. Pointed butterfly ginger (*H. spicatum*) presents creamy spikes of bloom accented with reddish stamens. The large leaves are slightly hairy beneath. In *H. ellipticum* yellowish blossoms combine with purple filaments.

🦋 *Pastels*

For the lover of warm pastels, there are delectable species of *Hedychium* and a vast, confusing array of hybrids. *H. aurantiacum* is orange in bud, opening peach, with reddish stamens. A popular older hybrid, *H. × kewense*, comes from the yellow Kahili and orange-red *H. coccineum*. It features rich, coral pink blossoms set against lush, blue-green foliage. The flesh-colored 'Kinkaku', the soft salmon 'Pink V', and the creamy rose 'Pradhani' are additional warm-toned hybrids. 'Samsheri' underscores coral blossoms with deeper coral stamens.

🦋 *Curcuma*

After these showy-flowering varieties, the hardiest and most commonly planted gingers are various forms of *Curcuma*. The soft, bananalike leaves of *Curcuma* give these heat lovers a very different character from *Hedychium*. Only the cone-like structure of the flowering stems reveals their family alliance. In some species this is borne at the tip of the leafy stalk during summer, but in others it appears separately, before the leaves emerge in spring.

These tough, deciduous plants grow from rounded, swollen rhizomes with wiry masses of brown roots and clusters of pungent, aromatic tubers. In India and Southeast Asia, several *Curcuma* are raised for these edible roots. Although the globular swellings contain food and moisture, helping the plants endure dormancy and drought, they do not have the capacity to form stems on their own. When dividing *Curcuma* for the garden, it is essential to have a piece of the crown rhizome, which carries the buds from which leaves may grow.

The wide, pleated blades of foliage rise directly from the ground, arranging themselves in opposite ranks like gigantic oriental fans. The leafstalks overlap to form a short false stem, giving these plants their bananalike character. Although tender in appearance, most *Curcuma* are hardy in the middle and lower South and will stand dry storage in winter.

The most common varieties in older Southern gardens are the giant plume of Burma (*Curcuma elata*) and the very similar Indian *C. latifolia*. When well grown, the robust, pale green leaves of giant plume reach four feet or more. The foliage of *C. latifolia* gets even taller and bears a light purplish stripe down the center. When touched on the undersides of the leaves, both species exhibit a silky, felted texture.

Before the foliage emerges in early summer, green, violet-topped cones sprout from the bare earth like fantastic mushrooms. These brilliant masses of colored bracts obscure the small, pale yellow true flowers, but the effect is spectacular and lasts for several weeks, until the leaves sprout from the ground. These robust plants announce spring with a uniquely exotic flair.

Zedoary (*C. zedoaria*) is a similar spring-flowering variety with slightly smaller leaves marked by dark purplish red stains. This is one of the *Curcuma* cultivated for food in the East Indies. The pungent leaves are used to wrap fish, imparting a pleasant, gingerlike flavor to food when steamed.

The favorite summer-flowering *Curcuma* is the hidden ginger, or queen lily (*C. petiolata*). This Burmese variety stays less than two feet tall and forms lovely masses of broad, pale green leaves. Gardeners may willingly sacrifice some of these to better reveal the rosy purple, pink, and green cones. Sitting on six-inch stems hidden down amongst the foliage, the cones last for many weeks in midsummer, while the pale yellowish flowers take turns emerging between the bracts.

The Indian saffron ginger (*C. domestica*) is a similar species with whitish cones, famous as the source of turmeric, an essential ingredient of curry powder. The rhizomes of *C. domestica* are bright yellow and are used as a dye in India.

Most fabulous of all is the pride of Burma (*C. roscoeana*). The fiery terra-cotta bracts of this magnificent Asian coalesce into tight, glistening spires up to eight inches long. These glow in the midst of graceful, emerald green leaves for many weeks of summer. Unlike other *Curcuma*, this queenly native of the Irrawaddy River delta prefers light, sandy soils. It is apt to rot away over winter if left in heavy ground. The pride of Burma is hardy only in the warmest parts of the South, but it thrives as a summer pot plant or bedding subject in a rich, loamy mix of peat, coarse sand, and compost.

❧ *Peacocks*

Perhaps because they are smaller, less-dramatic plants than *Hedychium* or *Curcuma*, the remarkably diverse *Kaempferia* are less widely planted. This is a foolish oversight from gardeners, for the beautifully marked foliage of these plants recommends them for wide use in shady borders. In the lower South, where shade perennials such as hostas sulk in heat and humidity, *Kaempferia* offers a lavish, leafy alternative. The many species come from Southeast Asia and tropical Africa and are known as peacock gingers. Nearly all have beautiful leaves variegated with zones of color. The rhizomes multiply at a rapid pace, so there are always plenty of tubers to share or experiment with in the garden.

The one modestly tall member of this genus is the resurrection lily, or tropical crocus (*Kaempferia rotunda*), reaching eighteen inches with its paired, long-stemmed leaves. These are deciduous and pleated like *Curcuma* but share the attractive markings common to their group. The underside is dark purple, with silver-toned variegations on the upper surface.

Costus sp.

Alpinia zerumbet 'Variegata'

Left to right: *Curcuma elata*,
Crinum procerum 'Splendens',
and *Crinum amabile*

Costus speciosus

Globba bulbifera

Globba winittii

In early spring this species carpets the ground with fragrant, white and lavender flowers, looking remarkably like colonies of soft-petaled crocuses. These blossoms have the gentle texture of African violets, making a beautiful scene in the foreground of a shady border. This is one of the hardiest *Kaempferia* and will endure hard frost if mulched over winter. In Southeast Asia the young leaves, shoots, and tender rhizomes are steamed and eaten with rice.

The dwarf species of *Kaempferia* hug the earth, making good groundcovers for rich, shady beds in the lower South. Small blooms appear sporadically through summer among the leaves and, though not spectacular, add to the quiet beauty of the plants. These plants are rarely without flower from early summer till frost.

K. roscoeana is typical, forming prostrate rosettes of six-inch, saucer-shaped leaves. Dark green and marked with pale bands, these leaves provide a backdrop to a succession of small, white blooms. The closely related *K. pulchra* has white-spotted leaves and purple flowers. Other species display charming foliage with white margins, bronze shadings, or wavy, rippled effects.

🦋 *Dancing Girls*

The fancifully named dancing girls (*Globba* spp.) enjoy the same generous growing conditions as the dwarf *Kaempferia*, but these small, leafy gingers develop upright stems more like *Hedychium*.

The yellow dancing girl (*Globba bulbifera*) offers long-lasting sprays of tiny, golden blooms, which carry through most of the summer. They are borne at the tips of twelve- to eighteen-inch stalks furnished with dusty, blue-green leaves. The pendulous flower clusters develop numerous small bulbils, which, gathered and planted, flower in less than a year.

The mauve dancing girl (*Globba winitii*) sports an even more vibrant combination of purplish bracts and cascading, yellow flowers. It lacks the thrifty bulbils, but the rhizomes multiply steadily and may be divided at any time. Other *Globba* varieties include purple globe (*G. globulifera*), with a rounded cluster of purple flowers, and narrow-leaf dancing girl (*G. marantina*), with red-spotted blooms.

🦋 *Spirals*

The spiral flags (*Costus* spp.) are made of stronger stuff than these *Globba* diminutives and enjoy positions in full or part sun. Their sturdy, helical stems carry aloft the terminal, sometimes colorful floral cones. From these emerge conspicuous, textured blossoms with gracefully formed lips. Innumerable *Costus* species occur in tropical Africa and Latin America. They adapt to a wide range of garden soils and propagate quickly from seed or division. Stem cuttings, which may be taken in summer, root easily in ordinary potting soil. Although naturally evergreen, the most vigorous *Costus* species resprout lustily when cut back by hard frost.

Crepe ginger (*Costus speciosus*) reaches a height of nearly ten feet when well grown, bearing especially rich, waxy foliage. Its five-inch flower heads are formed by masses of wine-purple bracts. Through several weeks of summer, the white, funnel-shaped blooms protrude from the cones, displaying delicate, crepe-textured lips. A creamy striped form, 'Variegata', is less vigorous but looks especially striking, with its gently curving stems of white-splashed leaves.

The orange-flowered fiery spiral of Brazil (*C. igneus*) is one of the few spiral gingers enjoying cool shade. It is hardier than most varieties but lacks the large, bracted cones. It makes up for this deficiency with especially vibrant blossoms.

Less hardy varieties include the blood spiral (*C. erythrophyllum*), one of several species with yellow, red-edged blossoms, and the red tower ginger (*C. barbatus*), which combines bronzy cones with yellow flowers. Bumpy cone (*C. spiralis*) is a stout, West Indian spiral flag with large, shiny foliage and rose red cones and flowers. The dwarf yellow trumpet (*Monocostus uniflorus*) is a related ginger with a delicate, short spiral and large, yellow blossoms.

🦐 *Pinecones*

Although not brilliant in flower, the most architecturally satisfying gingers belong to the genus *Zingiber*. These delightful perennials commonly bear flowers exerted from the scales of dense, bracted cones. The cones are borne on leafless shoots separate from the sheltering, overhanging, leafy stems.

A hardy member of this group, the Japanese ginger or mioga (*Zingiber mioga*) is a handsome, deciduous perennial with lance-shaped, aromatic leaves and pungent, edible rhizomes. In Hawaii the bracts of the conelike flower clusters are sliced as a relish, and in Japan the orchidlike, yellow flowers are savored in tempura. Although this species should thrive widely in the Southeast, it is rarely cultivated. A close cousin is the true culinary ginger, *Z. officinale*, which is hardy only in the warmest parts of the South.

For garden ornament the most decorative species is the red pinecone ginger (*Z. zerumbet*). In midsummer this splendid subtropical sends up numerous foot-high stems bearing the greenish flowering cones. When squeezed, these emit a sudsy, aromatic juice used in Southeast Asia as a shampoo. After the small, white flowers finish peeking from between the scales, the cone slowly turns vibrant red.

Pinecone gingers revel in filtered light, and the creeping roots will ramble freely among ferns or other loose groundcovers. Although the individual stems are several feet long, they bow back to the earth so that they rarely exceed three feet. Over time, a graceful sea of arching stems fills the background of a shady garden, building a serene vision of woodland exuberance.

There is a very beautiful variegated form of red pinecone ginger called 'Darcey'. Its glossy green leaves, edged with creamy marginal stripes, are worthy of a sheltered, shady nook.

Another herbal relation, the dwarf, or cluster, cardamom (*Amomum compactum*) makes an attractive, dense mound of dark green, cinnamon-scented leaves. These slender-stemmed plants, reaching two feet in height, give a cool green look to shady summer borders. Inconspicuous flowers appear on short stems held near the ground. In Java the pungent fruits are chewed to sweeten the breath.

❧ *Shells*

In the warm regions where they can be grown, the shell gingers (*Alpinia* spp.) are highly regarded for their foliage and flowers. Even the most cold-hardy *Alpinia* varieties suffer badly, however, if frozen to the ground, for their blooms appear only from the tips of second-year stems. Nevertheless, along the latitude of the Gulf, a surprising number of gardens hold sheltered positions suited to these grand perennials.

The pink porcelain lily (*Alpinia zerumbet*) is certainly worth any effort. Dense clumps of smooth, long-bladed, leathery leaves are held on its showy canes. Reaching upward to twelve feet, the leaves dispose themselves like flowers in a brimming vase. These majestic perennials show tremendous vigor and tolerate drought and sun better than most gingers. If given a mild winter or a frost-sheltered position, abundant flower buds appear in spring.

These buds hang from the tips of the outstretched stems like bunches of porcelain grapes. They open one at a time over several weeks, expanding bell-shaped, waxy lips, tipped with delicate red and yellow markings. The pendulous clusters of iridescent bloom underscore the cover-girl quality of the shell ginger, which has been the subject of countless photographs in books on tropical horticulture.

A creamy yellow-striped form of *A. zerumbet* possesses one of the most satisfying variegations of garden perennials. An extraordinary golden pin-striped ginger is a form of the closely related *A. formosana*.

Although these subtropical plants fall outside the realm of ordinary garden perennials, pushing horticultural boundaries often brings gardeners their greatest satisfactions. With modest encouragement, these exotics breathe renewed life into lusterless summer borders. Gingers, like all bulbous flowers, offer themselves as instruments of garden magic. Learning to create a symphony from their varied timbres is the pleasant challenge faced by the gardeners of the South.

Appendix

🌺 Southern Bulb Culture

The Southern climate offers occasional droughts, but rain is distributed more or less evenly through the year. A hurricane or similarly large deluge might visit anytime. Humidity remains high during the summer, and the ground holds warmth over a long season. Winters and springs are capricious and unpredictable, with a mix of cold, wetness, and wind. For the bulb gardener this environment presents certain challenges, but it may also present advantages to various plants. Cultivation follows in accordance with the origins of the bulb varieties.

🌺 Mediterranean Beds

Bulbs that come from southern Europe, Asia Minor, the Cape province of South Africa, and California usually accomplish most of their growth during winter and spring months, when moisture is readily available. They receive little rainfall during their long summer dormancy. These plants sometimes succumb to soil fungi or bacteria if kept moist through summer. A raised bed of gravelly earth, simulating the dry summer habitat of these winter-rainfall plants, affords them congenial homes in the humid South.

Where heavy clay soils prevail, it is a simple matter to construct raised beds of rubble, sand, or decomposed granite to accommodate these drought-loving varieties. Once built and planted, these "Mediterranean beds" require only minimum maintenance. They greatly extend the variety of bulbs that may be cultivated.

A bed eighteen to twenty-four inches tall is sufficient to accommodate a wide range of bulbs. Attractive edgings of stone flags or boulders can help consolidate the mounded plantings, as well as offer valuable niches and crevices in which to nestle dwarf corms and tubers like crocuses and oxalises. A thin mulch of composted bark, dried leaves, or stony gravel should be spread over the well-drained bed substrate to dress up the bed and get the plantings off to a good start. Since the purpose of these beds is discouragement of summer rot, nitrogen fertilizers and manures should be avoided.

Many bulbs enjoy these types of raised beds. Spring starflowers (*Ipheion uniflorum*) are easy and permanent on raised mounds of sand. These low-growing clumpers bear light blue flowers from late winter through spring and make good plants for an informal edging. Daffodils of the *Narcissus cyclamineus* section (Division VI), such as 'Peeping Tom', 'February Gold', and 'March Sunshine', enjoy deep beds of sand or crushed granite. The tiny, fragrant *N. jonqilla* is easy and permanent on sand, if well watered during its growing season.

Some subtropical bulbs also enjoy these Mediterranean beds—× *Amarcrinum*, *Lycoris africana*, and *Pancratium maritimum* all benefit from this type of culture.

🐚 *Bulbs for Hog Wallows*

It's a widely accepted and repeated horticultural myth that all bulbs require good drainage. Fortunately for Southerners who contend with tight clays, no claim could be more exaggerated. Many bulbs receive summer rains in their native habitats and seem to thrive on rich, mucky soils. The seasonal "buffalo wallows" of the American prairies and the temporary pans or *vleis* of African savannahs are examples of such environments. These habitats offer distinctively adapted bulbs geared to grow in concert with alternating surfeits and deficits of moisture.

Many spring-blooming bulbs come from soggy homes and have the capacity to grow in waterlogged soils during the cool spring months. Such flowers as summer snowflake (*Leucojum aestivum*), Dutch iris (*Iris* × *hollandica*), Naples onion (*A. neapolitanum*), large-flowered buttercup (*Ranunculus macranthus*), and jonquil hybrids such as 'Trevithian' will bloom happily even in standing water. The strong growing, old-fashioned campernelle narcissus, the tazetta variety 'Grand Primo', white French-Roman hyacinths, Byzantine gladioli, and virgin's spray (*Ornithogalum narbonense*) are also good on heavy ground.

Such summer bulbs as *Colocasia*, *Zephyranthes*, *Crinum*, *Hymenocallis*, and *Canna* develop fleshy roots especially adapted to waterlogged conditions. Many plants in the ginger and iris families also thrive on swampy ground. All of these may be freely fed with rich manures and composts.

A Review
of Garden Bulbs
for the South

ACHIMENES Pers. (Gesneriaceae)
Fifty species native to tropical
America
Achimenes candida
—coccinea
cv. 'Major'
—grandiflora
cv. 'Atropurpurea'
—longiflora

AGAPANTHUS L'Her. (Liliaceae)
Ten species native to southern
Africa
Agapanthus africanus
cv. 'Henryae'
cv. 'Mooreanus' ('Minor')
—campanulatus
cv. 'Headbourne Hybrids'
—orientalis (*A. umbellatus*)
cv. 'Albatross'
cv. 'Albus'
cv. 'Blue Skyrocket'
cv. 'Flore Pleno'
cv. 'Peter Pan'
cv. 'Variegatus'

ALLIUM L. (Liliaceae)
A genus with approximately five
hundred species native to the
northern hemisphere

White-flowered species
Allium canadense
—cepa
cv. 'Proliferum' ("Egyptian
onion")
—fraseri
—texanum

—tuberosum
—neapolitanum
cv. 'Grandiflorum' (*A. cowanii*)
—subhirsutum

Pink-flowered species
Allium ampeloprasum
cv. 'Elephant garlic'
cv. *porrum*
—drummondi
—ecristatum (*A. canadense* v. *ecristatum*)
—hyacinthoides (*A. canadense* v.
hyacinthoides)
—mobilense (*A. canadense* v. *mobilense*)
—sativum
—schoenoprasum
—sphaerocephalum
—stellatum
—zenobiae (*A. canadense* v. *zenobiae*)

Yellow-flowered species
Allium coryi
—flavum
—moly

ALOCASIA L. (Araceae)
Seventy species of tuberous
perennials native to tropical Asia
Alocasia macrorhiza
cv. 'Jungle Gold'
cv. 'Variegata'
—plumbea (*A. indica* v. *metallica*)
— × amazonica

ALOPHIA Herb. (Iridaceae)
About five species native to
Mexico, Guatemala, and the
southern United States

Alophia purpurea
—*veracruzana*

ALPINIA Roxb. (Zingiberaceae)
Over 250 species of tuberous
perennial herbs native to
tropical Asia
Alpinia formosana
cv. 'Variegata'
—*zerumbet*
cv. 'Variegata'

ALSTROEMERIA
L. (Alstroemeriaceae)
About fifty species native to
South America
Alstroemeria braziliensis
—*psittacina* (*A. pulchella*)

× **AMARCRINUM Coutts**
(Amaryllidaceae)
Bigeneric hybrid of *Crinum
moorei* and *Amaryllis belladonna*,
formerly called × *Crinodonna*
× *Amarcrinum*
cv. 'Fred Howard'

AMARYLLIS L. (Amaryllidaceae)
One species native to southern
Africa, closely related to and
sometimes included in *Brunsvigia*
Amaryllis belladonna
— × *parkeri*

AMIANTHIUM A. Gray
(Liliaceae)
One species native to eastern
North America, allied to *Zigadenus*
Amianthium muscaetoxicum

AMOMUM Roxb. (Zingiberaceae)
Over one hundred species of
tuberous, aromatic perennials
native to tropical Asia
Amomum compactum

AMOREUXIA DeCandolle
(Cochlospermaceae)
A genus of seven species native
to warm parts of the Americas
Amoreuxia wrightii

AMORPHOPHALLUS Blume ex
Decne (Araceae)
About ninety species of tuberous
perennials native to the Old
World tropics
Amorphophallus rivieri (*Hydrosme
rivieri*)
cv. 'Konjac'

ANDROSTEPHIUM Torr.
(Liliaceae)
Two species of cormous flowers
native to western North
America
Androstephium coeruleum

ANEMONE L. (Ranunculaceae)
A large genus including 150
species worldwide, with
tuberous varieties native to the
Mediterranean region and to the
grasslands of North and South
America
Anemone appenina
—*biflora*
—*blanda*
—*caroliniana*
—*coronaria*
cv. 'De Caen'
cv. 'St. Brigid'
—*edwardsiana*
—*heterophylla*
—*hortensis*
cv. 'St. Bavo'
—*nemorosa*
— × *fulgens*

**ANEMONELLA Spach.
(Ranunculaceae)**
>One species native to eastern
>North America
>*Anemonella thalictroides*

ANREDERA Juss. (Basellaceae)
>Ten species of tuberous vines
>native to the warm parts of the
>Americas
>*Anredera cordifolia*

ARISAEMA Mart. (Araceae)
>About 150 species native to
>temperate Asia and North
>America
>*Arisaema candidissimum*
>—*draconitum*
>—*flavum*
>—*macrospathum*
>—*quinatum*
>—*triphyllum*

ARISTEA Aiton (Iridaceae)
>About fifty species of
>fibrous-rooted African perennials
>*Aristea ecklonii*

ARUM L. (Araceae)
>Fifteen species native to Europe
>and the Mediterranean region
>*Arum creticum*
>—*italicum*
>>cv. 'Marmoratum'
>—*maculatum*
>>var. *immaculatum*
>—*palestinum*
>—*pictum*

ASPARAGUS L. (Liliaceae)
>Three hundred species of
>tuberous perennials native to
>the Old World

Asparagus densiflorus
>cv. 'Myers'
>cv. 'Sprengeri'
—*falcatus*
—*filicinus*
—*officinalis*
>var. *pseudoscaber*
>cv. 'Spitzenschleier'
—*setaceus*
—*tenuifolius*
—*virgatus*

BEGONIA L. (Begoniaceae)
>Over 900 species in the warm
>regions of the world
>*Begonia crassicaulis*
>—*grandis* (*B. evansiana*)
>—*heracleifolia*
>>cv. 'Selph's Mahogany'

BELAMCANDA Adans. (Iridaceae)
>Two species of tuberous,
>clumping perennials native
>to the Far East
>*Belamcanda chinensis*

BESSERA Schult. f. (Liliaceae)
>Two species of cormous herbs
>native to western and southern
>Mexico
>*Bessera elegans*

BLETILLA Rchb. f. (Orchidaceae)
>Nine species of terrestrial herbs
>with tuberous rhizomes native to
>China and Japan
>*Bletilla striata*

BOMAREA Mirb. (Alstroemeriaceae)
>More than one hundred species
>of twining, rhizomatous
>perennials native to the
>highlands of tropical America
>*Bomarea edulis*

BRODIAEA (L. see *TRITELEIA,*
DICHELOSTEMMA)

CALADIUM Venten (Araceae)
 About fifteen species native to
 tropical America
Caladium albanense
—*bicolor*
—*humboltii* (*C. argyrites*)
— × *hortulanum*
 cv. 'Candidum'

CALOSTEMMA R. Br.
(Amaryllidaceae)
 Three or four species of
 Australian bulbs related to
 Pancratium
Calostemma purpurea

CAMASSIA Lindl. (Liliaceae)
 Five species native to North
 America, related to Old World
 genus *Scilla;* one species native
 to the South
Camassia scilloides

CANNA L. (Cannaceae)
 About sixty species native to
 warm parts of Asia and the
 Americas
Canna childsii
 cv. 'Cleopatra'
—*edulis*
—*flaccida*
—*glauca*
 cv. 'Erebus'
—*indica*
—*iridiflora*
 cv. 'Ehemanni'
—*limbata* (*aureo-vitatta*)
 cv. 'Striped Beauty'
 cv. 'Pretoria'

—*liliflora*
—*warscewiczii*
 cv. 'Robusta'

CIPURA Aubl. (Iridaceae)
 Two or three species native to
 tropical America
Cipura paludosa

COLCHICUM L. (Liliaceae)
 Seventy species native to
 Europe and the Near East
Colchicum autumnale
—*psaridis*

COLOCASIA Fabr. (Araceae)
 About six species of tuberous
 perennials native to tropical Asia
Colocasia esculenta
 cv. 'Chicago Harlequin'
 cv. 'Illustris'
 cv. 'Jet Black Wonder'
 cv. 'Red Dot'
—*esculenta*
 var. *aquatilis*

COMMELINA L. (Commelinaceae)
 Over one hundred species of
 tuberous perennials spread
 widely around the world
Commelina erecta

COSTUS L. (Zingiberaceae)
 About 150 species of tuberous
 perennial herbs native to the
 tropics of the world
Costus barbatus
—*erythrophyllum*
—*igneus*
—*speciosus*
—*spiralis*
 cv. 'Variegata'

CRINUM L. (Amaryllidaceae)

About one hundred and thirty species native to warm regions around the world

Species with slender, spreading flowers (subgenus *Crinum*)

Crinum americanum
    var. *loddigessianum*
—*amoenum*
—*asiaticum*
—*erubescens* (*C. americanum* 'Robustum')
    cv. West Indies Mini-Crinum
—*flaccidum*
—*japonicum*
—*pedunculatum*
—*pratense*
—*procerum*
    cv. 'Splendens'
—*xanthophyllum*
— × *amabile* (*C. augustum*)

Species with trumpet-shaped flowers (subgenus *Codonocrinum*)

Crinum bulbispermum (*C. capense*, *C. longifolium*)
    cv. 'Alba'
    cv. 'Sacramento'
—*jagus*
    cv. 'Christopher Lily'
    cv. 'Maya Moon'
    cv. 'Rattrayi'
—*macowanii*
—*moorei*
    var. *Schmidtii*
—*scabrum*
—*yemense*
—*zeylanicum*
— × *baconi*
— × *digweedii*
— × *goweni*
— × *herbertii* (*C. sanderianum*, *C. kunthianum*)
    cv. 'Carroll Abbott'

— × *powellii*
    cv. 'Album'
    cv. 'Cecil Howdyshel'
— × *worsleyi*

CROCOSMIA Planchon (Iridaceae)

Six species native to southern Africa, formerly included in *Tritonia*

Crocosmia aurea
—*masoniorum*
—*pottsii*
— × *crocosmiiflora*
    cv. 'Solfatere'
— × *Curtonus paniculatus*
    cv. 'Lucifer'

CROCUS L. (Iridaceaea)

About eighty species of dwarf cormous herbs native to southern Europe and Asia

Spring-flowering species

Crocus ancyrensis
—*angustifolius* (*C. susianus*)
—*biflorus*
—*chrysanthus*
—*corsicus*
—*flavus* (*C. aureus*)
    cv. 'Dutch Yellow'
—*seiberi*
—*tomasinianus*
    cv. 'Albus'
    cv. 'Lilac Beauty'
    cv. 'Roseus'
    cv. 'Ruby Giant'

Fall-flowering species

Crocus goulimyi
—*kotschyanus* (*C. zonatus*)
    var. *leucopharynx*
—*laevigatus*
—*medius*
—*ochroleucus*
—*sativus*

C. speciosus
cv. 'Aitchisonii'
cv. 'Cassiope'

CURCUMA Roxb. (Zingiberaceae)
About seventy species of rhizomatous perennials native to tropical Asia

Curcuma elata
—*domestica*
—*latifolia*
—*petiolata*
—*roscoeana*
—*zedoaria*

CYCLAMEN L. (Primulaceae)
About fifteen species native to Europe and the Near East, all growing from large, flattened tubers

Cyclamen hederifolium (C. neapolitanum)
—*persicum*

CYPELLA Herb. (Iridaceae)
Twenty species of *Tigridia*-like bulbs native to warm parts of the Americas

Cypella herbertii
—*plumbea*
—*rosei*

CYRTANTHUS Aiton (Amaryllidaceae)
Fifty species of bulbs native to eastern and southern Africa

Cyrtanthus obrienii

DAHLIA L. (Compositae)
Twenty species native to Mexico and Central America

Dahlia coccinea
—*imperialis*
—*merckii*

DICHELOSTEMMA Heller (Liliaceae)
Six species native to western North America

Dichelostemma pulchellum

DICHORISANDRA Mikan f. (Commelinaceae)
Thirty species native to tropical America

Dichorisandra thyrsiflora

DIETES Salisb. ex Klatt. (Iridaceae)
About five species of rhizomatous perennials native to tropical and southern Africa

Dietes bicolor
—*vegeta (Moraea iridioides)*
cv. 'Lemon Drops'
cv. 'Orange Drops'

DIOSCOREA L. (Dioscoreaceae)
More than five hundred species of tuberous vines native to warm regions

Dioscorea batatas
—*bulbifera*
—*elephantipes*
—*glauca*
—*macrostachya*
—*sylvatica*

DRACUNCULUS Miller (Araceae)
Three species native to Europe and the Mediterranean region

Dracunculus vulgaris

DRIMIOPSIS (Liliaceae)
Small genus of *Scilla*-like bulbs native to southern Africa

Drimiopsis maculata

ELEUTHERINE (Iridaceae)
Two species of night-flowering bulbs native to tropical America,

now widely naturalized around
the world

Eleutherine plicata

ENDYMION (see HYACINTHOIDES)

ERYTHRONIUM L. (Liliaceae)

A small genus with about
twenty-five species in North
America and one in Eurasia

Erythronium albidum

—americanum

—rostratum

EUCHARIS Planch. (Amaryllidaceae)

About a dozen species of leafy,
bulbous herbs native to Central
and South America

Eucharis grandiflora (E. amazonica)

EUCOMIS L'Her. (Liliaceae)

About ten species native to
southern Africa

Eucomis bicolor

—pole-evansii

—punctata (E. comosa)

FREESIA Klatt (Iridaceae)

About ten species of cormous
herbs native to southern Africa

GALANTHUS L. (Amaryllidaceae)

A dozen species native to
Europe and Asia

Galanthus byzantinus

—elwesii

—nivalis

cv. 'Sam Arnott'
cv. 'Scharlockii'

GLADIOLUS L. (Iridaceae)

About 300 species native to Africa
and the Mediterranean basin

Gladiolus byzantinus

cv. 'Alba'

—callianthus (Acidanthera bicolor)

cv. 'Murielae'

—cardinalis

—communis

—imbricatus

—natalensis (G. psittacinus)

—papilio

—primulinus

—segetum

—tristis

— × colvillei

GLOBBA L. (Zingiberaceae)

Seventy species of rhizomatous
perennials native to tropical Asia

Globba bulbifera

—globulifera

—marantina

—winitii

GLORIOSA L. (Liliaceae)

Five species of tuberous
climbers in Africa and India

Gloriosa carsoni

—rothschildiana

—simplex (G. plantii)

—superba (G. virescens)

cv. 'Lutea'

— × greenei

cv. 'Wilhelmina Green'

GYNANDRIRIS Parl. (Iridaceae)

About twenty species of
cormous perennials in southern
Africa, one native to the
Mediterranean region

Gynandriris sisrynchium

HABRANTHUS Herb. (Amaryllidaceae)

About forty species distributed
from South America to Mexico
and Texas

Habranthus brachyandrus
—*cardinalis* (*Zephyranthes bifolia*)
—*concolor*
—*gracilifolius* (*H. estensis*)
—*howardii* (*Zephyranthes howardii*)
—*immaculatus*
—*juncifolius*
—*martinezii*
—*robustus*
   cv. 'Russel Manning'
—*tubispathus*
   var. *texensis*
   var. *roseus*
—*vittatus*
—× *floryi*

HAEMANTHUS (see *SCADOXUS*)

HAYLOCKIA Herb.
(Amaryllidaceae)
Four species native to Bolivia
and Uruguay
Haylockia americana

HEDYCHIUM J. König.
(Zingiberaceae)
About fifty species of perennial
herbs native to tropical Asia and
the Himalayas
Hedychium aurantiacum
—*coccineum*
   var. *augustifolium*
   var. *carneum*
—*coronarium*
—*greenei*
—*ellipticum*
—*flavescens* (*H. flavum*)
—*gardnerianum*
—*spicatum*
—*thyrsiforme*
—× *kewense*

HERBERTIA Sweet (Iridaceae)
About ten species of blue-
flowered bulbs native to warm
parts of the Americas

Herbertia amatorum
—*lahue*
   var. *drummondii*
—*pulchella*

HERMODACTYLUS Salisb.
(Iridaceae)
One species native to the
Mediterranean region
Hermodactylus tuberosus (*Iris tuberosa*)

HIPPEASTRUM Herb.
(Amaryllidaceae)
About seventy-five species
native mostly to South America,
formerly *Amaryllis*

Subgenus *Macropodastrum*
—*brasiliensis*
—*parodii*
   cv. 'Germa'
—× *Johnsonii*

Subgenus *Lais*
—*blossfeldiae*
—*petiolatum*
—*striatum*
   cv. 'Fulgida'
—*vittatum*

Subgenus *Aschamia*
—*puniceum* (*Amaryllis belladonna*)
   cv. 'Charm'
   cv. 'Semiplenum' ('Albertii')
—*evansiae*
   cv. 'Yellow Pioneer'
—*reginae*
—*reticulatum*
   var. *striatifolium*
   cv. 'Mrs. Garfield'
—*traubii*
   var. *doranianum*

Subgenus *Omphalissa*
—*angustifolium*
—*aulicum*
—*bukasovii*

—*calyptratum*
—*iguazuanum*
—*papilio*
—*psittacinum*
—× *Ackermannii*

Subgenus *Cephaleon*
—*cybister*
—*leopoldii* (*H. neoleopoldii*)
  cv. 'Sumac Pinini' ('Spotty')
—*pardina*

× *HIPPESTRALIA*
(Amaryllidaceae)
  Bigeneric hybrid of *Hippeastrum*
  and *Sprekelia*
× *Hippestralia*
  cv. 'Mystique'

HOMERIA **Vent. (Iridaceae)**
  About forty species native to
  southern Africa
Homeria breyniana (*H. collina*)

HYACINTHOIDES **Medicus**
(Liliaceae)
  Three species in western
  Europe, formerly included in
  Scilla
Hyacinthoides hispanica (*Scilla
  campanulata, Endymion hispanica*)
—*non-scripta*

HYACINTHUS **L. (Liliaceae)**
  Three species native to central
  Asia and the eastern
  Mediterranean
Hyacinthus orientalis
  var. *albulus*

HYMENOCALLIS **Salisb.**
(Amaryllidaceae)
  Seventy or more species native
  to tropical and warm temperate
  America

**South American species (*Ismene
and Elisena*)**
Hymenocallis amancaes
  cv. 'Sulfur Queen'
—*heliantha*
—*longipetala*
  cv. 'Festalis'
—*narcissiflora* (*Ismene calathina*)
  cv. 'Advance'
—*pedunculata* (*Ismene macleana*)

Tropical Carribean species
Hymenocallis acutifolia
  var. *riparia*
—*caribaea*
—*imperialis*
—*latifolia* (*H. pedalis*)
  cv. 'Variegata' (*H. caribaea*
  'Variegata')
—*littoralis*
  cv. 'The Clumper'
—sp. "Tropical Giant"
—*speciosa*
  cv. 'Daphne'
—*tenuiflora*

Mexican deciduous species
Hymenocallis araniflora
—*azteciana*
—*cleo* (*H. chiapasiana*)
—*eucharidifolia*
—*glauca* (*H. choretis*)
—*guerreroensis*
—*harrisiana*
—*leavenworthii*
—*maximiliani*
—*sonorensis*

Southeastern U.S. species
Hymenocallis caroliniana
—*coronaria*
—*floridana*
—*galvestonensis* (*H. eulae, Choretis
  galvestonensis*)
—*liriosme*
—*palmeri*

—*rotata*
—*traubii*
   cv. 'Excelsior'

HYPOXIS L. (Hypoxidaceae)
Over one hundred species,
mostly native to the southern
hemisphere
Hypoxis hirsuta
—*decumbens*

IPHEION Raf. (Liliaceae)
Ten or twenty species of
onion-scented bulbs native to
South America
Ipheion uniflorum
   cv. 'Alba'
   cv. 'Froyle Mill'
   cv. 'Rolf Fielder'
   cv. 'Violaceum'
   cv. 'Wisley Blue'

IRIS L. (Iridaceae)
Three hundred species of
bulbous and tuberous flowers
distributed over the northern
hemisphere

Beardless irises
Iris brevicaulis (*I. foliosa*)
—*crocea* (*I. aurea*)
—*ensata*
—*foetidissimma*
   cv. 'Lutea'
   cv. 'Variegata'
—*fulva*
—*giganticaerulea*
—*graminea*
—*hexagona*
—*lazica*
—*monnieri*
—*nelsonii*
—*orientalis* (*I. ochroleucus*)

—*pseudacorus*
   cv. 'Flore Pleno'
   cv. 'Variegata'
—*sambucina*
—*siberica*
—*unguicularis*
—*verna*
—*virginica*

Crested irises
Iris confusa
   cv. 'Nada'
—*cristata*
—*japonica*
   cv. 'Uwodu'
   cv. 'Variegata'
—*tectorum*
   var. *alba*

Bearded irises
Iris albicans
   cv. 'Madonna'
—*florentina*
—*germanica*
   cv. 'Nepalensis'
   ('Atropurpurea')
—*kochii*
—*pallida*
   cv. 'Dalmatica'
   cv. 'Variegata'
—*susiana*
—*variegata*

Bulbous irises
Iris danfordiae
—*latifolia*
—*persica*
—*reticulata*
—*tingitiana*
   cv. 'Wedgwood'
—*vartanii*
   cv. 'Alba'
—*xiphium*
— × *hollandica*

IXIA L. (Iridaceae)
Sixty species of cormous perennials native to southern Africa

JATROPHA L. (Euphorbiaceae)
About 130 species of perennial herbs and shrubs native to tropical America, Africa, and Asia, several species developing large, succulent tubers
Jatropha cathartica

KAEMPFERIA L. (Zingiberaceae)
More than fifty species of dwarf, tuberous perennials native to tropical Asia and Africa
Kaempferia pulchra
—*roscoeana*
—*rotunda*

LAPEIROUSIA Tourn. (Iridaceae)
Fifty species native to Southern Africa and the highlands of east Africa
Lapeirousia laxa (*Anomatheca cruenta*)
cv. 'Alba'

LEOPOLDIA (Liliaceae)
A small genus of bulbs related to *Muscari* and native to the Mediterranean and western Asia
Leopoldia comosum (*Muscari comosum*)
cv. 'Plumosum' (*Muscari plumosum*)

LEUCOCORYNE Lindl. (Liliaceae)
Six species native to South America, principally Chile
Leucocoryne ixiodes

LEUCOJUM L. (Amaryllidaceae)
Eleven species native around the Mediterranean and the Near East

Leucojum autumnale
—*aestivum*
cv. 'Gravetye Giant'
—*vernum*

LILIUM L. (Liliaceae)
Eighty species distributed around the northern hemisphere

Division I: Asiatic hybrids
Division II: Hybrids of
L. martagon and L. hansonii
Division III: Candidum hybrids
Division IV: American hybrids
Division V: Hybrids of
L. longiflorum and L. formosanum
Division VI: Aurelian hybrids
Division VII: Oriental hybrids
Division VIII: Miscellaneous hybrids

Division IX: Species
Lilium auratum
—*brownii*
—*candidum*
cv. 'Limerick'
cv. 'Uprising'
—*catesbyi*
—*chalcedonicum*
—*formosanum* (*L. philippinense* v. *formosanum*)
—*grayi*
—*henryi*
cv. 'White Henryi'
—*iridollae*
—*lancifolium* (*L. tigrinum*)
cv. 'Fortunei'
—*leichtlinii*
—*leucanthum*
—*longiflorum*
cv. 'Croft'
var. *eximium*
—*michauxii*
—*sargentiae*
—*speciosum*
var. *rubrum*

—*sulfureum*
—*superbum*
—*regale*
— × *maculatum*
— × *testaceum*

LITTONIA Hook. (Liliaceae)

One species, a *Gloriosa*-like perennial native to southern Africa

Littonia modesta
  cv. 'Keitii'

LYCORIS Herb. (Amaryllidaceae)

Twenty or more species native to Japan, Korea, China, and Burma, often confused with *Nerine*

Spring-foliage species

Lycoris chinensis
—*haywardii*
—*incarnata*
—*sanguinea*
—*sprengeri*
—*squamigera*
—*straminea*

Fall-foliage species

Lycoris africana (*L. aurea*)
—*albiflora*
—*caldwellii*
—*elsiae*
—*howdyshelii*
—*radiata*
—*traubii*
— × *Jacksoniana*

MANFREDA Salisb. (Agavaceae)

Thirty species of succulent perennials native to the southern United States and Mexico

Manfreda longiflora
—*maculosa*
—sp. 'Maculata Gigantea'
—*sileri*

—*undulata*
—*variegata*
—*virginica*

MELANTHIUM L. (Liliaceae)

Five species native to North America

Melanthium virginicum

MILLA Cav. (Liliaceae)

About seven species of cormous herbs native to Mexico, Guatemala, and the southwest United States

Milla biflora
—*magnifica*

MONOCOSTUS (Zingiberaceae)

Rhizomatous tropical perennials related to *Costus*

Monocostus uniflorus

MONTBRETIA (see CROCOSMIA)

MORAEA L. (Iridaceae)

One hundred species of cormous herbs native to southern Africa, formerly included in *Iris*

Moraea polystachya

MUSCARI Miller (Liliaceae)

A genus of about sixty species native to Europe and western Asia

Muscari ambrosiacum
—*armeniacum*
—*botryoides*
  cv. 'Album'
—*neglectum* (*M. racemosum*, *M. atlanticum*)
—*tubergenianum*

MUSCARIMIA (Liliaceae)

Two or three species of Greek and Turkish bulbs related to *Muscari*

Muscarimia ambrosiacum (*Muscari ambrosiacum*)

—*moshatum* (*Muscari moschatum*)

NARCISSUS L. (Amaryllidaceae)

About forty species native around the Mediterranean and hundreds of garden forms

Division I: Trumpet narcissus

Division II: Large-cupped narcissus

Division III: Small-cupped narcissus

Division IV: Double narcissus

Division V: Triandrus narcissus

Division VI: Cyclamineus narcissus

Division VII: Jonquilla narcissus

Division VIII: Tazetta narcissus

Division IX: Poeticus narcissus

Division X: Species and wild hybrids

Subgenus *Eunarcissus*

Section *Jonquilleae*

Narcissus calcicola

—*fernandesii*

—*jonquilla*

cv. 'Queen Anne'

—*rupicola*

—*scaberulus*

—*viridiflorus*

Section *Ganymedes*

Narcissus triandrus

var. *albus*

var. *loiseleurii*

Section *Hermione*

Narcissus elegans

—*poeticus*

—*serotinus*

—*tazetta*

cv. 'Avalanche' ('Compressus')

cv. 'Grand Monarque'

cv. 'Grand Primo'

cv. 'Minor Monarque' (*N. tazetta* var. *italicus*)

cv. 'Pearl'

cv. 'Scilly White'

—*tazetta* var. *aureus*

cv. 'Soleil d'Or'

—*tazetta* var. *lacticolor*

cv. 'Canaliculatus'

—*tazetta* var. *orientalis*

cv. 'Double Roman' ('Constantinople')

—*tazetta* var. *papyraceus*

Subgenus *Ajax*

Narcissus cyclamineus

—*pseudonarcissus*

var. *moschatus* (*N. cernuus*)

Subgenus *Corbularia*

Narcissus bulbocodium

cv. 'Tenuifolius'

var. *citrinus*

var. *conspicuus*

var. *obesus*

—*cantabricus*

var. *foliosus*

cv. 'Nylon'

cv. 'Jessamy'

cv. 'Taffeta'

—*romieuxii*

cv. 'Julia Jane'

Wild hybrids

Narcissus × *biflorus*

— × *incomparabilis*

cv. 'Orange Phoenix' ("Eggs and Bacon")

× *intermedius*

— × *odorus* ('Campernelli')

— × *tenuior* ('Gracilis')

NEMASTYLIS Nutt. (Iridaceae)
Five species native to Mexico
and the southern United States
Nemastylis acuta (*N. geminiflora*)
—*floridana*
—*revoluta*

NEOMARICA T. Sprague
(Iridaceae)
Fifteen species of rhizomatous
perennials native to tropical
South America and west Africa
Neomarica caerulea
—*gracilis*
—*northiana*

NOTHOSCORDUM Kunth
(Liliaceae)
About thirty-five species of
onionlike, yet not odorous, bulbs
native to South America, with
one species ranging to North
America
Nothoscordum arenarium
—*bivalve*
—*inodorum* (*N. fragrans*)
—*montevidense*
—*nocturnum*

ORNITHOGALUM L. (Liliaceae)
Over 150 species in Europe,
southwest Asia, and southern
Africa
Ornithogalum arabicum
—*dubium*
—*maculatum*
—*narbonense* (*O. pyramidale*)
—*nutans*
—*saundersii*
—*thyrsoides*
—*umbellatum*

OXALIS L. (Oxalidaceae)
Over eight hundred species
native around the world, five
hundred in southern Africa

Pink- and white-flowered species
Oxalis corymbosa (*O. martiana*)
cv. 'Variegata'
—*crassipes*
cv. 'Alba'
—*deppei*
—*drummondii*
var. *vespertilionis*
—*latifolia*
—*nelsonii*
—*regnellii*
cv. 'Triangularis'
—*tetraphylla*
—*versicolor*
—*violacea*

Yellow-flowered species
Oxalis corniculata
—*pes-caprae* (*O. cernua*)
—*priceae*

PANCRATIUM L.
(Amaryllidaceae)
Twenty species native to coasts
of the Mediterranean, the
Canary Islands, Africa, and
tropical Asia
Pancratium canariense
—*illyricum*
—*maritimum*

× *PARDANCANDA* (Iridaceae)
Bigeneric cross of *Belamcanda
chinensis* and *Pardanthopsis
dichotoma*

PHILODENDRON Schott.
(Araceae)
About two hundred species of
vining herbs native to tropical
America, some with succulent,
thickened stems and roostocks
Philodendron selloum

PINELLIA (Araceae)

Five species of dwarf, rhizomatous herbs native to China and Japan

Pinellia pedatisecta
—*ternata*
—*tripartita*

POLIANTHES L. (Agavaceae)

Fifteen species native to western and southern Mexico

Polianthes geminiflora
—*howardii*
—*nelsoni*
—*palustris*
—*pringlei*
—*tuberosa*
    cv. 'Mexican Single'
    cv. 'Pearl'
    cv. 'Variegata'
— × *blissii*
— × *bundrandtii*

POLYGONATUM Mill. (Liliaceae)

About fifty species in the northern hemisphere

Polygonatum biflorum (*P. giganteum*)
—*falcatum* (*P. japonicum*)
    cv. 'Variegatum'

PYROLIRION Herb. (Amaryllidaceae)

Ten species in Peru and Bolivia

Pyrolirion aureum
—*flammeum*

RANUNCULUS L. (Ranunculaceae)

Around four hundred species in the northern hemisphere, tuberous varieties native to the Mediterranean and southwestern North America

Ranunculus asiaticus
—*macranthus*

RHODOHYPOXIS Nel. (Hypoxidaceae)

About six species of cormous herbs native to southern Africa

Rhodohypoxis baurii

RHODOPHIALA Pres. (Amaryllidaceae)

Thirty-five species native to Chile and Argentina, with one species ranging east into Brazil

Rhodophiala bifida (*Hippeastrum advenum*)
    var. *spathaceae*
    var. *granataflora*

RIGIDELLA Lindl. (Iridaceae)

Four species of *Tigridia*-like flowers native to Mexico, Guatemala, and Peru

SANDERSONIA Hook (Liliaceae)

One species of climbing perennial similar to *Gloriosa*; native to Natal

Sandersonia aurantiaca

SAUROMATUM Schott. (Araceae)

Six or seven species native to tropical Africa, India, and Malaysia

Sauromatum guttatum
    var. *venosum*

SCADOXUS Raf. (Amaryllidaceae)

Nine species native to eastern and southern Africa

Scadoxus multiflorus (*Haemanthus katherinae*)

SCHOENOCAULON Gray (Liliaceae)
A genus of a dozen species
native from Mexico and Texas
south to Peru
Schoenocaulon drummondii
—*texanum*

SCHOENOLIRION Durand
(Liliaceae)
Four species of fleshy rooted
perennials native to North
America
Schoenolirion croceum

SCILLA L. (Liliaceae)
About one hundred species
native to Europe, Asia, and
southern Africa
Scilla hyacinthoides
—*litardieri* (*S. pratensis*,
S. amethystinus)
—*natalensis*
—*peruviana*
cv. 'Alba'

SISYRINCHIUM L. (Iridaceae)
Seventy-five species of clumping
herbs native to the western
hemisphere
Sisyrinchium bellum
cv. 'Album'
—*californicum*
—*striatum*
cv. 'Aunt May'

SPARAXIS Ker-Gawl. (Iridaceae)
Six species of cormous herbs
native to the Cape region of
Africa

SPHENOSTIGMA Bak. (Iridaceae)
Thirteen species of bulbs native
to warm parts of the Americas,
related to *Cipura*
Sphenostigma coelestinum

SPREKELIA Heist
(Amaryllidaceae)
Two or three species in Mexico
and South America
Sprekelia formosissima
cv. 'Orient Red'
cv. 'Peru'
cv. 'Superba'

STENANTHIUM (Gray) Kunth
(Liliaceae)
One species native to North
America
Stenanthium gramineum

STERNBERGIA Waldst. & Kit.
(Amaryllidaceae)
Five species native around the
eastern Mediterranean
Sternbergia candida
—*clusiana*
—*fischerana*
—*lutea*
—*sicula*

TIGRIDIA Juss. (Iridaceae)
About a dozen species in
Mexico and Central America
Tigridia ehrenbergii
—*pavonia*

TOLFIELDIA Huds. (Liliaceae)
Fourteen species of rhizomatous
perennials native to North and
South America, Europe, and
Asia
Tolfieldia racemosa

TRILLIUM L. (Liliaceae)
Thirty species in North America
and Asia
Trillium gracile (*T. ludovicianum*)
var. *luteum*

—*pusillum*
—*recurvatum*
—*sessile*

TRIMEZIA Salisb. ex Herb. (Iridaceae)

Nine species of cormous perennials native to tropical America
Trimezia martinicensis

TRITELEIA Dougl. ex Lindl. (Liliaceae)

Fifteen species of cormous herbs native to western North America; formerly included in *Brodiaea*
Tritelia hyacinthina
—*laxa*
cv. 'Queen Fabiola'
—*peduncularis*
— × *tubergenii*
—*uniflora* (see *Ipheion uniflorum*)

TRITONIA Ker-Gawl. (Iridaceae)

About thirty species of cormous perennial herbs native to the Cape region of Africa; formerly included in *Crocosmia*

TULBAGHIA L. (Liliaceae)

About twenty species native to southern Africa
Tulbaghia fragrans
—*violacea*
cv. 'Silver Lace'

TULIPA L. (Liliaceae)

About one hundred species of bulbs native mainly to central Asia

Division I: Single early tulips
Division II: Double early tulips
Division III: Triumph tulips

Division IV: Darwin Hybrid tulips
Division V: Single late tulips
Division VI: Lily-flowered tulips
Division VII: Fringed tulips
Division VIII: Viridiflora tulips
Division IX: Rembrandt tulips
Division X: Parrot tulips
Division XI: Double late (peony-flowered) tulips
Division XII: Kaufmanniana tulips
Division XIII: Fosteriana tulips
Division XIV: Greigii tulips

Division XV: Species
Tulipa acuminata
—*batalanii*
—*clusiana*
cv. 'Cynthia'
var. *chrysantha*
var. *stellata*
—*eichleri*
—*gesnerana*
—*linifolia*
—*saxatilis* (*T. bakeri*)
cv. 'Lilac Wonder'
—*sylvestris* (*T. florentina odorata*)
var. *australis*
cv. 'Major'
cv. 'Tabris'

VAGARIA Herb. (Amaryllidaceae)

Three species native to the Mediterranean region
Vagaria parviflora

XANTHOSOMA Schott. (Araceae)

About forty species of tuberous perennials native to tropical America
Xanthosoma muffata
cv. 'Aurea'
—*saggittifolium*
—*violacea*

ZANTEDESCHIA **Sprengel**
(Amaryllidaceae)

Six species native to southern
Africa

Zantedeschia albo-maculata

—*elliottiana*

—*ethiopica*

cv. 'Godfrey'

cv. 'Green Goddess'

—*pentlandii*

—*rehmanii*

ZEPHYRANTHES **Herb.**
(Amaryllidaceae)

About seventy-five species in
warm parts of the Americas

White-flowered species

Zephyranthes albiella

—*atamasco*

var. *simpsonii*

var. *treatiae*

—*candida* (*Argyropsis candida*)

—*chlorosolen* (*Cooperia drummondii*)

—*drummondii* (*Cooperia pedunculata*)

—*insularum*

—*minima*

—*puertoricensis*

—*subflava*

—*traubii*

Pink- and rose-flowered species

Zephyranthes bella

—*chichimeca*

—*crociflora*

—*erubescens*

—*fosteri*

—*grandiflora* (*Z. robusta*)

—*latissamafolia*

—*lindleyana* (*Z. clintiae*)

cv. 'Horsetail Falls'

—sp. "Labuffarosea"

—*macrosiphon*

—*morrisclintii*

—*rosea*

—*verecunda*

— × *flaggii*

Yellow-flowered species

Zephyranthes citrina (*Z. sulfurea*)

—*flavissima*

—*jonesii*

—*katherinae*

—*longifolia*

—*nymphaea*

—*primulina*

—*pulchella*

—*refugiensis*

—*reginae*

—*smallii*

ZIGADENUS **Michx. (Liliaceae)**

About twenty species of bulbous
or tuberous plants in North
America and Asia

Zigadenus glabberrimus

—*leimanthoides*

—*nutallii*

ZINGIBER **Boehmer.**
(Zingiberaceae)

About ninety species of aromatic
perennial herbs native to
tropical Asia

Zingiber mioga

—*officinale*

—*zerumbet*

cv. 'Darcey'

Resources

🐚 *Sources of Bulbs*

Brudy's Exotics
P.O. Box 820874
Houston, TX 77282-0874
(713) 963-0033
Gingers, cannas

Coastal Gardens and Nursery
4611 Socastee Blvd.
Myrtle Beach, SC 29575
(803) 293-2000
Irises, asparagus

Cruickshank's, Inc.
1015 Mt. Pleasant Road
Dept. MAN94
Toronto, Ontario M4P 2M1
Canada
*Van Tubergen's representative in
North America*

Daffodil Mart
Rte. 3, Box 794
Gloucester, VA 23061
(804) 693-3966
*Wide range of hardy bulbs, many old
varieties of narcissuses*

Fancy Plants Farms
88-5 Knox Lane
Lake Placid, FL 33852
(800) 869-0953
Caladiums

Florida Market Bulletin
Mayo Building
407 South Calhoun Street
Tallahassee, FL 32304

Flowers & Greens
P.O. Box 1802
Davis, CA 95617
(916) 756-9238
Alstroemeria, Freesia, Gladiolus

Kelly's Plant World
10266 East Princeton
Sanger, CA 93657
(209) 292-3505
Cannas

Louisiana Market Bulletin
P.O. Box 44365
Capitol Station
Baton Rouge, LA 70804

Louisana Nursery
Rte. 5, Box 43 (Hwy. 182)
Opelousas, LA 70576
(318) 948-3696
Louisiana irises, crinums, collector plants

McClure & Zimmerman
108 West Winnebago Street
P.O. Box 368, Dept. MAN94
Freisland, WI 53935-0368
Hardy bulbs

Grant Mitsch Novelty Daffodils
P.O. Box 218C
Hubbard, OR 97032

Old House Gardens
536 Third Street
Ann Arbor, MI 48103-4957
(313) 995-1486
Antique tulips, hyacinths, and daffodils

The Onion Man
Mark McDonough
30 Mt. Lebanon Street
Pepperell, MA 01463
Alliums and quarterly newsletter,
G.A.R.L.I.C.

Plant Delights Nursery
9241 Sauls Road
Raleigh, NC 27603
(919) 772-4794
Amorphophallus, Pinellia,
Belamcanda, Bletilla, Crocosmia,
Eucomis, Polygonatum,
Sauromatum, Sisyrinchium

Plumeria People
910 Leander Drive
Leander, TX 78641
(512) 259-0807
Gingers and subtropical bulbs

Poest Gladiolus
Box 55, Dept. FG
Zeeland, MI 49464
(616) 772-6049

John Scheeper's, Inc.
P.O. Box 700
Bantam, CT 06750
(203) 567-0838
Illustrated color catalog of hardy bulbs

Siskiyou Rare Plant Nursery
Dept. 1, 2825 Cummings Road
Medford, OR 97501
(503) 772-6846
Dwarf rock garden bulbs

Sister's Bulb Farm
Rte. 2, Box 170
Gibsland, LA 71028
Heirloom daffodils

Skittone Bulb Company
1415 Eucalyptus, Dept. 702
San Francisco, CA 94132
(415) 753-3332
Many botanical bulb varieties

Southern Exposure
35 Minor at Rusk
Beaumont, TX 77702-2414
(409) 835-0644
Subtropical aroids

Van Bourgondien Bros.
P.O. Box 1000-4607
Babylon, NY 11702-0598
(800) 622-9997
Wide range of bulbs and perennials

William R.P. Welch
Garzas Road
Carmel Valley, CA 93924
(409) 659-3830
Tazetta narcissi, Amaryllis
belladonna, Scilla peruviana

Nancy R. Wilson
Species and Miniature Narcissus
571 Woodmont Avenue
Berkeley, CA 94708

Guy Wrinkle Exotic Plants
11610 North Addison Street
North Hollywood, CA 91601
(213) 766-3643
South African bulbs

Tom Wood
P.O. Box 100
Archer, FL 32818
(904) 485-9168
Over 150 gingers

Yucca-Do Nursery
Peckerwood Gardens
P.O. Box 655
Waller, TX 77484
(409) 829-6363
Zephyranthes, Dahlia, Arisaema,
Pinellia, Cypella, Tigridia

❧ Societies and Publications

American Daffodil Society
Miss Leslie E. Anderson,
Executive Director
Rte. 3, 2302 Byhalia Road
Hernando, MS 38632

American Iris Society
Mrs. Larry D. Stayer, Secretary
7414 East 60th Street
Tulsa, OK 74145

American Rock Garden Society
P.O. Box 67
Millwood, NY 10546

North American Lily Society
P.O. Box 272, Dept. F
Otowonna, MN 55060

International Bulb Society
U.C.I. Arboretum
University of California
Irvine, CA 92717
(Formerly the American
Amaryllis Society)

Royal Horticultural Society
Vincent Square
London SW1P 2PE
United Kingdom

Southern Garden History Society
Old Salem, Inc.
Drawer F, Salem Station
Winston-Salem, NC 27108

The Society for Louisiana Irises
Marie Caillet
1216 Cedar Pine Lane
Little Elm, TX 75068-3060

❧ Labels

Paw-Paw Everlast Label Co.
P.O. Box 93-C
Paw Paw, MI 49079-0093

Bulb Savers
Box 3024
Princeton, NJ 08543-3024

Bibliography

Allen, C.L. *Bulbs and Tuberous Rooted Plants*. New York: Orange Judd, 1915.

Bailey, Liberty Hyde, and Ethel Joe Bailey. *Hortus Third*. New York: Macmillan, 1976.

Baron, Robert C., ed. *The Garden and Farm Books of Thomas Jefferson*. Golden, Colorado: Fulcrum, 1987.

Barre, Peter. *Ye Narcissus or Daffodil Flowre, and hys Roots*. London, 1884. Reprint American Daffodil Society, Washington, DC, 1968.

Caillet, Marie, and Joseph K. Mertzweiller. *The Louisiana Iris*. Waco, Texas: Texas Gardener Press, 1988.

Correl, Donovan Stewart, and Marshall Conring Johnston. *Manual of the Vascular Plants of Texas*. Richardson: University of Texas at Dallas, 1979.

Eliovson, Sima. *South African Flowers for the Garden*. Cape Town: Howard Timmins, 1957.

Gorer, Richard. *The Development of Garden Flowers*. London: Eyre and Spottiswoode, 1970.

Hannibal, L.S., "Garden Crinum." *Bulletin of The Louisiana Society For Horticultural Research*, Vol. 3, No. 5, 1970–71.

Herbert, William H. *Amaryllidaceae*, 1837. Reprint J. Kramer, 1966.

Herbertia, *The Journal of the International Bulb Society*, Vols. 1–46, 1936–1990.

Johnson, Hugh. *The Principles of Gardening*. New York: Simon and Schuster, 1979.

Killingback, Stanley. *Tulips*. Secaucus, New Jersey: Chartwell Books, 1990.

Kohlein, Fritz. *Iris*. Portland, Oregon: Timber Press, 1987.

Lane Publishing. *Sunset Western Garden Book*. Menlo Park, California: Lane, 1988.

Lawrence, Elizabeth. *The Little Bulbs*. New York: Criterion Books, 1957.

————. *A Southern Garden*. Chapel Hill: University of North Carolina Press, 1991.

Lee, George S. "Daffodil Handbook." *The American Horticultural Magazine*, Vol. 45, No. 1, January 1966.

Linnegar, Sidney, and Jennifer Hewitt. *Irises*. London: Cassel/The Royal Horticultural Society, 1990.

Mallary, Peter, and Frances Mallary, with Joan Waltermire and Linney Levin. *A Redouté Treasury*. New York: The Vendome Press, 1986.

Matthew, Brian. *Dwarf Bulbs*. New York: Arco, 1973.

McFarland, J. Horace, with R. Marion Hatton and Daniel J. Foley. *Garden Bulbs in Color*. New York: Macmillan, 1941.

Miles, Bebe. *Bulbs for the Home Gardener*. New York: Grosset & Dunlap, 1976.

Mitchell, Sydney B. *Gardening in California*. New York: Doubleday, Page, 1924.

Parkinson, John. *Paradisi in Sole, Paradisus Terrestris*, 1629. Latest ed. 1976.

Phillips, Roger, and Martyn Rix. *The Bulb Book*. London: Pan Books, 1981.

Rix, Martyn. *Growing Bulbs*. Portland, Oregon: Timber Press, 1983.

Robinson, Benjamin Lincoln, and Merrit Lyndon Fernald. *Gray's New Manual of Botany*. New York: American Book Company, 1908.

Scott, George Harmon. *Bulbs*. Tucson, Arizona: HP Books, 1982.

Scruggs, Mrs. Gross R., and Margaret Ann Scruggs. *Gardening in the Southwest*. Dallas: Southwest Press, 1932.

Stearn, William T. *Stearn's Dictionary of Plant Names for Gardeners*. London: Cassel, 1992.

Stern, Sir Frederick C. *A Chalk Garden*. London: Thomas Nelson and Sons, 1960.

Thomas, Graham Stuart. *Perennial Garden Plants*. London: J.M. Dent and Sons, 1982.

Verdoorn, I.C. "The Genus *Crinum* in Southern Africa." *Bothalia,* Vol. 11, Nos. 1 & 2, 27–52, 1973.

Warburton, Bee. *The World of Irises*. Wichita, Kansas: American Iris Society, 1978.

Welch, William C. *Perennial Garden Color*. Dallas: Taylor Publishing, 1989.

Wilder, Louise Beebe. *Adventures in a Suburban Garden*. New York: Macmillan, 1931.

————. *Adventures with Hardy Bulbs*. New York: Macmillan, 1990.

Wills, Mary Motz, and Howard S. Irwin. *Roadside Wildflowers of Texas*. Austin: University of Texas Press, 1969.

Woodard, Marcus. *Leaves from Gerard's Herbal*. New York: Dover, 1969.

Index

Note: **Boldface** page numbers refer to illustrations.